298

MAKING USEFUL THINGS OF WOOD

Conestoga wagon model with full equipment (see p. 170).

MAKING
USEFUL THINGS
of WOOD

FRANKLIN H. GOTTSHALL

BONANZA BOOKS • NEW YORK

To MR. WILLIAM C. BRUCE

President and Editor in Chief of The Bruce Publishing Co., Without Whose Encouragement and Courteous Consideration My Earliest Efforts Would in All Probability Never Have Been Committed to Print.

Foreword

A BOOK containing simple projects of good design and with plenty of boy appeal has always been a shop teacher's dream. Periodically, the need arises for books which provide new and unique projects, and those which utilize a wide variety of materials, processes, and techniques; also projects suited to various degrees of skill.

The author submits this collection, to be added to the many other fine projects made available in recent years by teachers and craftsmen, with the sincere hope that it will meet the most exacting requirements of shop teachers, students, and home craftsmen.

In planning, selecting, and working up this collection of projects, the following objectives have been kept in mind constantly:

1. To provide a wide variety of projects.
2. To provide designs in which utility and beauty have been properly combined.
3. To provide designs which are in many cases unique, and adapt themselves to the conditions generally prevailing in school and home workshops.
4. To provide a large number of simple projects, easily within the ability range of the very young and inexperienced.
5. To provide other projects which, though they conserve valuable materials, nevertheless are designed to challenge the skills of craftsmen who have had considerable training.
6. To provide a collection of projects sufficiently varied to furnish opportunities to engage in ordinary cabinetmaking, wood turning, wood carving, designing, wood finishing, inlaying, handwork, machine work, etc. This fosters the acquisition of a wide variety of skills and interests.
7. To provide adequate illustrations, instructions, and visual aids of the most advanced type so far developed by either industry or pedagogical science for the training of beginners in this art.

8. To introduce the learner to as many new techniques, processes, materials, and skills as is possible within the limited scope of a book such as this.
9. To provide projects, many of which, by actual testing, have proven to be equally well adapted to the needs of beginners in junior and senior high schools, colleges, and universities, as well as to those who do not have access to any formal instruction such as is provided in the classroom.

It is never possible, perhaps, to acknowledge or thank everybody who has extended help or assistance in the compilation of a book. If any who have had a share in the preparation of this one, have been overlooked, it is due to an oversight and not to any lack of appreciation.

The author is sincerely grateful to all who have in any way extended aid in the compilation of this material, but especially to the following:

1. To the Brodhead Garrett Co., Cleveland, Ohio, and to Mr. R. C. Stucker, sales manager, in particular, for information and assistance.
2. To the X-Acto Crescent Products Co., New York, and to Mr. David Goldberg, advertising manager, in particular, for photographs and other valuable help and information useful in the preparation of this book.
3. To the editors of *Popular Science Monthly* for permission to use the projects on pages 10, 63, 70, and 74, formerly published by the author in *Popular Science Monthly* and other publications sponsored by them.
4. To Mr. H. J. Hobbs, editor of *The Homecraftsman Magazine,* for permission to use material formerly published by the author in the *Homecraftsman* magazine.
5. To Mr. John J. Metz, editor of *Industrial Arts and Vocational Education,* for valu-

able aid and assistance in the preparation of this material.

6. To Mr. Frank Updegrove, of Boyertown, Pa., who built the conestoga wagon shown in the frontispiece and from whose model the plans for the one shown in this book were adapted.

To all others who have in any way contributed to the success and completion of this venture, the author extends his sincere and grateful thanks.

FRANKLIN H. GOTTSHALL

Boyertown, Pa.
April, 1950

Contents

MAKING USEFUL THINGS OF WOOD

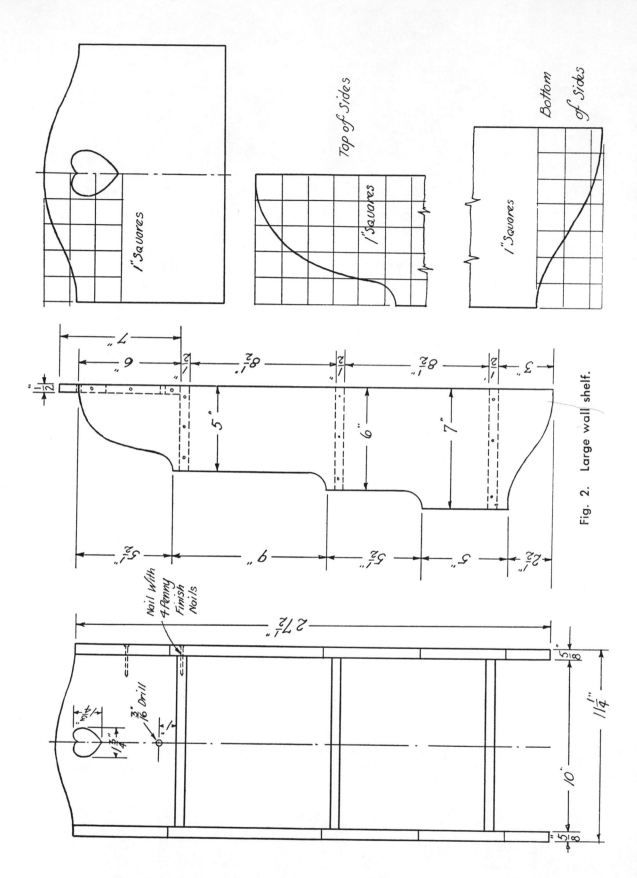

Fig. 2. Large wall shelf.

Small and Large Wall Shelves

SINCE both of these projects are made alike, except for size, the details of their construction will be treated here as though they were one project. Sometimes it is desirable to save ma-

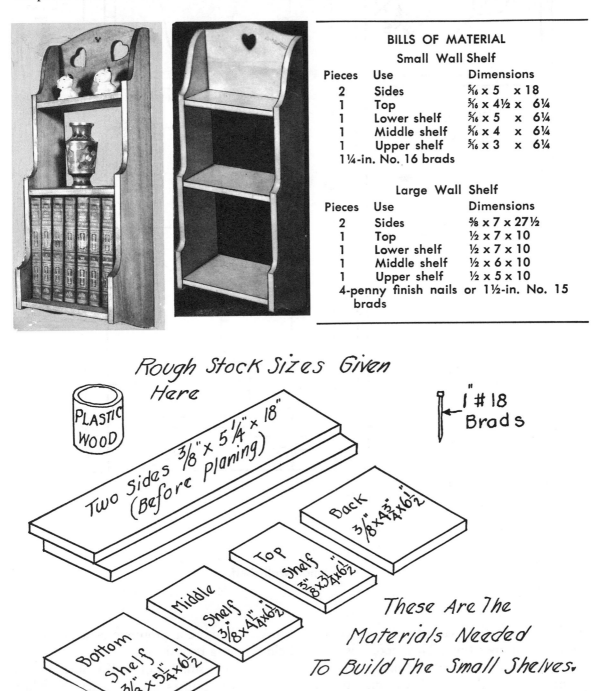

BILLS OF MATERIAL

Small Wall Shelf

Pieces	Use	Dimensions
2	Sides	⁵⁄₁₆ x 5 x 18
1	Top	⁵⁄₁₆ x 4½ x 6¼
1	Lower shelf	⁵⁄₁₆ x 5 x 6¼
1	Middle shelf	⁵⁄₁₆ x 4 x 6¼
1	Upper shelf	⁵⁄₁₆ x 3 x 6¼

1¼-in. No. 16 brads

Large Wall Shelf

Pieces	Use	Dimensions
2	Sides	⅝ x 7 x 27½
1	Top	½ x 7 x 10
1	Lower shelf	½ x 7 x 10
1	Middle shelf	½ x 6 x 10
1	Upper shelf	½ x 5 x 10

4-penny finish nails or 1½-in. No. 15 brads

Rough Stock Sizes Given Here

PLASTIC WOOD

Two Sides $\frac{3}{8}$" x $5\frac{1}{4}$" x 18" (Before Planing)

1" #18 Brads

Back $\frac{3}{8}$" x $4\frac{3}{4}$" x $6\frac{1}{2}$"

Top Shelf $\frac{3}{8}$" x $3\frac{1}{4}$" x $6\frac{1}{2}$"

Middle Shelf $\frac{3}{8}$ x $4\frac{1}{4}$" x $6\frac{1}{2}$"

Bottom Shelf $\frac{3}{8}$" x $5\frac{1}{4}$" x $6\frac{1}{2}$"

These Are The Materials Needed To Build The Small Shelves.

Fig. 3.   Materials for small wall shelves.

1

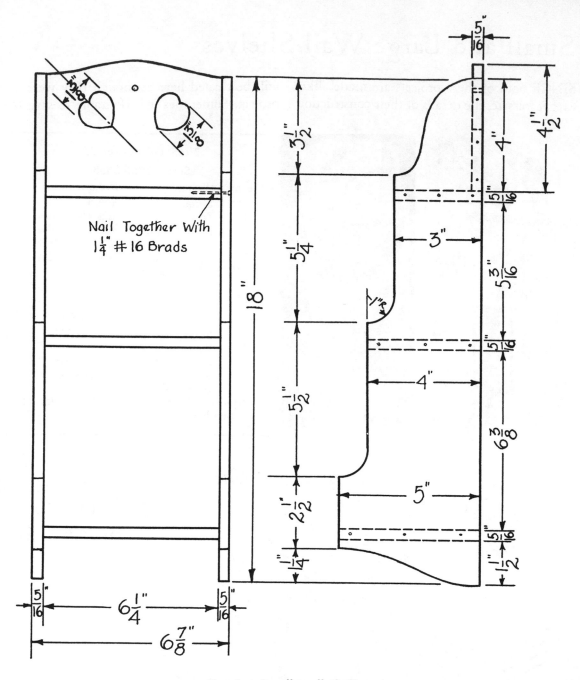

Fig. 1. Small wall shelf.

Nail Together With 1¼" #16 Brads

terial, and yet, at the same time, teach certain fundamental operations. Then, too, it is often desirable to have two similar projects in different sizes. While small books may be put on the shelves of the smaller project, as shown

above, it is more appropriate as a bric-a-brac holder than a bookshelf.

Because the small wall shelf is such a good project for beginners, a step-by-step procedure for making it has been worked out.

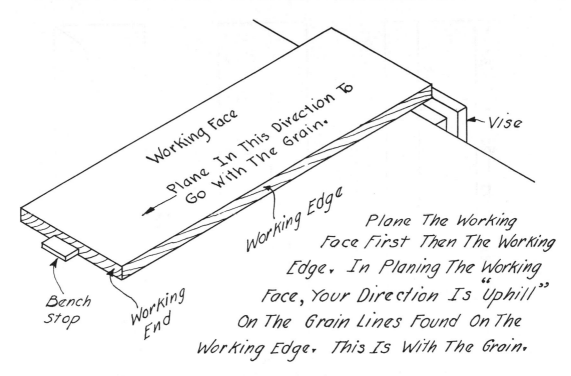

Working Face

Plane In This Direction To Go With The Grain.

Working Edge

Vise

Plane The Working Face First Then The Working Edge. In Planing The Working Face, Your Direction Is "Uphill" On The Grain Lines Found On The Working Edge. This Is With The Grain.

Bench Stop

Working End

Fig. 4.   Directions for planing.

PROCEDURE

A. SIDES.

1. Plane and square boards for the sides to the sizes given in the bill of material.

2. Make a full-size pattern of the side, and lay it out on the boards as directed in **Figures** 6 and 7.

Boards Are Marked, To Determine Width Or Thickness, With A Gauge. The Gauge Is Used Only With (Parallel To) The Grain Never Across The Grain.

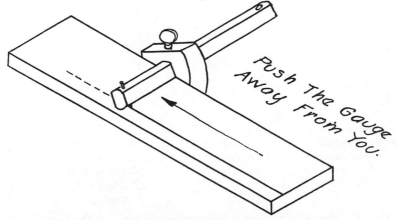

Push The Gauge Away From You.

Fig. 5.   Marking board with gauge.

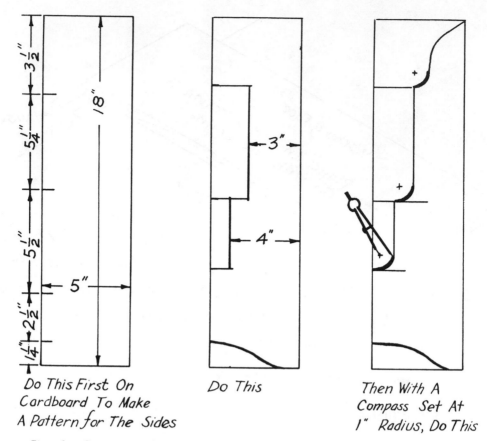

Fig. 6. Steps in making a pattern for the sides of the small wall shelves.

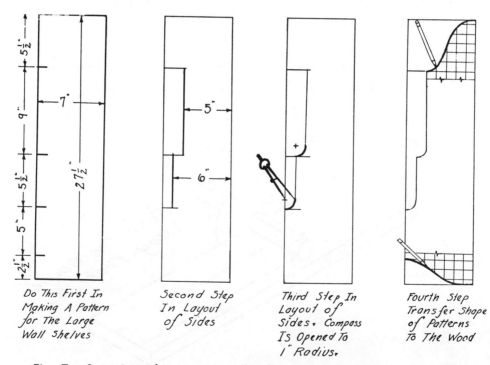

Fig. 7. Steps in making a pattern for the sides of the large wall shelves.

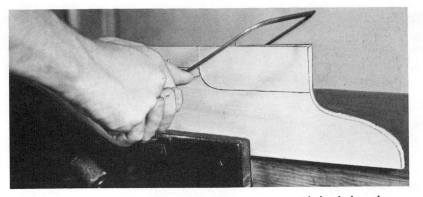

Fig. 8.   Grasp the handle of the coping saw with both hands —
one hand over the other, as shown. Hold the saw level, and
saw close to the line.

3. Saw the pieces to shape with a coping saw. Saw the upper curve first, then the middle two, and finally the lower end. See Figure 8.

4. Pare with a chisel (Fig. 9); then file and sandpaper the sawed edges (Fig. 10). Sandpaper all surfaces before assembling the project.

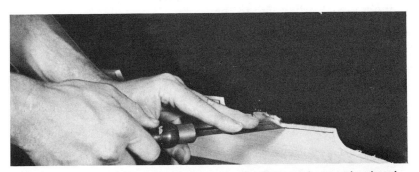

Fig. 9.   Pare the flat edges away to the line with a wide chisel.
Hold the chisel at this angle. Pare away the shavings to the line.

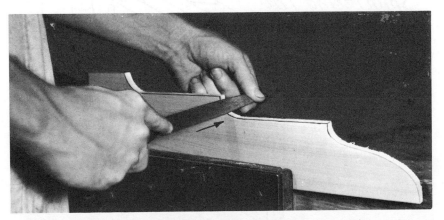

Fig. 10.   File the curved parts with a half-round file. File away
from you, rolling the file.

5

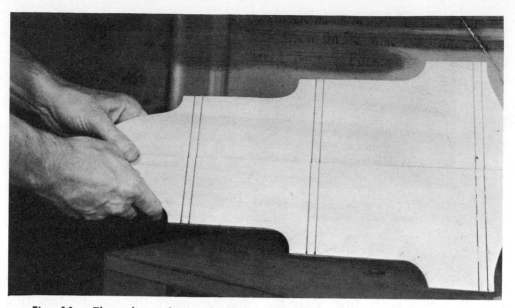

Fig. 11. These lines show where the shelves go. To make a pair, the lines must appear on the same side when the sides are placed back to back.

5. On the inner surface of the sides, lay out two lines where each shelf is to be fastened. On the outside, square light lines across the sides as a guide for nailing.

B. SHELVES.

Square and plane the shelves to size.

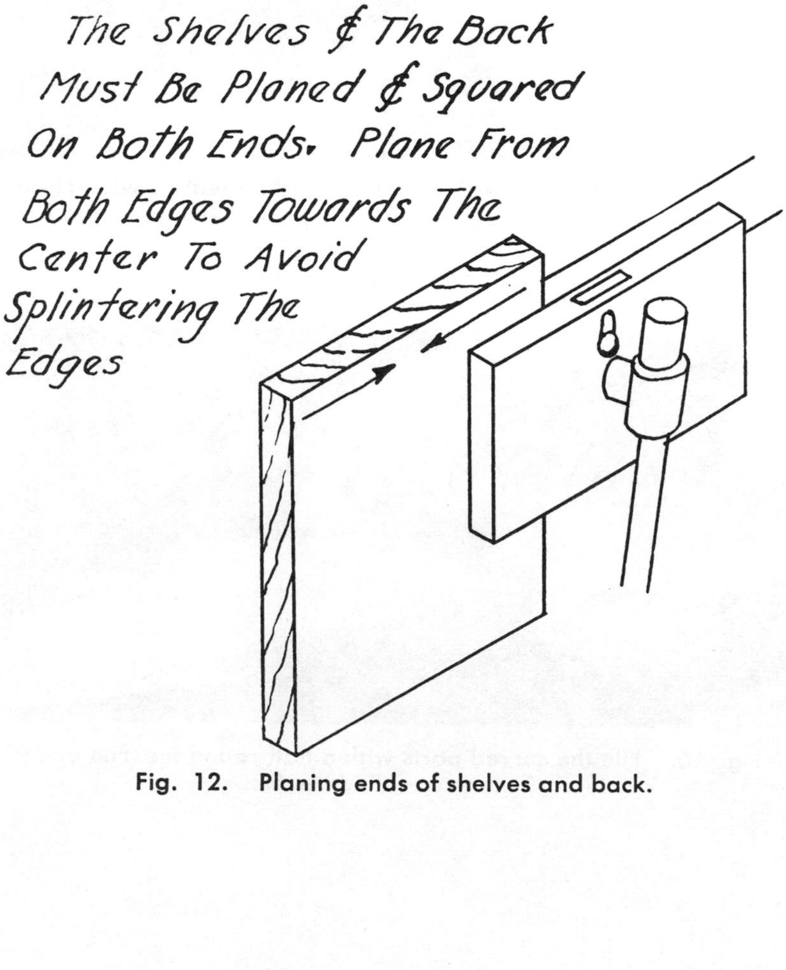

The Shelves & The Back Must Be Planed & Squared On Both Ends. Plane From Both Edges Towards The Center To Avoid Splintering The Edges

Fig. 12. Planing ends of shelves and back.

6

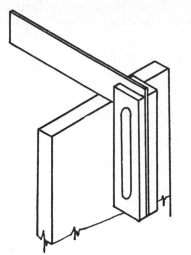

Square The Ends & Edges
To The Working Face

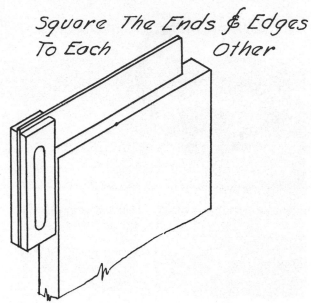

Square The Ends & Edges
To Each   Other

Fig. 13.   Squaring ends and edges.

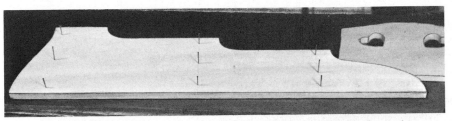

Fig. 14.   Square lines across the opposite face of the side and
drive 1-in. brads into the side as shown here.

Fig. 15.   The points of the brads stick out far enough so that the
ends of the shelves may be pressed into place in this manner.

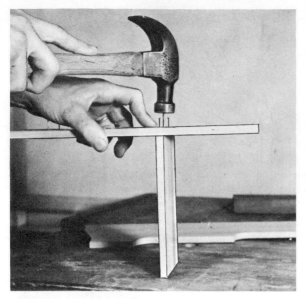

Fig. 16. The brads then are driven in and set with a nail punch.

C. ASSEMBLE THE SIDES AND SHELVES.

1. Start the nails through one side until the ends just protrude on the inside (Fig. 14).

2. Press the first shelf against these protruding points (Fig. 15); then, resting the opposite end of the shelf upon the workbench,

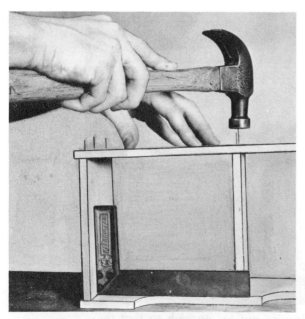

Fig. 17. Nail the other side squaring the shelves in this manner.

drive the nails home (Fig. 16). Proceed in this manner until all shelves have been nailed to one side.

3. Turn the nailed side down on the bench top, and nail the other side to the shelves (Fig. 17).

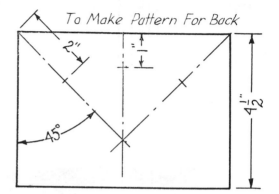

To Make Pattern For Back

2"

45°

$4\frac{1}{2}$"

On A Piece of Cardboard
Do This First

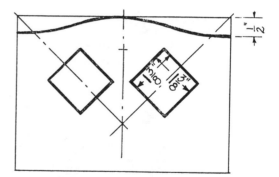

$1\frac{1}{2}$"

$\frac{3}{8}$" $\frac{3}{8}$"

Then Do This Second

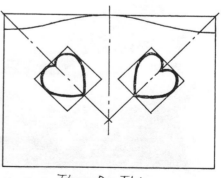

Then Do This

Fig. 18. Pattern for back.

Fig. 19. Drill three holes with a
¾₆-in. drill.

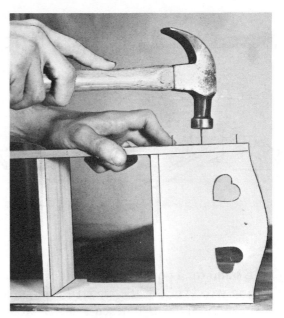

Fig. 21. Fasten the back, and the
shelves are completed.

D. THE TOP.

1. Plane and square the top. When the second end of the top is to be squared, place the squared working end in its proper position against the side, and, with a sharp pencil, mark its exact length inside the opposite side. By doing this, a tight-fitting joint will be assured.

2. Draw the curve of the top from a pattern (Fig. 18), making sure, however, that the ends of the curve do not fall above or below the upper ends of the sides.

3. Saw the top to shape; use a spokeshave and a file to true it up to the line, and then sandpaper the edge smooth.

4. Saw out the heart or hearts, as the case may be, first drilling holes to insert the coping-saw blade (Figs. 19 and 20). True up with a file and sandpaper.

E. NAIL THE TOP TO THE SIDES AND TOP SHELF (FIG. 21).

F. GIVE THE PROJECT A SUITABLE FINISH.

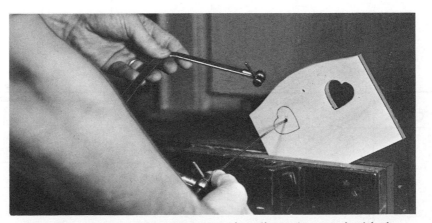

Fig. 20. Unscrew the coping-saw handle and insert the blade.
The teeth of the blade should point toward the handle.

Stand for a Potted Plant

BILL OF MATERIAL		
Pieces	Use	Dimensions
1	Top	¾ x 6 x 6
4	Feet	¾ x 1 x 3½
8 Wood screws, 1-in. No. 8 f.h.		

THE stand for a potted plant is a good project in hand woodwork. Little material is required to make it, and yet it teaches many woodworking operations. The plant stand also may be used as a hot-dish mat.

PROCEDURE

A. TOP.

1. Plane and square the board to the size given in the bill of material.

2. Lay out and plane a 45-deg. chamfer around the edges.

3. Sandpaper the top.

B. FEET.

1. The four feet may be sawed from one stick of wood ¾ by 1 by 15 in. A long stick is easier to plane to width and thickness than four short ones would be.

2. Make a full-size pattern like the one shown in Figure 2.

3. Transfer the design of the feet to the ¾-in. sides of the stick from this pattern.

4. Saw the feet to shape with a coping saw. Sawing with a coping saw is quite simple if the teeth of the blade are pointed toward the handle. Hold the saw level. Grip the handle of the saw with the right hand, and place the left hand over the right hand. This is the proper position for sawing with a coping saw. Saw as close to the line as possible without crossing the line.

5. File every sawed edge. Do this carefully, holding the file level. Keep the profile exactly like the pattern, making the corners sharp and the curves rounded.

6. Drill two ⁵⁄₃₂-in. holes into each foot, and countersink the holes for No. 8 screwheads.

If the screwhead is held upside down, its diameter will determine the diameter and depth of the countersinking.

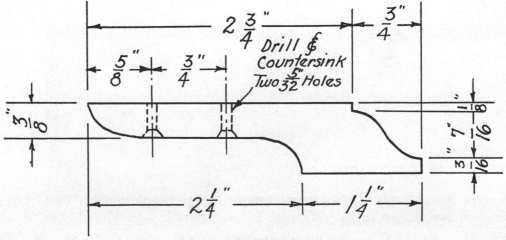

Fig. 2. Detail of foot.

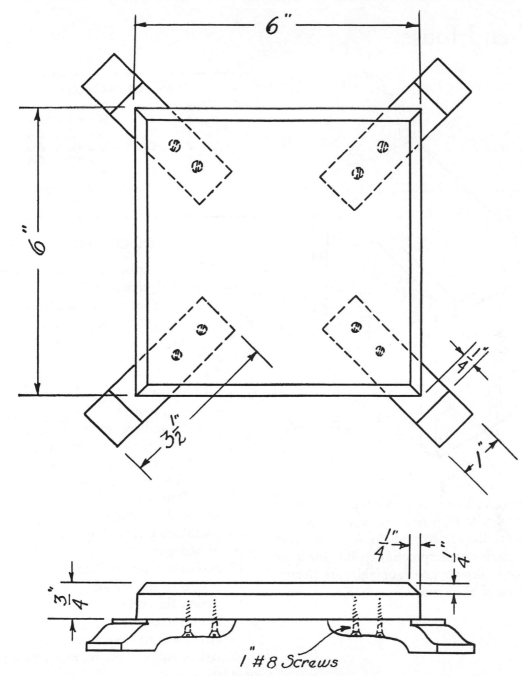

Fig. 1.   Stand for a potted plant.

C. FASTEN THE FEET TO THE TOP.

1. Lay the top upon the workbench, bottom upward.

2. Draw lines diagonally from corner to corner. These are center lines to line up the feet. Draw four more lines, ½ in. away from the center lines on each side and parallel to them.

3. Between these last four lines, fasten the feet. Let ¼ in. of the flat upper part of the foot protrude as shown in Figure 1. With the foot held in this position, mark its other end under the top. With this mark as a guide, screw the foot to the top.

D. GIVE THE PLANT STAND A SUITABLE FINISH.

Wren House

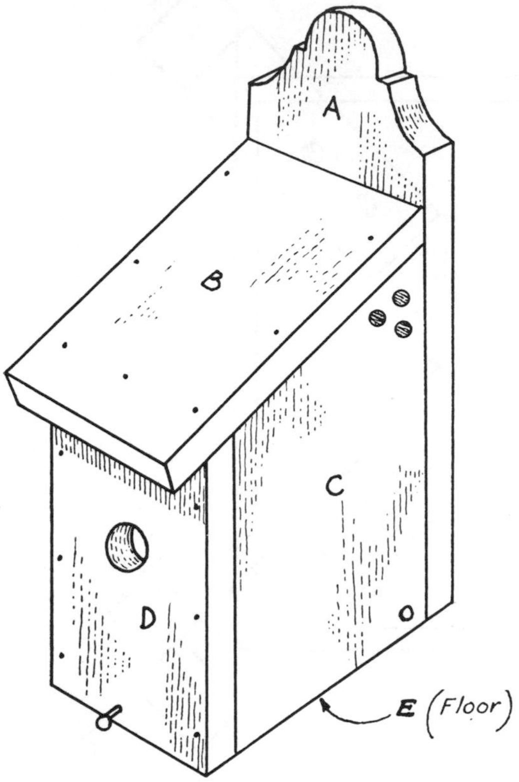

THE wren house is a good project. Birds prefer to build their nests in houses which are not too brilliantly colored. So, while red may be a good weatherproofing paint, birds do not like it. Brown, green, or white are suitable colors for a birdhouse.

BILL OF MATERIAL

Pieces	Use	Dimensions
1	A	⅝ x 4½ x 10⅝
1	B	⅝ x 4½ x 6½
2	C	⅝ x 4½ x 7½
1	D	⅝ x 4½ x 5⅞
1	E	⅝ x 3¼ x 4$\frac{7}{16}$

Three 3-penny common nails
4-penny finish nails

PROCEDURE

1. Plane and square all pieces to the sizes given in the bill of material.
2. Make a layout on the wood for the top of *A,* and saw the piece to shape.
3. Lay out the angle at the top of *C,* and saw and plane it to shape.
4. Lay out the angle at the end of *B* (set sliding T bevel at 70 deg.), and saw and plane it as shown in Figure 1.
5. Lay out and cut the angle at the end of *D* (set sliding T bevel at 70 deg.).
6. Locate and bore the ⅞-in. hole.
7. Drill the ventilating holes in pieces *C.*
8. Nail *D* to sides *C.*
9. Check the flatness of the top of these three assembled pieces. True them up with a plane, if necessary.
10. Nail *A* to the assembled parts.
11. Nail *B* to the assembled parts.
12. Round the end of *E* as shown in Figure 1, and nail it to the assembled pieces.
13. Give the birdhouse a suitable finish. Use a nontoxic wood preservative rather than paint or stain.

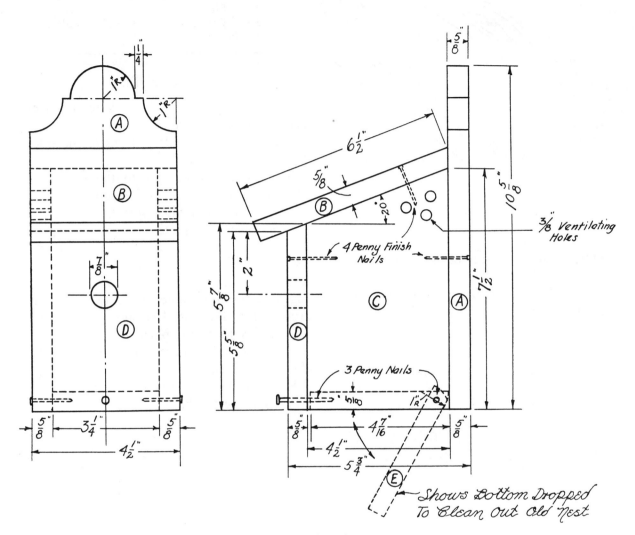

Fig. 1.   Wren house.

Small Serving Tray

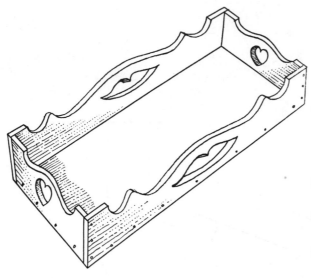

ONLY a small amount of material is necessary for this project, and yet it teaches many fundamental operations. It serves as an excellent sandwich tray.

BILL OF MATERIAL

Pieces	Use	Dimensions
1	Bottom	⅜ x 5½ x 14¼
2	Sides	⅜ x 2 x 15
2	Ends	⅜ x 2 x 5½

Brads — ¾ and 1 in., No. 18

PROCEDURE

1. Plane and square all stock to the sizes given in the bill of material.

2. Draw full-size half patterns of the sides and ends as shown.

3. Transfer the designs to the sides and ends, and saw them out with a coping saw.

4. File all sawed edges smooth.

5. Sandpaper all parts.

6. Cut the head off a 1-in., No. 18 brad, and use it as a drill to make holes in the sidepieces and lower edges of the ends to nail the parts together. Drilling holes prevents the nails from going in crooked; it also prevents the ends and sides from splitting.

7. Nail the sides to the ends first; then fit the bottom inside.

8. Sandpaper all joints level; then give the tray a suitable finish.

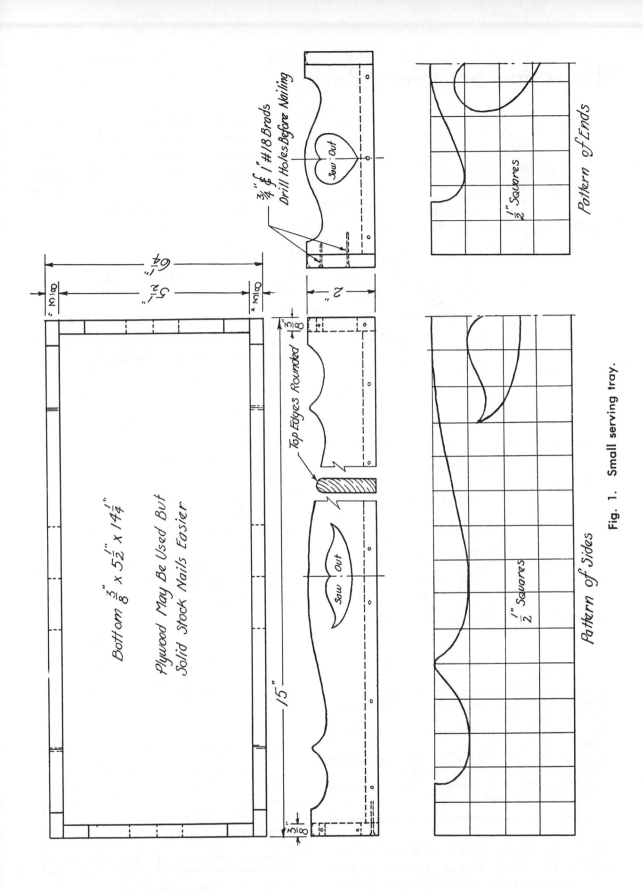

Fig. 1. Small serving tray.

15

Book and Stationery Rack

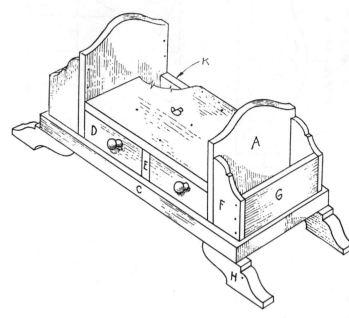

which a boy usually keeps in his room. The end pockets are for stationery, while the main section above the drawers will hold a number of books. While turned wooden drawer pulls are shown in the drawings, bright brass knobs also will be appropriate.

PROCEDURE

A. MAIN PART OF THE RACK.

1. Plane and square pieces *A, B, C,* and *E* to the sizes given in the bill of material.

2. Make a full-size pattern as shown in Figure 2.

3. The right-hand side of this pattern is for the top of piece *A.*

4. Saw the tops of pieces *A* to shape. File the sawed edges.

5. Sandpaper the pieces.

6. Assemble the parts.

a) First, draw lines to locate the places where *E* is joined to *B* and *C.*

b) On the opposite sides of *B* and *C,* draw lines to locate the nail holes.

c) Nail *B* and *C* to *E.*

BILL OF MATERIAL

Pieces	Use	
2	A	¾ x 6½ x 8½
1	B	¾ x 6½ x 16½
1	C	¾ x 7 x 23
4	D	½ x 1¹⁵⁄₁₆ x 7¹³⁄₁₆
1	E	¾ x 2 x 6
4	F	½ x 2 x 6
2	G	½ x 4 x 5½
4	H	¾ x 1½ x 6
4	I	¼ plywood x 1¹⁵⁄₁₆ x 5½
2	J	¼ plywood x 5 x 7⁵⁄₁₆
1	K	½ x 2 x 16½

Eight 1¼-in., No. 8 f.h. bright wood screws to fasten feet

1¼-in., No. 18 brads to assemble pockets

4-penny finish nails or 1½-in., No. 15 brads to assemble rack

1-in., No. 18 and ¾-in., No. 20 brads to assemble drawers

2 pieces ⅞-in. diameter x ⅞-in. long for drawer pulls (turn two from a longer piece)

Two 1-in., No. 6 f.h. bright wood screws to fasten drawer pulls

THIS is a project with a great deal of boy appeal. The small drawers may be used to hold pencils, erasers, and all kinds of trifles

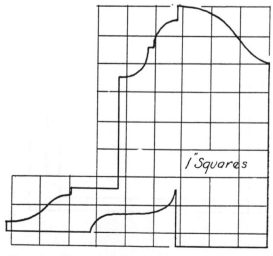

Fig. 2. Plywood pattern of foot and ends.

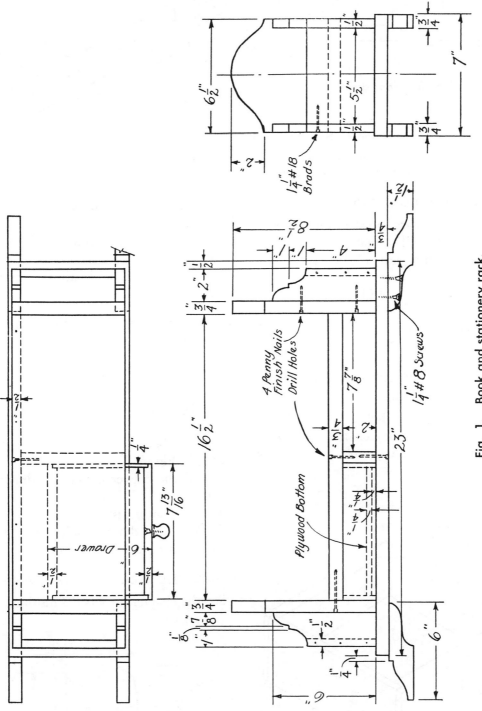

Fig. 1. Book and stationery rack.

17

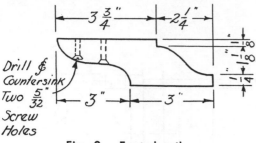

Fig. 3. Foot detail.

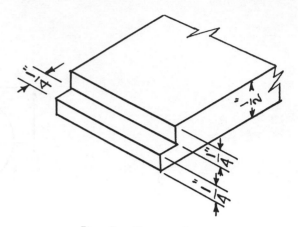

Fig. 5. Drawer front.

d) Nail pieces *A* to *B* and *C*. Be sure when you fasten them, that pieces *A* make right angles with *B* when they are nailed together.

B. POCKETS FOR EACH END.

1. Plane and square pieces *F* and *G* to the sizes given in the bill of material.

2. The left-hand side of the pattern in Figure 2 is for the top of *F*.

3. Saw *F* to shape, and file the curves.

4. Sandpaper the pieces, but do not sandpaper the ends of pieces *G*.

5. Nail pieces *F* to *G*.

C. FASTEN THE POCKETS TO THE MAIN PART OF THE RACK.

1. Locate the nail holes, and drill for 4-penny finish nails or for 1½-in., No. 15 brads, ¼ in. from the edges of *A*.

2. Nail the pockets to pieces *A*, as shown in Figure 1.

3. Put a few nails through the bottom into pieces *F* and *G*.

4. Make piece *K*, and nail it to pieces *A*, *B*, *C*, and *E*.

D. MAKE AND FASTEN THE FEET AS SHOWN IN FIGURE 3.

E. MAKE THE DRAWERS.

1. Plane and square pieces *D*, *J*, and *I* (Fig. 4) to the sizes given in the bill of material.

2. Cut rabbets on the ends of pieces *D* as shown in Figure 5.

3. Nail the drawer sides to the drawer front and back.

4. Nail *J* to pieces *I*.

5. Turn the drawer pulls (Fig. 6), and screw them to the drawer fronts.

F. GIVE THE RACK A SUITABLE FINISH.

See the chapter on wood finishing.

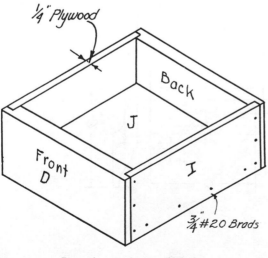

Fig. 4. Drawer detail.

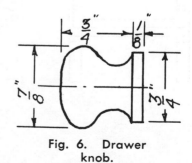

Fig. 6. Drawer knob.

18

Book Ends to Carve or Inlay

Glue Felt To Base

BILL OF MATERIAL		
Pieces	Use	Dimensions
2	Body	1¾ x 5 x 7¼
2	Base	¾ x 2½ x 6½
Pig lead or lead shot to weight book ends		
Wood screws — six 1½-in. No. 10 f.h.		
Green felt for base — 2 pieces 2½ x 6½		

THESE book ends are not only simple to make, but they are excellent for teaching various processes of decoration. They may be carved; inlaid with wood of a contrasting color; overlaid with a silhouette cut from metal, plastics, or some other material; or they may be painted with water colors, oil paints, or decalcomania transfers. Many who make these book ends prefer to leave them plain, giving them only an ordinary finish.

Whichever type of decoration is used, several designs are given here as suggestions. Other designs, of course, may be substituted. The alphabet shown may be used on other projects as well.

PROCEDURE

A. BODIES OF THE TWO BOOK ENDS.

1. Plane and square the blocks of wood to the size given in the bill of material for the bodies.

2. Lay out and cut the angles for the tops. Saw them on a miter box and plane them smooth.

3. Locate and bore two holes into the bottoms so that they can be weighted with lead. The depth of these holes, as shown in Figure 1, is 1 in. The holes may be bored deeper if so desired.

4. Lay out the design and do the decorating.

a) If a monogram or other design is carved, the background may be gouged out in a pleasing manner as shown in Figure 2. All gouge cuts should be made in the same direction to look well.

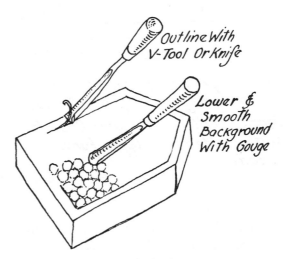

Outline With V-Tool Or Knife

Lower & Smooth Background With Gouge

Fig. 2. Method of carving.

b) If the design is to be inlaid, contrasting wood or veneer may be used. If veneer is used, first glue it to a piece of heavy wrapping paper. Then cut out the design. Lay the design on the book end in its proper position, and carefully transfer its outline to the wood with the point of a sharp knife. Rout out the space the design is to occupy; then glue the design to the place prepared for it with the paper

19

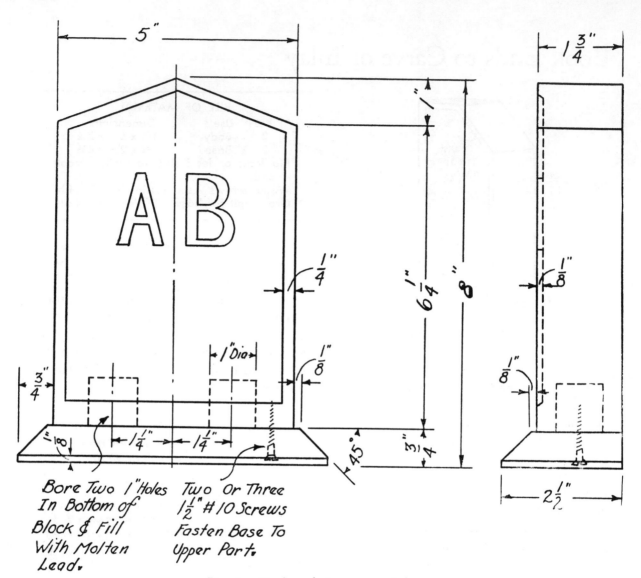

Bore Two 1" Holes In Bottom of Block & Fill With Molten Lead.

Two Or Three 1½" #10 Screws Fasten Base To Upper Part.

Fig. 1. Book ends to carve or inlay.

side up. After the glue has hardened, remove the paper backing with sandpaper.

c) If an overlay is to be superimposed, first cut it out on a jig saw or with a jeweler's saw, depending upon the nature of the material; then nail it on with escutcheon pins.

d) If a decalcomania transfer is to be used to decorate the book ends, follow the directions that accompany these designs in transferring them to the book ends.

B. BASES.

1. Plane and square the bases to the size that is given in the bill of material.

2. Lay out and plane the 45-deg. bevel on three edges.

3. Drill and countersink holes for the screws.

C. WEIGHT THE BOOK ENDS.

1. If pig lead is melted down to be poured with a ladle into the holes, make the bottoms of the holes slightly larger in diameter with a gouge before pouring. This prevents the lead from coming loose when it has cooled.

20

Fig. 3.   Designs for inlaying the book ends.

2. If pig lead or the means for melting it are not available, lead shot may be substituted.

D. SCREW THE BASE TO THE BODY.

E. GIVE THE BOOK ENDS A SUITABLE FINISH AS DIRECTED IN THE CHAPTER ON WOOD FINISHING.

Do not finish the bottom.

F. GLUE A PIECE OF FELT TO THE BOTTOM OF EACH BOOK END.

21

Fig. 4.   An alphabet suitable for carving or inlaying.

22

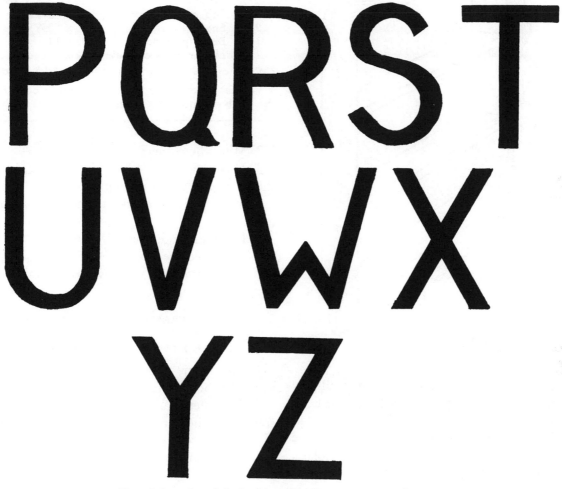

Fig. 4-A. An alphabet suitable for carving or inlaying.

Shadow Box

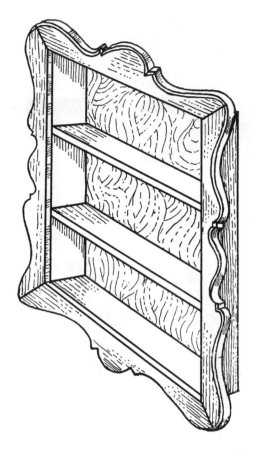

BILL OF MATERIAL

Pieces	Use	Dimensions
2	Frame	½ x 2 x 20½
2	Frame	½ x 2 x 14½
2	Sides	½ x 3½ x 18
2	Top and bottom	½ x 3⅛ x 11
2	Shelves	⅜ x 3⅛ x 11
1	Back (plywood)	⅜ x 11 x 18
1	Mirror (blue or plain)	⅛ x 11 x 17

Finish nails, 3-penny, or 1¼-in., No. 15 brads

NOTE: If a mirror is to be placed in back of the shelves, make the shelves only 3 in. wide.

2. Miter the corners.

3. Make patterns of the side and end as shown in the graph in Figure 1.

4. Make a layout on the frame, and saw it to shape.

5. File and sandpaper all sawed edges.

6. Assemble the frame. See Figure 4, page 55, for instructions on how to assemble a picture frame.

C. NAIL THE FRAME TO THE BOX.

D. PAINT AND ENAMEL THE SHADOW BOX.

1. The frame may be painted or finished to match the furniture.

2. The interior usually is painted a different color from the outside; generally a pastel tint. If a blue mirror is to be placed back of the shelves, the color used should harmonize with blue.

3. Give the box at least two coats of enamel undercoat, followed by one or two coats of enamel.

E. PLACE THE MIRROR INTO THE BOX.

F. NAIL THE BACK IN PLACE.

Be careful not to crack the mirror.

SHADOW boxes are in reality small display cases made to be hung on a wall. They usually serve to hold a small collection of objects in miniature, such as knicknacks. Many of these boxes have a mirror back, either blue or plain, in which the pieces displayed on the shelves are reflected.

PROCEDURE

A. BOX AND SHELVES.

1. Plane and square all pieces except those for the frame.

2. Nail the sides, shelves, top, and bottom pieces together.

B. FRAME.

1. Plane and square the pieces to size.

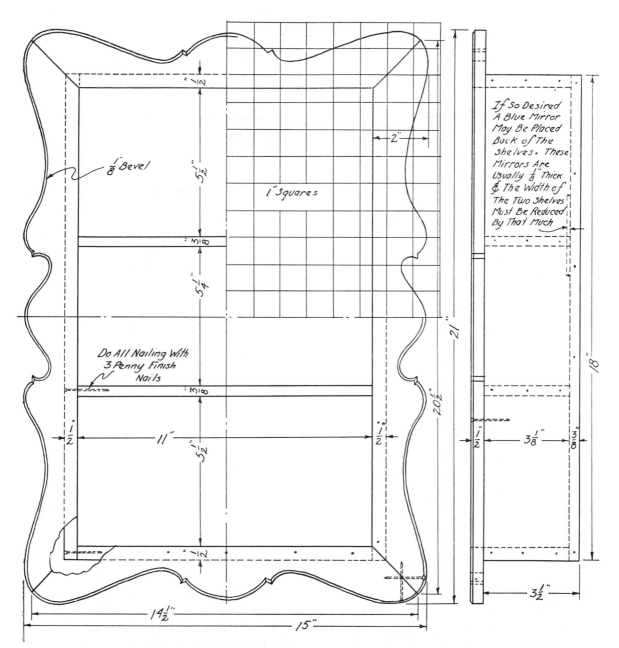

Fig. 1. The frame of the shadow box may be painted or finished to match the furniture, but the inside should be enameled in some pleasing pastel tint.

25

Colonial Electric Candle Lamp

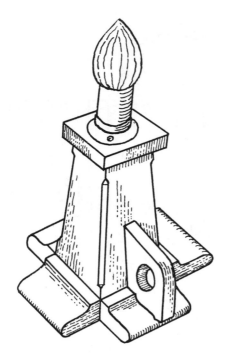

BILL OF MATERIAL

Pieces	Use	Dimensions
2	A and B	¾ x 2 x 5
1	C	2 x 2 x 4½
1	D	½ x 2 x 4⅜
1	E	½ x 2 x 2

One metal flange plate
¾-in. piece of ⅛-in. continuous thread pipe
One candle electric-light socket
Electric-lamp cord, length to suit
One wall plug

THIS makes a nice little bedroom lamp. A higher candle socket than the one shown may be used. With a different type of bulb, a small lamp shade also may be placed over the lamp.

This little lamp is an excellent project in joinery. It requires quite a lot of skill and care to fit the pieces together properly. Very little material is needed to make it, however.

PROCEDURE

A. PIECES A AND B.

1. Plane and square these two pieces to size.
2. Lay out and cut the half-lap joint. Cut the shoulders with a backsaw, and chisel out most of the waste. Then complete the job by smoothing the bottom of each with a router plane.
3. Lay out and cut the groove for the handle in A, Figure 2. This is a stopped groove, or gain, at one end. This end must be chiseled, but the other may be cut like the half lap.

4. Bore the ¾-in. hole shown at A. Drill or bore a hole in B, at the same place as in A. Saw out the square hole with a coping saw, and complete it with a chisel or file.
5. From a pattern made beforehand, lay out and shape the ends of A, as shown in Figure 1.
6. Drill the hole for the electric-lamp cord at one end of B; then shape the ends of B like the ends of A.
7. Glue pieces A and B together.
8. Lay off and cut the handle groove in B.

B. PIECE C.

1. Plane and square the piece to the size given in the bill of material.
2. Lay out and cut the tenon on the bottom; then fit it to the mortise in B.
3. Lay out and cut the through-mortise for the handle in C. Saw the vertical cuts; then trim out the waste with a chisel.
4. Make a layout for tapering the piece C. Rip and plane two opposite sides first; then do the adjacent sides.
5. Lay out and chisel the chamfers on each corner.

NOTE: Do not glue C to the base until the handle has been made and fitted.

C. MAKE AND FIT THE HANDLE, PIECE D.

1. Plane and square the piece of wood to size. Fit it to C.

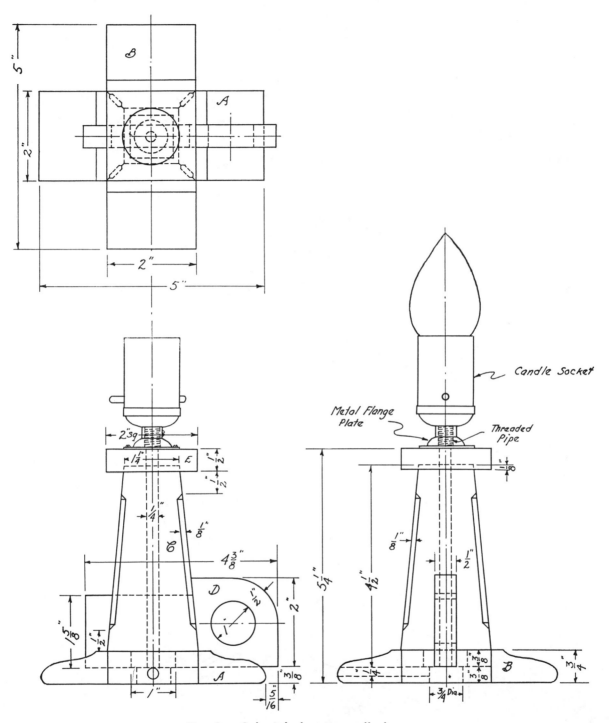

Fig. 1.   Colonial electric candle lamp.

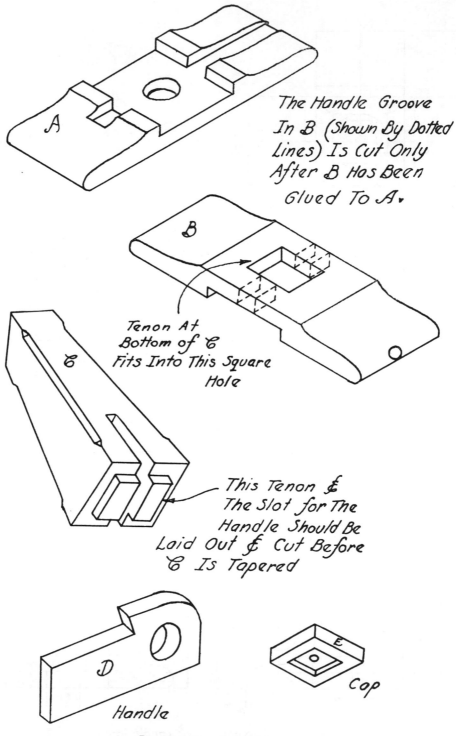

The Handle Groove
In B (Shown By Dotted
Lines) Is Cut Only
After B Has Been
Glued To A.

Tenon At
Bottom of C
Fits Into This Square
Hole

This Tenon &
The Slot for The
Handle Should Be
Laid Out & Cut Before
C Is Tapered

Handle

Cap

Fig. 2.   Details of lamp.

2. Locate and bore the 1-in. hole. In order not to split the handle when this is done, first drill a small pilot hole nearly as large in diameter as the lead screw of the bit. Bore only halfway through the handle from each side.

3. Make a layout, and cut the haunch on the top of the handle.

4. Round the end of the handle.

D. ASSEMBLE AND GLUE THE PARTS THUS FAR COMPLETED.

E. DRILL OR BORE A $\frac{1}{4}$-IN. HOLE VERTICALLY THROUGH THE ASSEMBLED PARTS FOR THE LAMP CORD, AS SHOWN IN THE SIDE AND END VIEWS IN FIGURE I.

F. MAKE THE CAP E, AND FIT IT TO THE TOP OF C.

1. Plane and square the piece to size.
2. Lay out and cut the shallow mortise.
3. Drill or bore the $\frac{1}{4}$-in. hole.
4. Glue the cap to the top of C.

G. GIVE THE PROJECT A SUITABLE FINISH.

See the chapter on wood finishing.

H. FASTEN THE FLANGE PLATE TO THE TOP OF THE CAP WITH SCREWS.

Screw the threaded pipe to the flange plate.

I. WIRE THE LAMP FOR ELECTRICITY.

Screw the base of the socket to the threaded pipe while the socket is separated from the base to prevent twisting the wire.

Spool Rack for the Sewing Room

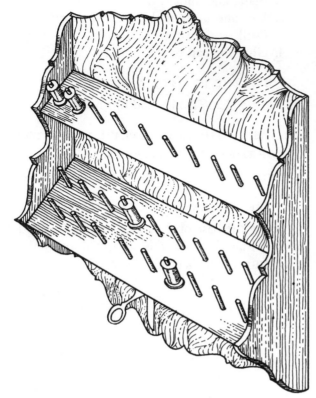

BILL OF MATERIAL

Pieces	Use	Dimensions
2	Sides	⅝ x 5 x 14¾
1	Bottom shelf	⅝ x 6¼ x 18
1	Upper shelf	⅝ x 4⅜ x 18
1	Back	⅜ plywood x 18¾ x 18¾
26	Dowels	¼ diameter x 2⅜

4-penny finish nails
⅝ in. brass cup hooks or screw hooks (as many as necessary)

THIS practical project is attractive and should be welcomed by mother as a gift, on some appropriate occasion, for her sewing room.

PROCEDURE

1. Plane and square the sides and shelves to the sizes given in the bill of material.

2. Lay out and plane 45-deg. angles on the back edges of the shelves.

3. Locate and drill or bore holes into the shelves for the dowels.

4. Cut the dowels, and glue them in place. Clean off the glue around the joints after it has dried.

If the glue is put into the holes with a small stick, with proper care, very little glue will have to be removed later.

5. Lay out and cut the rabbet on the back edge of each side.

6. Make a full-size pattern of the sides as shown in Figure 2.

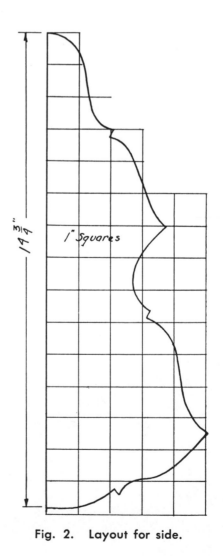

1" Squares

14¾"

Fig. 2.   Layout for side.

30

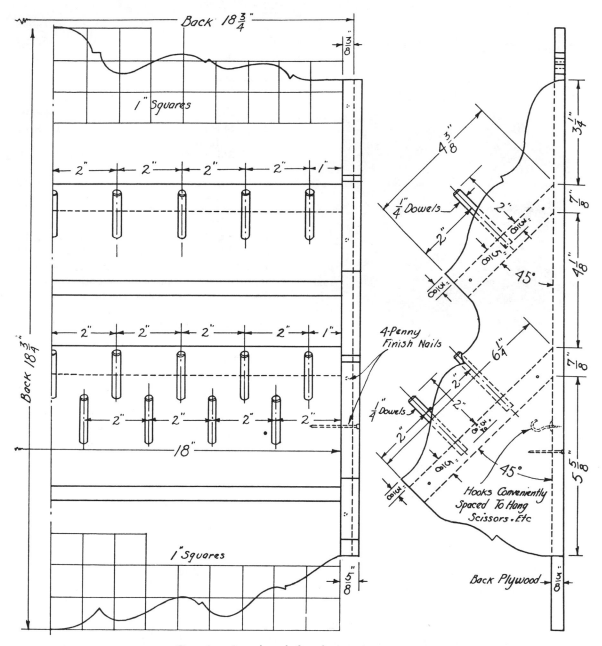

Fig. 1. Spool rack for the sewing room.

7. Saw the sides to shape with a coping saw, or by some other means.

8. File all sawed edges. Sandpaper all filed edges.

9. Assemble the shelves and sides with 4-penny finish nails or with 1½-in., No. 15 brads.

10. Plane and square the edges of the back.

11. Sandpaper the back.

12. Make full-size half patterns of the top and bottom of the back as shown in Figure 1.

13. Transfer these designs to the back.

14. Saw the top and bottom to shape.

15. File and sandpaper all sawed edges.

16. Nail the back to the assembled parts.

17. Give the rack a suitable finish. See the chapter on wood finishing.

Magazine Holder

BILL OF MATERIAL

Pieces	Use	Dimensions
2	Stiles for middle frame	¾ x 3 x 11¼
4	Stiles for outside frames	¾ x 3 x 9½
3	Top rails for all frames	¾ x 4 x 12
3	Bottom rails for all frames	¾ x 2 x 12
1	Floor	⅝ x 7 x 17
2	Feet	¾ x 1½ x 11

Nine 1¼-in., No. 8 f.h. bright wood screws
Four 1-in., No. 8 f.h. bright wood screws

THE magazine holder is a good handwork project. It will hold the largest as well as the smallest magazines. The heart-shaped cutout at the top of the middle frame makes a convenient handle for moving it about from place to place.

PROCEDURE

A. FRAMES.

1. Square the rails and stiles, planing them to size.

2. Lay out and cut the mortises (Fig. 1). Bore holes close together for mortises; then clean them out with chisels.

3. Lay out and cut the tenons on all rails (Fig. 2).

a) Square lines around all rails with a try square for the shoulder cuts. Make gauge lines for the cheek cuts.

b) Clamp a square-edged block to the shoulder line, and saw the shoulder cut with a backsaw.

c) Chisel away the waste to make the cheek cut, completing it by chiseling across the grain of the wood.

d) Lay off the width of the tenon with a gauge.

e) Saw along these lines with a backsaw from the end of the tenon to the shoulder.

f) Saw off the waste exactly to the shoulder line, or leave a little to chisel off to the shoulder line. Be sure the shoulder is perfectly square before assembling the frame.

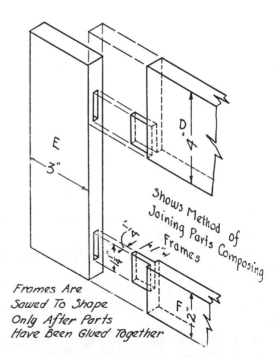

Frames Are
Sawed To Shape
Only After Parts
Have Been Glued Together

Fig. 2.   Joining parts of frames.

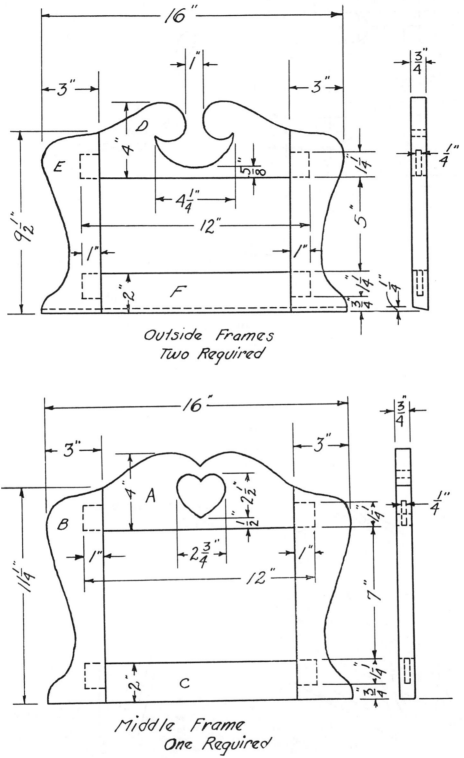

Outside Frames
Two Required

Middle Frame
One Required

Fig. 1. Outside and middle for magazine holder.

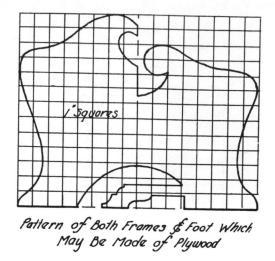

Pattern of Both Frames & Foot Which
May Be Made of Plywood

Fig. 3. Frame and foot pattern.

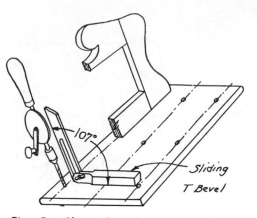

Fig. 5. Shows how holes are drilled.

4. Make a trial assembly of all frames.

5. Glue all frames.

6. Plane the joints on both sides of all frames to make them perfectly flat and smooth; then sandpaper the sides and inside edges of each frame.

7. Plane the angles on the lower edges of the outside frames (Fig. 1).

a) Draw a horizontal line ¼ in. up from the bottom on one side of the outside frame.

b) Set the sliding T bevel to the angle shown at the bottom of the outside frame, and use it to test the angle as you plane it.

8. Draw a full-size pattern like the one shown in Figure 3. The left half is a half pattern of the large middle frame, while the right half is a half pattern of the outside frame. At the bottom is a pattern of the foot.

9. Lay these patterns on the frames, and trace the designs thereon.

10. Saw the frames to shape.

11. File the edges smooth; then sandpaper the edges.

B. FLOOR.

1. Plane the board to the sizes given in Figure 4.

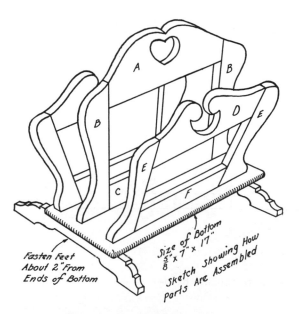

Fasten Feet About 2" From Ends of Bottom

Size of Bottom ⅝" x 7" x 17"

Sketch Showing How Parts Are Assembled

Fig. 4. Assembled parts.

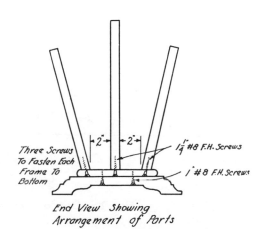

Three Screws To Fasten Each Frame To Bottom

1¼" #8 F.H. Screws

1" #8 F.H. Screws

End View Showing Arrangement of Parts

Fig. 6. End view of parts.

34

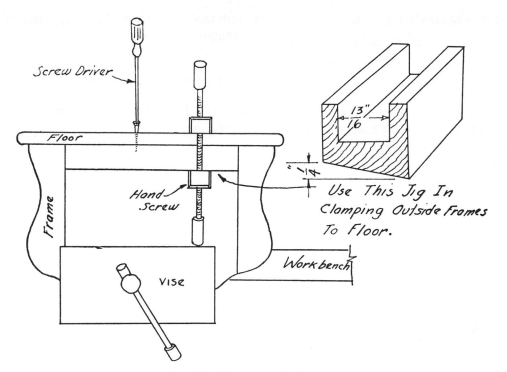

Fig. 7. Clamping jig in use.

2. Draw lines ⅛ in. in from the edges of both sides, and round these edges to the lines with a hand plane, file, and sandpaper.

3. On the floor, draw three center lines to mark the position of each frame, as shown in Figures 5 and 6. These center lines will be 2¾ in. apart.

4. Set the sliding T bevel to an angle of 107 deg., and at this angle drill three holes for each outside frame for 1¼-in., No. 8 f.h. wood screws.

5. Drill holes for the middle frame perpendicular to the floor.

6. Countersink these holes underneath the floor.

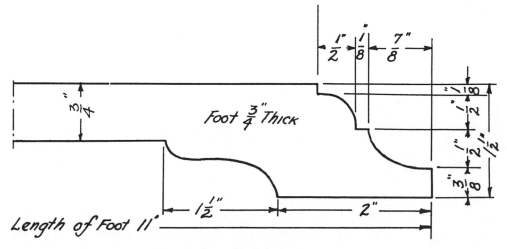

Fig. 8. Detail of foot.

C. SCREW FRAMES TO FLOOR.

1. Clamp the middle frame to the floor; then fasten these parts to a vise as shown in Figure 7, and screw them together.

2. Clamp the outside frames to the floor, each in its turn. Use the jig to help hold the clamp straight on the frames, and screw the frames to the floor.

D. FEET.

Square up the stock, lay out the pattern, and saw it to shape (Fig. 8); then file and sandpaper the feet.

E. FASTEN THE FEET TO THE FLOOR ABOUT 2 IN. FROM EACH END.

F. GIVE THE PROJECT A SUITABLE FINISH. See the chapter on wood finishing.

Pump Lamp

THE mechanical action involved whereby the handle of the pump switches on the light makes this project appeal to grownups as well as boys. When completed, it is a nice lamp for a boy's or a girl's room.

PROCEDURE

A. BASE.

1. Plane and square the base to the size given in the bill of material.
2. Bevel the edges.
3. Bore the holes to wire the base.

B. SIDES.

1. Plane and square the sides.
2. Lay out and chisel the chamfers on the wide sides.
3. Make the hole for the pump handle in one of the narrow sides.

BILL OF MATERIAL

Pieces	Use	Dimensions
1	Base	¾ x 4⅝ x 9¼
2	Sides of pump	⅜ x 2¼ x 8¼
2	Sides of pump	⅜ x 3 x 8¼
1	Top of pump	¾ x 3½ x 3½
1	Pump handle	⅜ x 1⅛ x 7
		(This is slightly larger than the finished size)
2	Sides of trough	3⁄16 x 1½ x 4
		(This is slightly larger than the finished size)
1	Large end of trough	¼ x 1⅝ x 1½
1	Small end of trough	¼ x 1¼ x 1½

Dowel — ½ in. diameter by 2 in. long, for spout
Pull-chain brass-shell socket threaded for ⅛-in. pipe
Continuous threaded pipe, ⅛ x 1 in. long
Brads — 1¼ in., No. 16; ¾ in., No. 20; 1 in., No. 18
One 1¾-in., No. 15 brad to pivot pump handle
Lamp cord, length to suit
Wall plug
Lamp shade, largest diameter about 12 in.

a) Drill or bore a hole, and saw it to the previously laid out shape with a coping saw.

b) Chisel or file the 30-deg. angle at the bottom of this hole.

4. Bore the hole for the spout.
5. Nail the sides together with 1-in., No. 18 brads.

C. TOP.

1. Plane and square the block.
2. Chamfer the edges.
3. Drill the hole for the threaded pipe, as shown in the front view, Figure 1.

D. HANDLE AND TROUGH SIDES.

1. Make full-size patterns for these pieces, as shown in Figure 3.
2. Plane the wood to thickness, and transfer the patterns to the wood.
3. Saw, file, and sandpaper the pieces to shape.
4. Fasten the handle to the hole which was made for it.

37

E. FASTEN THE HANDLE TO THE PUMP.

1. Drill as far as the hole from one side.

2. Fit the handle to the hole so it will swing low enough to pull the lamp chain and switch off the light.

3. Drive the 1¾-in., No. 15 brad into the side and through the handle, into the opposite side of the hole.

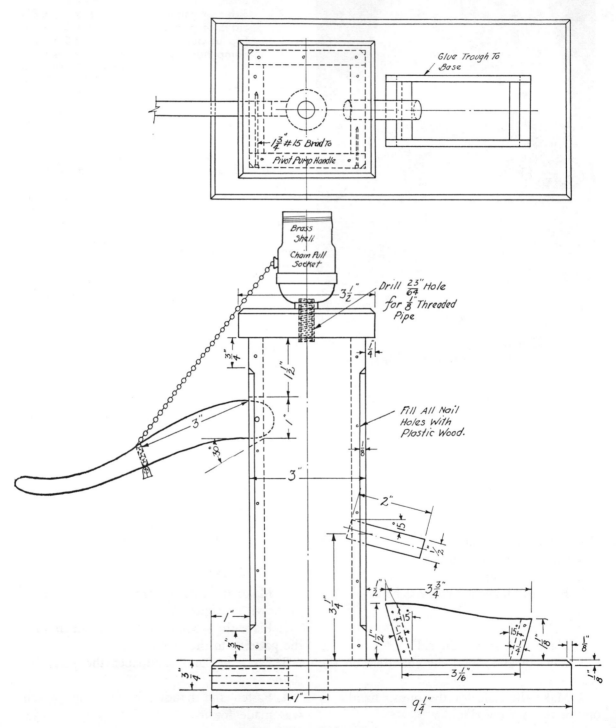

Fig. 1. Pump lamp.

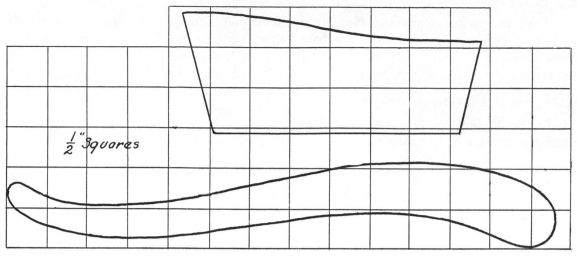

$\frac{1}{2}$" Squares

Fig. 3.   Details of pump handle and trough side.

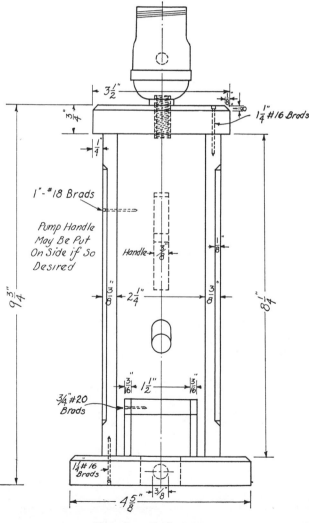

Fig. 2.   End view.

F. GLUE THE SPOUT TO THE PUMP.

G. FASTEN THE PUMP TO THE BASE.

1. Locate the place where the pump will be nailed onto the base by placing the pump on the base in its proper position.

2. Trace around the sides of the pump with a pencil, thus marking the position on the base.

3. Remove the pump from the base, and ³/₁₆ in. in from these lines, drill nail holes through the base.

4. Nail the base to the assembled sides.

H. FASTEN THE TOP TO THE SIDES.

1. Locate and drill nail holes as was done on the base.

2. Nail the top to the assembled sides.

I. MAKE THE TROUGH, AND FASTEN IT TO THE BASE.

1. Cut the ends to size, and plane the angles.

2. Assemble the trough.

3. Glue the trough to the base.

J. WIRE THE LAMP FOR ELECTRICITY.

1. Screw the threaded pipe to the top as shown in the front view, Figure 1.

2. Thread the wire through from the base to the socket.

3. Take the socket apart, and fasten the wires. Reassemble the socket. Screw the base of the socket to the pipe before reassembling the socket to avoid twisting the wires.

K. FASTEN THE CHAIN TO THE HANDLE.

1. Locate the hole on the handle at a place where the chain will just clear the top. The dimension given in Figure 1 is approximately right, but may have to be changed a little.

2. Drill the hole.

3. Remove the bell-shaped end from the ball at the end of the chain. Slip the chain through the hole and refasten the bell.

L. GIVE THE LAMP A SUITABLE FINISH.

Combination Bathroom Seat and Clothes Hamper

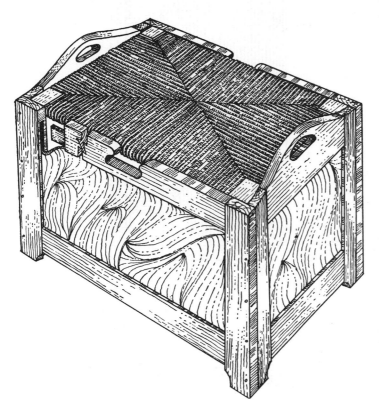

THIS project is a cross between the small paneled wastebasket project and the rush-seated stool project.

As with the small paneled wastebasket project, it is advisable to have the grooves in the rails and stiles made with a dado head on a circular saw when rough-dimensioned stock is used. In the author's classes it has been the custom to issue stock for such projects with thicknesses ranging from ⅟₁₆ to ⅛ in. thicker, from ⅛ to ¼ in. wider, and about ¼ in. longer than the dimensions given in the bill of material. Such stock always should be prepared well in advance and stored until needed, to prevent warping, waste of material, and waste of valuable time.

BILL OF MATERIAL

Pieces	Use	Dimensions
4	Rails	¾ x 3 x 15½
2	Rails	¾ x 3 x 11½
2	Rails (with handles)	¾ x 5 x 11½
4	Stiles	¾ x 1½ x 16¾
4	Stiles	¾ x 2¼ x 16
1	Floor	⅝ x 12½ x 16½
2	Seat-frame stretchers	¾ x 1¾ x 16½
2	Seat-frame stretchers	¾ x 1¾ x 12½
4	Corner blocks for seat frame	¼ x 1¾ x 1¾
4	Strips to support seat frame	½ x ½ x 6½ (Long sides)
2	Strips to support seat frame	½ x ½ x 11½
2	Plywood panels	¼ x 9¾ x 14¼
2	Plywood panels	¼ x 9¾ x 10¼

Approximately 1½ lb. ³⁄₁₆-in. multicolored art-fiber weaving material for the seat

1-in., No. 8 f.h. wood screws
4-penny finish nails or 1½-in., No. 15 brads

PROCEDURE

A. SQUARE UP THE STILES AND RAILS, PLANING THEM TO THE SIZES GIVEN IN THE BILL OF MATERIAL.

If the grooves have been cut before squaring begins, be sure to leave ¼ in. on each side of the groove when planing the stock to thickness.

B. LAY OUT THE MORTISES ON THE STILES.

C. CUT THE MORTISES.

Bore ¼-in. holes close together where the mortises are to go; then clean out the mortises with chisels.

D. LAY OUT AND CUT THE TENONS ON THE RAILS.

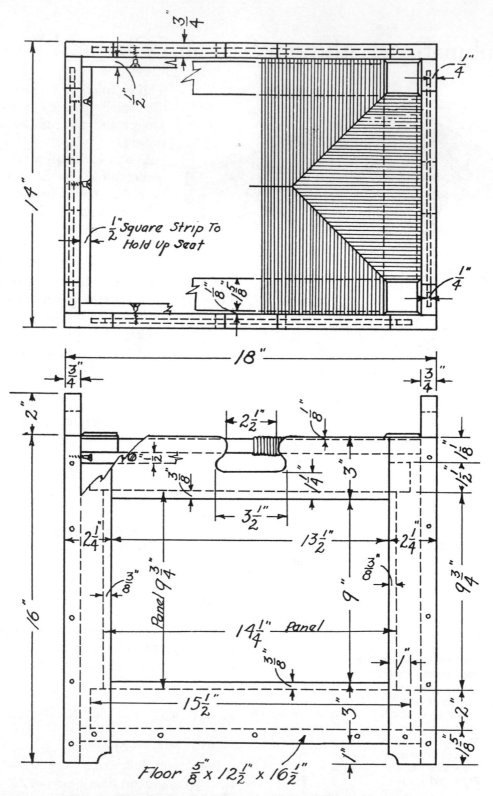

Fig. 1. Combination bathroom seat and clothes hamper.

1. For the shoulder cuts, square lines around the ends of the rails with a try square.

2. Gauge lines around the edges and ends of the rails for the cheek cuts.

3. Clamp a square-edged block of wood to the shoulder line, and saw the shoulder cut with a backsaw.

4. Make the cheek cuts with a chisel, completing them by chiseling across the grain.

5. Cut the tenons to the proper width, and fit them to the mortises.

E. CUT THE PANELS TO SIZE, AND SANDPAPER THEM.

F. AFTER MAKING TRIAL ASSEMBLIES OF ALL FRAMES, GLUE THEM UP.

Put glue on mortises and tenons only. Do not glue the panels into the grooves, but leave them free.

G. PLANE ALL JOINTS TO MAKE THEM SMOOTH AND EVEN, IF NECESSARY, THEN SANDPAPER BOTH SIDES OF EACH FRAME.

H. SQUARE UP ALL FRAMES, MAKING OPPOSITE SIDES EQUAL IN SIZE.

I. LAY OUT THE SHAPES AT THE TOP AND BOTTOM OF EACH FRAME, INCLUDING THE HANDLES.

J. CUT THE FRAMES TO SHAPE.

1. Bore ¾-in. holes at each end of the handle, and saw out the remainder with a coping saw.

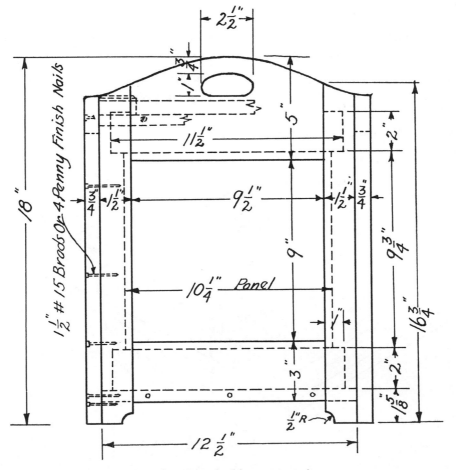

Fig. 2.   Detail of hamper ends.

2. Saw the curves at the top and bottom, file them smooth, and sandpaper them.

K. NAIL THE FOUR FRAMES TOGETHER WITH 4-PENNY FINISH NAILS.

L. PLANE BOTH SIDES OF THE FLOOR.

M. PLACE THE FEET OF THE ASSEMBLED FRAMES UPON ONE SIDE OF THE FLOOR BOARD, AND MARK EACH CORNER WITH A WELL-POINTED PENCIL.

Connect these corners with lines drawn with a straightedge. Plane the edges to these lines.

N. SLIP THE FLOOR INTO POSITION, AND NAIL IT FIRMLY WITH 4-PENNY FINISH NAILS.

O. SET ALL NAILS, AND FILL THE HOLES WITH PLASTIC WOOD.

P. CUT AND SQUARE STRIPS TO SUPPORT THE SEAT FRAME, AND SCREW THE STRIPS TO THE SIDES AND ENDS.

Drill and countersink screw holes.

Q. MAKE THE SEAT FRAME.

1. Cut each rail to length; then make end-lap joints at each corner. Glue the end-lap joints.

2. Plane a strip of wood to the width and thickness of the corner blocks; then cut four blocks from this strip on the miter box. File the edges smooth, and glue the blocks to the top of the seat frame as shown in Figure 3.

3. Saw off ⅛ in. on each side of the seat frame to make place for the weaving material, as shown in Figure 3. This may best be done on a band saw. Soften the sharp corners of the seat frame.

R. STAIN, OR PAINT AND ENAMEL THE PROJECT.

S. WEAVE THE SEAT.

Clamp the seat frame in a metalworker's vise, and proceed weaving according to instructions O and P in the directions for making the rush-seated stool, pages 51 and 52.

T. IF THE STOOL WAS STAINED, PUT ON THE REMAINING FINISHING COATS.

Rub the final coat of varnish with pumice stone and oil.

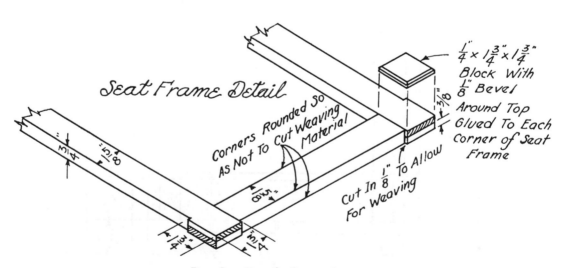

Fig. 3. Detail of seat frame.

Small Paneled Wastebasket

BILL OF MATERIAL

Pieces	Use	Dimensions
4	Stiles	¾ x 2¼ x 13½
4	Stiles	¾ x 1½ x 13½
8	Rails	¾ x 3 x 7½
1	Floor	⅝ x 8½ x 8½
4	Plywood panels	¼ x 6¼ x 7¾
4-penny finish nails		

PROCEDURE

A. SQUARE UP THE STILES AND RAILS, AND PLANE THEM TO THE SIZES GIVEN IN THE BILL OF MATERIAL.

If the grooves have been cut before squaring begins, be sure to leave ¼ in. on each side of the groove when planing the stock to thickness.

B. LAY OUT THE MORTISES ON THE STILES.

C. CUT THE MORTISES.

Bore ¼-in. holes close together where the mortises are to go; then clean out the mortises with chisels.

D. LAY OUT AND CUT THE TENONS ON THE RAILS.

1. Square lines around the ends of the rails for the shoulder cuts, with a try square.

2. Gauge lines around the edges and ends of the rails for the cheek cuts.

3. Clamp a square-edged block of wood to the shoulder line, and saw the shoulder cut with a backsaw.

This operation also may be performed on a miter box. Care must be taken to work exactly to the line.

4. Make the cheek cuts with a chisel, completing them by chiseling across the grain.

5. Cut the tenons to the proper width, and fit them to the mortises.

E. CUT THE PANELS TO SIZE, AND SAND-PAPER THEM.

THE small paneled wastebasket does not take quite as long a time to build as the rush-seated stool, but it compares favorably with it in other respects as an ideal project.

It has been found advisable, in cutting stock for this project, first to make the grooves in the rails and stiles on a variety saw with a dado head, since this operation is rather difficult to perform properly with hand tools. It might be well to practice grooving one frame with hand tools to become acquainted with the proper procedure.

The wastebasket has a great many features to recommend it as a good project. It does not require a great deal of material, and is attractive and useful when made. While the many operations in its construction teach a variety of skills, it is not too difficult to make.

This also is an excellent project to decorate with decalcomania, stenciled designs, or hand-painted designs.

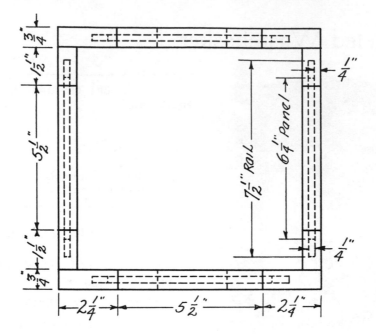

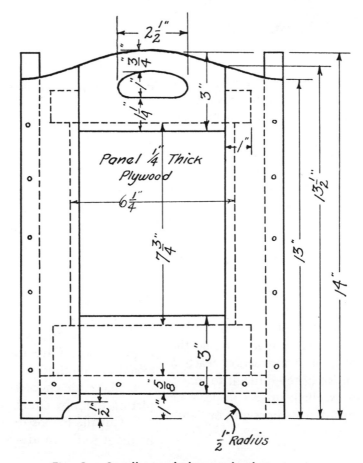

Fig. 1. Small paneled wastebasket.

46

F. AFTER MAKING TRIAL ASSEMBLIES OF ALL FRAMES, GLUE THEM UP.

Put glue on mortises and tenons only. Do not glue the panels into the grooves, but leave them free.

G. PLANE ALL JOINTS TO MAKE THEM SMOOTH AND EVEN; THEN SANDPAPER BOTH SIDES OF EACH FRAME.

H. SQUARE UP ALL FRAMES, MAKING OPPOSITE SIDES EQUAL IN SIZE.

I. LAY OUT THE SHAPE OF THE TOP AND BOTTOM OF EACH FRAME, INCLUDING THE HANDLES ON TWO SIDES.

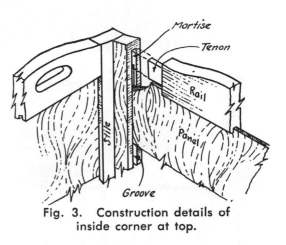

Fig. 3. Construction details of inside corner at top.

J. CUT THE FRAMES TO SHAPE.

1. Bore ¾-in. holes at each end of the handle, and saw out the remainder of the opening with a coping saw.

2. Saw the curves at the top and bottom, file them smooth, and sandpaper them.

K. NAIL THE FOUR FRAMES TOGETHER WITH 4-PENNY FINISH NAILS.

L. PLANE BOTH SIDES OF THE FLOOR.

M. PLACE THE FEET OF THE ASSEMBLED FRAMES UPON ONE SIDE OF THE FLOOR BOARD.

Mark each corner with a well-pointed pencil. Connect these corners with lines drawn with a straightedge. Plane the edges to these lines.

N. SLIP THE FLOOR INTO POSITION, AND NAIL IT FIRMLY WITH 4-PENNY FINISH NAILS.

O. SET ALL NAILS, AND FILL THE HOLES WITH PLASTIC WOOD.

P. SANDPAPER WHERE NECESSARY, AND GIVE THE WASTEBASKET A SUITABLE FINISH.

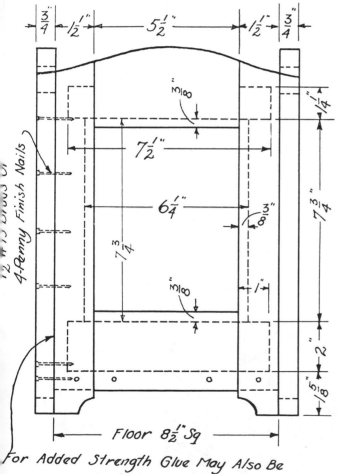

Fig. 2. Detail of sides.

Rush-Seated Stool

BILL OF MATERIAL

Pieces	Use	Dimensions
4	Legs	1⅝ x 1⅝ x 16½
4	Rails	¾ x 3 x 12½
4	Rails	¾ x 1½ x 12½
4	Seat stretchers	¾ x 1¾ x 13¼
4	Blocks (corners of seat)	¼ x 1¾ x 1¾

1 lb. of ³⁄₁₆-in. multicolored art fiber for seat weaving

This art fiber is manufactured of kraft paper, and is widely used as a satisfactory substitute for genuine rush for seat weaving. It may be purchased in 1-lb. boxes or in rolls containing approximately 25 lb. Seats made of this material have been in constant use in the author's home for the past twenty years and are still in as good condition as when originally put on.

THE rush-seated stool makes a comfortable seat, and the woven seat makes it an attractive piece of furniture. Learning to weave such a seat is a worth-while project. The stool also is a good project from which to learn how to make mortise-and-tenon joints.

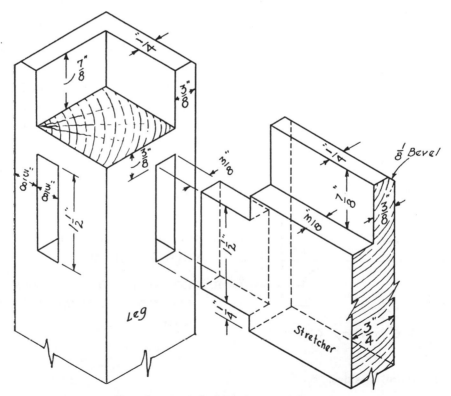

Fig. 2. Detail of joint at top of stool.

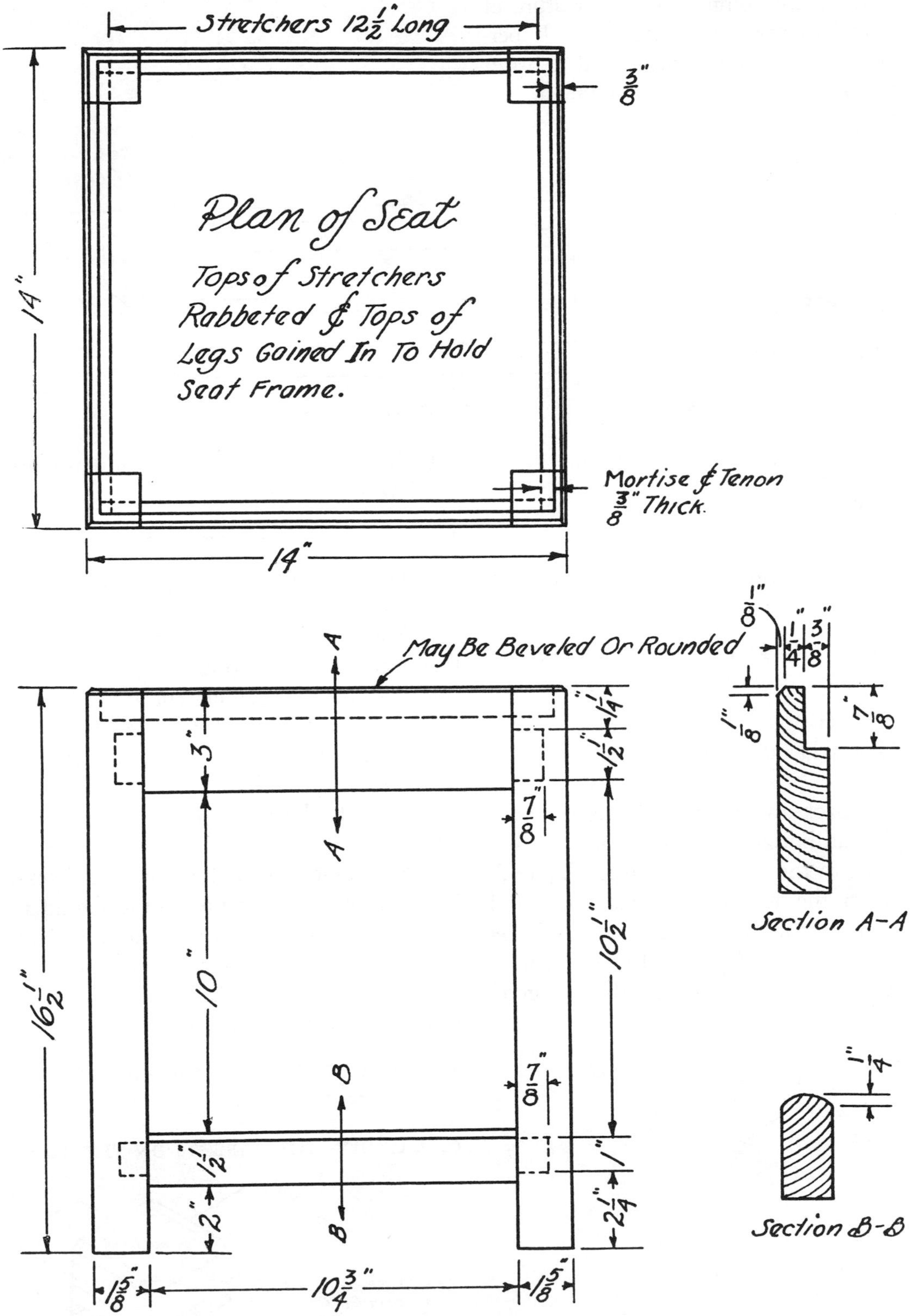

Stretchers 12½" Long

3/8"

Plan of Seat

Tops of Stretchers
Rabbeted & Tops of
Legs Gained In To Hold
Seat Frame.

14"

14"

Mortise & Tenon
3/8" Thick.

May Be Beveled Or Rounded

A

1/8"

1/8" 1/4" 3/8"

3"

1/4"
1/2"

7/8"

A

1/8"

7/8"

Section A-A

16½"

10"

10½"

B

7/8"

B

½"

2"

1"

2¼"

1/4"

1⅝"

10¾"

1⅝"

Section B-B

Fig. 1.   Rush-seated stool.

49

The legs and rails on this stool are flush on the outside at the joints. This is a feature of all fine early American cabinetwork. It permits making the tenon longer and a better dressing of the joint after gluing. It also permits easier application of finish, especially where hand rubbing is done.

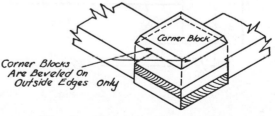

Fig. 4. Chiseling the corner of the leg.

PROCEDURE

A. SQUARE UP THE LEGS.

B. LAY OUT ALL MORTISES.

Use a try square across the grain; gauge with the grain.

C. CUT THE MORTISES.

Use a ⁵⁄₁₆-in. bit to bore the holes; then chisel them out.

D. LAY OUT AND REMOVE THE CORNERS AT THE TOPS OF THE LEGS AS SHOWN IN FIGURE 2.

1. Make a layout with a gauge and a try square.
2. Use a backsaw to saw across corners both vertically and horizontally (Fig. 3).
3. Chisel to the line as shown in Figure 3.
4. Clamp the leg to the bench top, and remove the remainder of the waste from the corner as shown in Figure 4. Be sure to have the end of the leg clamped firmly to a good solid bench top, and then, with a sharp chisel, the job will be easy.

E. LAY OUT AND CUT THE TENONS.

1. Use a gauge and a try square to make the layout.
2. Make the shoulder cut on the side of the tenon first. Clamp a square-edged block to the line, and saw the shoulder cut with a backsaw.
3. Chisel away the waste to make the cheek cut, completing it by chiseling directly across the grain of the wood.
4. Lay off the width of the tenon with a gauge.
5. Saw along these lines with a backsaw from the end of the tenon to the shoulder.
6. Saw off the waste exactly to the shoulder line, or leave a little to chisel off to the shoulder line. Be sure the shoulder is perfectly square before assembling the project.

F. MAKE A TRIAL ASSEMBLY TO CHECK ALL JOINTS.

G. LAY OUT THE RABBETS ON THE TOP IN-

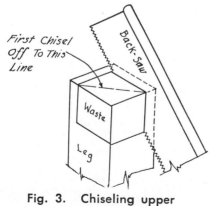

Fig. 3. Chiseling upper end of leg.

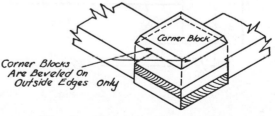

Fig. 5. Shaping corner blocks.

Fig. 6. Using router plane.

SIDE EDGES OF THE SEAT STRETCHERS AS SHOWN IN FIGURE 2.

H. CLAMP TWO OF THESE SEAT STRETCHERS SIDE BY SIDE ON TOP OF THE WORKBENCH BETWEEN THE VISE DOG AND THE BENCH STOP (FIG. 3, P. 54).

Cut along the rabbet line on the inside of the stretcher with a knife, using a straight-edge to keep the knife line straight.

I. CUT THE RABBETS ON BOTH STRETCHERS SIMULTANEOUSLY WITH A ROUTER PLANE (FIG. 6).

J. ROUND THE UPPER EDGES OF THE BOTTOM STRETCHERS.

K. GLUE UP THE STOOL.

1. The best procedure is to first glue up two opposite sides.

2. The joints may be further strengthened by drilling holes through them and driving in wooden pegs, if so desired. This was a feature of early colonial craftsmanship.

L. MAKE THE SEAT FRAME.

1. Cut each rail to length; then make end-lap joints at each corner. Glue the end-lap joints.

2. Plane a strip of wood to the width and thickness of the corner blocks; then cut four from this strip on the miter box. File the edges of the blocks smooth, and glue them to the top of the seat frame as shown in Figure 7. Note that these corner blocks must not be beveled nor rounded on the inside edges.

3. Saw off ⅛ in. on each side of the seat frame to make place for the weaving material

as shown in Figure 7. This may best be done on a band saw.

M. DRESS ALL JOINTS ON THE OUTSIDE WITH A PLANE UNTIL THEY ARE PERFECTLY LEVEL AND SMOOTH. ALSO REMOVE ANY GLUE AT THE JOINTS ON THE INSIDE SURFACES.

Then sandpaper the entire stool thoroughly.

N. STAIN THE STOOL.

O. WEAVE THE SEAT.

1. Clamp one rail of the seat frame in a metalworker's vise, with the top of the frame facing out, and proceed to weave according to the following directions, as shown in Figure 8:

a) Tie a slip knot at 1.

b) Go from the bottom of rung 9 to the top of rung 2.

c) Go around rung 2 to the top of rung 3.

d) Go around rung 3 to the top of rung 4.

e) Go around rung 4 to the top of rung 5

f) Go around rung 5 to the top of rung 6

g) Go around rung 6 to the top of rung 7

h) Go around rung 7 to the top of rung 8

i) Go around rung 8 to the top of rung 9

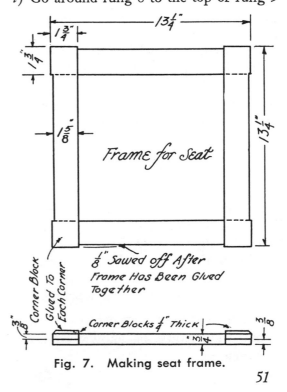

Fig. 7. Making seat frame.

51

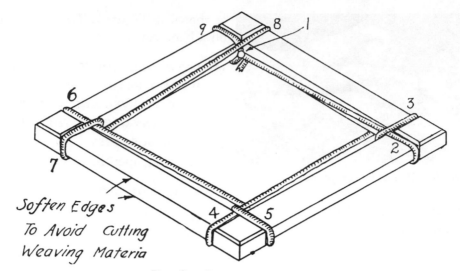

Soften Edges
To Avoid Cutting
Weaving Materia

Fig. 8. Steps in weaving.

j) Go around rung 9. Then repeat all operations until the seat has been completed.

2. Before beginning to weave, it is best to wrap about three layers of the art fiber around a stick about 12 or 14 in. long. Drill a small hole into each end of the stick. Insert the end of the cord through one hole, and wrap on three or four layers.

3. Let two people do the weaving. The one who holds the stick should stand to the left of the one who does the actual weaving. Every time the cord is passed around a seat rung, the person holding the stick passes it through the opening in the seat frame from back to front. It is also his job to keep the twist of the cord properly regulated as the weaving proceeds. When the end of one piece of cord has been reached, tack it to the bottom of a stretcher. Tack on a new end, and proceed in this way until the entire seat has been woven. When the opening in the center of the seat becomes too small to pass the stick through it, pull the end of the cord through instead until all of the weaving has been done. When the weaving has proceeded to a point shown in Figure 9, where the jaws of the metalworker's vise will be too wide, then fasten one corner of the frame in a woodworker's vise to complete the weaving.

P. STUFF THE SEAT UNDERNEATH WITH OLD NEWSPAPER OR BROWN WRAPPING PAPER.

This tightens the seat, and helps to give it a better shape.

This is best accomplished with a thin-bladed paddle-shaped stick of wood. Cut the paper into long strips before inserting it between the two bottom layers of the seat. (There will be three layers when the seat has been woven.)

Q. SHELLAC THE SEAT AND THE REST OF THE STOOL.

R. GIVE THE STOOL TWO COATS OF FLOOR VARNISH, RUBBING THE FINAL COAT DOWN WITH PUMICE STONE AND OIL.

Fig. 9. Frame in vise to complete weaving.

52

Tilting Photograph Frame

patience, and the need for observing care and being exact when learning the art of cabinetmaking.

PROCEDURE

A. SELECT THE STOCK.

Use mahogany, maple, or walnut, preferably.

B. PLANE AND SQUARE ALL STOCK.

1. Leave the frame stock at least ½-in. extra length.

2. Supports and the top need not be planed on all sides.

C. BASE.

1. Cut a shallow rabbet around one edge and two ends of the base to start forming the molding, as shown in Figures 1 and 1-A.

a) Run gauge lines 1 in. in and ¹⁄₁₆ in. down on the long side. Mark with a knife and a try square instead of a gauge across the sides and edges at each end.

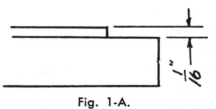

Fig. 1-A.

b) Clamp a straightedge to the gauge line, and score deeply with a knife.

c) Plane a rabbet with a router plane or a rabbet plane.

2. Round the edge of the base to form the molding, using a wide chisel, plane, file, and sandpaper.

BILL OF MATERIAL

Pieces	Use	Dimensions
1	Base	⅞ x 3 x 16¾
2	Supports	½ x 3½ x 10½
2	Frame	½ x ¾ x 11
2	Frame	½ x ¾ x 9
1	Top	¼ x 2¾ x 8¾
1	Glass	8 x 10
1	Cardboard	8 x 10
2	Small glue blocks	

Two 1¼-in., No. 8 f.h. wood screws
Two 1-in., No. 6 r.h. brass screws
1-in., No. 18 brads for frame
¾-in., No. 20 brads to fasten top

THE photograph frame, although it appears to be a simple project, requires considerable painstaking effort to build.

The frame itself is intended for a standard 8 by 10-in. portrait-size photograph. All other parts of the frame have been proportioned to this size.

Some difficult operations will be encountered in working with pieces of wood as light and small as this. However, this will teach

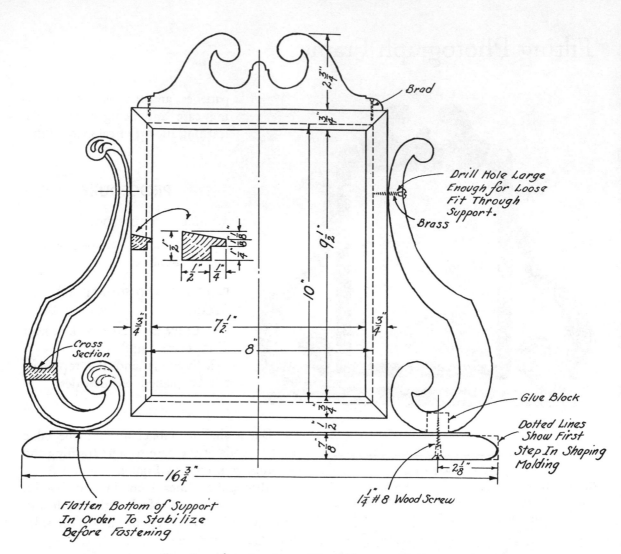

Brad

Drill Hole Large
Enough for Loose
Fit Through
Support.

Brass

Cross
Section

Glue Block

Dotted Lines
Show First
Step In Shaping
Molding

Flatten Bottom of Support
In Order To Stabilize
Before Fastening

$1\frac{1}{4}$" #8 Wood Screw

Fig. 1.   Sheraton-type tilting photograph frame.

D. FRAME.

1. Rabbet the frame material.

Clamp two strips to the bench, and fasten them between a vise dog and a bench stop, as shown in Figure 3. Cut rabbets in both strips at the same time with a router plane.

2. Lay out the angle or slope on the face side of the strips. See the cross section in Figure 1.

3. Plane the faces to this angle.

4. Saw miters to make the joints, using a 45-deg. angle on the miter box.

The rabbeted side must be down when cutting the miters.

5. Assemble the frame as shown in Figure 4.

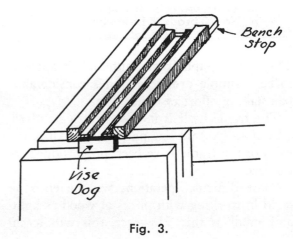

Bench
Stop

Vise
Dog

Fig. 3.

54

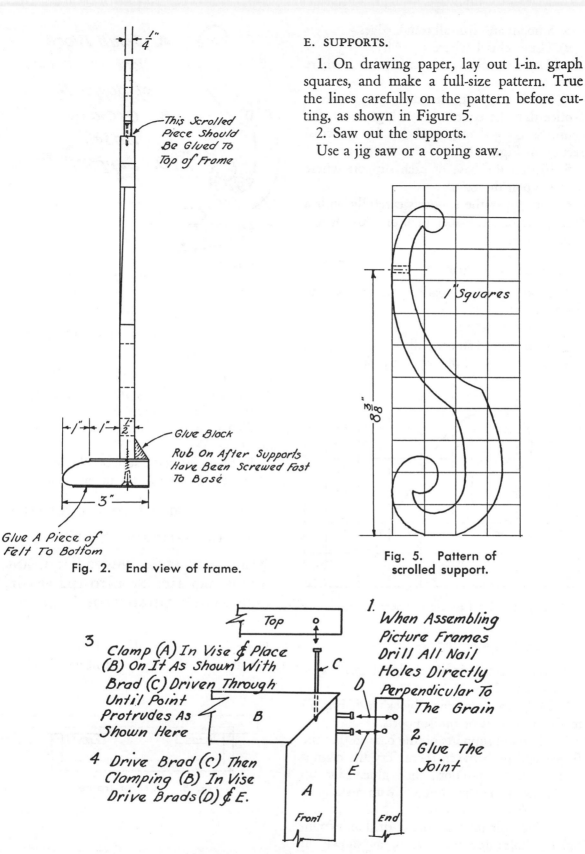

$\frac{1}{4}$"

This Scrolled Piece Should Be Glued To Top of Frame

E. SUPPORTS.

1. On drawing paper, lay out 1-in. graph squares, and make a full-size pattern. True the lines carefully on the pattern before cutting, as shown in Figure 5.

2. Saw out the supports.

Use a jig saw or a coping saw.

1" Squares

$8\frac{13}{8}$"

1"   1" $\frac{7}{2}$

Glue Block

Rub On After Supports Have Been Screwed Fast To Base

3"

Glue A Piece of Felt To Bottom

Fig. 2.   End view of frame.

Fig. 5.   Pattern of scrolled support.

Top

3   Clamp (A) In Vise & Place (B) On It As Shown With Brad (C) Driven Through Until Point Protrudes As Shown Here

C

B

D

E

A

Front

End

1. When Assembling Picture Frames Drill All Nail Holes Directly Perpendicular To The Grain

2 Glue The Joint

4 Drive Brad (C) Then Clamping (B) In Vise Drive Brads (D) & E.

Fig. 4.   Assembling the frame.

3. Smooth and true all rough edges.

a) Use a chisel where possible.

b) Use a file and sandpaper where necessary.

4. Make a layout, and carve the supports. Notice that the edges are left high when the center is gouged out, as shown by the cross section in Figure 1.

5. Flatten the base of each support where it rests upon the base.

6. Sandpaper the supports carefully with a fine grade of sandpaper (1/0 or 2/0), or 4/0 garnet paper.

F. ORNAMENTAL TOP.

1. Make a paper pattern, as shown in Figure 6.

2. Saw out the top.

3. True up and smooth all edges with a file.

4. Glue and brad the top to the frame.

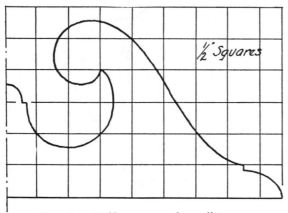

Fig. 6. Half pattern of scroll top.

G. FASTEN THE SUPPORTS TO THE BASE.

1. Make two small wedge-shaped glue blocks (Fig. 2).

2. Make two clamping blocks (*A*, Fig. 7) to fit the curves of the supports.

3. Place the supports on the base so that the frame will go between them. Try the clamps and mark the position; then glue. Line up the backs of the two supports with a straight-edge as shown in Figure 8.

4. When the glue has dried, drill and countersink holes for the screws, as shown in Figure 1, to further strengthen this joint.

56

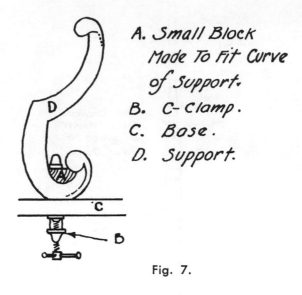

A. Small Block Made To Fit Curve of Support.

B. C-Clamp.

C. Base.

D. Support.

Fig. 7.

H. LAY THE SUPPORTS FLAT UPON THE BENCH TOP.

Place the frame in its proper position between them. Lay off a line parallel to the base, thus lining up screw holes which are to be drilled through the supports to fasten the frame (Fig. 1).

Make the holes in the supports large enough to allow the screws to turn in them easily.

I. SCREW THE FRAME TO THE SUPPORTS.

J. GIVE THE FRAME A PROPER FINISH.

K. PLACE THE GLASS, PHOTOGRAPH, AND CARDBOARD BACKING INTO THE FRAME, AND FASTEN THEM WITH ½-IN., NO. 20 BRADS.

These may quite easily be hammered into the frame with the edge of a heavy chisel.

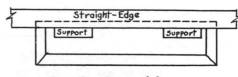

Fig. 8. Base of frame.

Telephone or Bedside Table

BILL OF MATERIAL

Pieces	Use	Dimensions
4	Legs	1¾ x 1¾ x 29¼
3	Sides and back	¾ x 6 x 14½
1	Stretcher under drawer	¾ x 1¾ x 14½
1	Stretcher above drawer	¾ x 1 x 14½
2	Drawer guides	1 x 1½ x 12½
2	Drawer runs	¾ x 1 x 14½
2	Strips to fasten top	¾ x ¾ x 12½
1	Table top	¾ x 18 x 18
1	Drawer front	¾ x 3 15/16 x 12 7/16
2	Drawer sides	½ x 3 15/16 x 15
1	Drawer bottom (plywood)	¼ x 11 15/16 x 14¾
1	Drawer back (plywood)	¼ x 3 5/16 x 11 15/16

Four 1½-in., No. 10 f.h. wood screws
Fourteen 1¼-in., No. 8 f.h. wood screws
1 drawer pull, oval type, antique finish brass, 2½- to 3-in. bail plate
Inlay banding for drawer and metal feet optional

THIS table is another interesting project. It will take more time to make the legs with the spade-type foot than the tapered leg shown above, but the spade-type foot makes a more attractive table. Four blocks of wood could be glued to the bottom of the tapered leg to make the spade foot, instead of doing it as described in the procedure. The method described, however, is best from the standpoint of fine craftsmanship. The table shown above was made of poplar and had not yet received a finish when the picture was taken.

In Figure 6 are suggestions for hardware which may be made in the shop. The pierced designs could be omitted if so desired.

PROCEDURE

A. LEGS.

Spade Type:

1. Cut stock to length and square it to the size given in the bill of material.

2. Lay out the mortises with a try square and a gauge, and cut the mortises.

Bore 5/16-in. holes close together for the mortises; then clean them out with chisels.

3. Square lines around the legs 2⅜ in. from the floor, and others 18 in. from the floor.

4. On the miter box, or with a backsaw, make saw cuts ⅜ in. deep on the lines which are 2⅜ in. from the floor.

5. Draw lines for the taper from the lines which are 18 in. from the floor to the saw cuts you have just made. Saw the taper on two opposite sides with a ripsaw or on a band saw, leaving enough to plane and chisel the sides to get a smooth surface. Square the first two tapered sides to those which remain to be tapered.

6. Draw lines to taper the last two sides; saw, plane, and chisel them, squaring them to the first two. The table leg now should appear as in Figure 2.

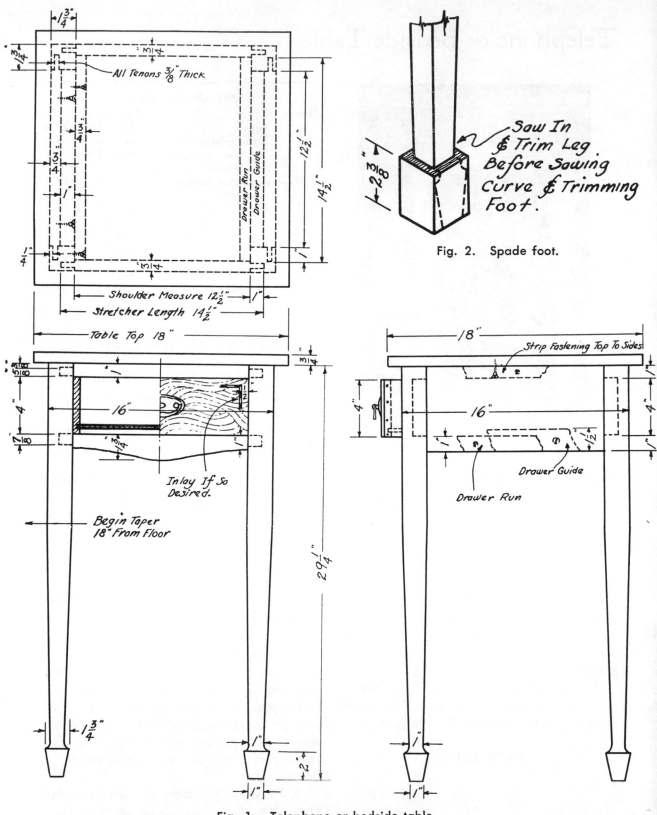

All Tenons ⅜" Thick

Drawer Run

Drawer Guide

12½"

14½"

Shoulder Measure 12½"

Stretcher Length 14½"

Table Top 18"

Saw In & Trim Leg Before Sawing Curve & Trimming Foot.

2⅜"

Fig. 2.   Spade foot.

16"

Inlay If So Desired.

Begin Taper 18" From Floor

1¾"

29¼"

2"

1"

18"

Strip Fastening Top To Sides

4"

16"

Drawer Guide

Drawer Run

½"

1"

Fig. 1.   Telephone or bedside table.

7. Set the marking gauge at ⅜ in., and gauge lines on the bottom of the foot from every side.

8. Square lines around the foot 2 in. up from the floor.

9. Clamp the foot in a vise with the leg in a vertical position.

10. Saw the curves at the top of the foot with a coping saw, beginning at the top and sawing toward the bottom.

11. File these curves, being careful not to thin the narrow section above the foot in the process.

12. Plane the taper of the foot to the gauge lines on the bottom.

Taper-Type Leg:

1. Cut stock to length, and square it to the sizes given in the bill of material.

2. Lay out the mortises.

3. Cut the mortises.

Bore 5/16-in. holes as close together as possible, and chisel the holes to size.

4. Set the marking gauge at ⅜ in., and gauge lines from each side on the foot end of the leg.

5. Lay out the lines for the taper on two opposite sides of each leg. Begin the taper 18 in. from the floor.

6. Plane the taper on the first two sides, squaring to the sides not yet tapered.

7. Plane the taper on the last two sides (Fig. 3).

B. STRETCHERS, BACK, AND SIDES.

1. Plane and square them to size.

2. Lay out all tenons.

a) Mark for all shoulder cuts with a try square.

b) Mark for all cheek cuts with a marking gauge.

3. Clamp a straight, square-edged block to the shoulder lines, and with a backsaw make shoulder cuts on the sides of the boards and stretchers.

This operation also may be performed on the miter box if care is taken to saw exactly to the line.

4. Chisel cheek cuts, completing them by chiseling across the grain.

5. With a gauge, mark lines for the width of the tenons.

6. Saw to these lines, making the shoulder cuts last. It is a good idea to chisel this part of the shoulder square and to the line, so do not saw too close to the shoulder line.

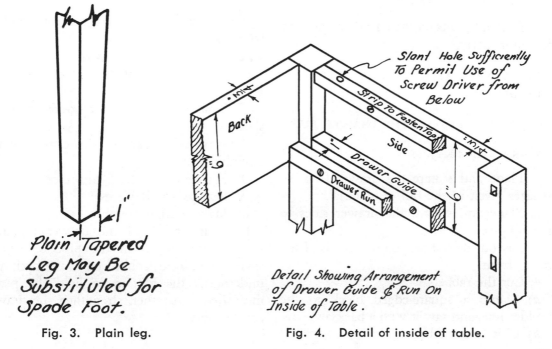

Plain Tapered Leg May Be Substituted for Spade Foot.

Fig. 3. Plain leg.

Slant Hole Sufficiently To Permit Use of Screw Driver from Below

Strip To Fasten Top

Back

Side

Drawer Guide

Drawer Run

Detail Showing Arrangement of Drawer Guide & Run On Inside of Table.

Fig. 4. Detail of inside of table.

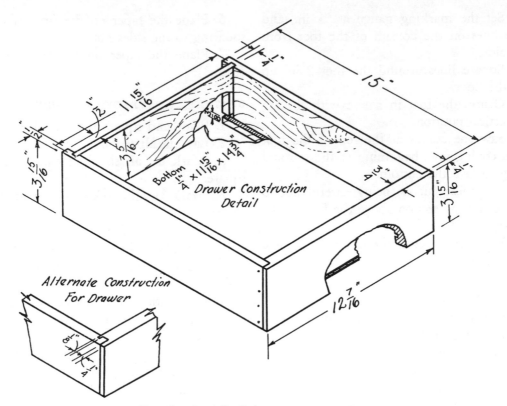

Fig. 5. Detail of drawer construction.

C. MAKE A TRIAL ASSEMBLY OF ALL
JOINTS.

D. GLUE UP THE FRAME.

Smooth all joints on the outside by planing
and sandpapering.

E. MAKE AND FASTEN THE DRAWER
GUIDES.

F. MAKE AND FASTEN THE DRAWER RUNS.

G. MAKE THE DRAWER.

1. Plane and square the drawer front to
the sizes given in the bill of material.

2. Plane and square the drawer sides to
the sizes given.

3. Lay out the rabbets on both ends of the
drawer front.

4. Cut the rabbets.

a) Clamp a square-edged block to the
shoulder line, and saw it with a backsaw.

b) Chisel the rabbet.

5. Lay out grooves in the drawer front and
in the drawer sides.

a) Horizontal grooves are laid out with a
gauge.

b) Vertical grooves are laid out with a
try square.

6. Cut along all lines with a sharp knife;
then cut the grooves with a router plane (see
Fig. 6, p. 51).

7. Square up the drawer bottom to exact
size.

This is what squares the drawer when
assembling.

8. Square up the back to the exact size.

9. Sandpaper all pieces.

10. Make a trial assembly.

11. Glue and brad the drawer together,
keeping it squared in the process. Several
small glue blocks, rubbed on at the back and
underneath the bottom to hold the pieces
more firmly together, strengthen the drawer
considerably.

H. MAKE THE TOP.

The top usually is glued up, then is planed and squared to size.

I. MAKE AND SCREW ON THE STRIPS TO FASTEN THE TOP (FIG. 4).

J. FASTEN THE TOP TO THE TABLE.

1. Place the table top with the best side down on the bench top.

2. Place the table frame on it in proper position for fastening.

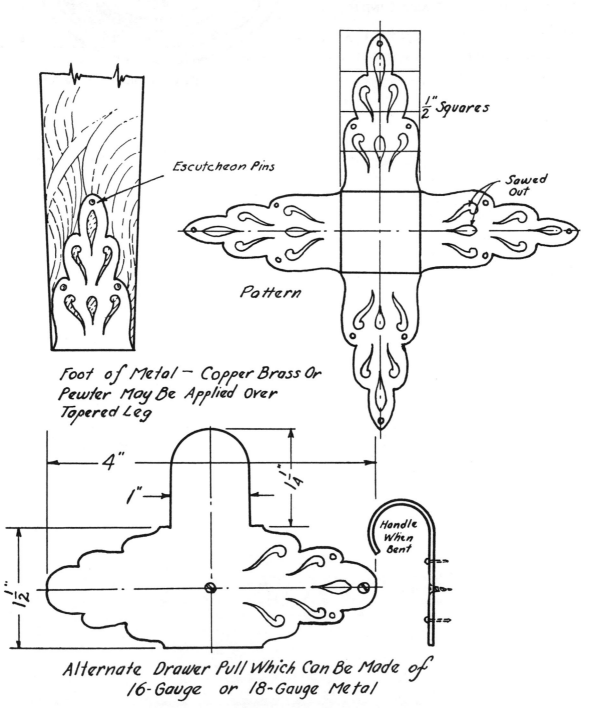

Escutcheon Pins

Pattern

½" Squares

Sawed Out

Foot of Metal — Copper Brass Or Pewter May Be Applied Over Tapered Leg

4"

1"

1¼"

1½"

Handle When Bent

Alternate Drawer Pull Which Can Be Made of 16-Gauge or 18-Gauge Metal

Fig. 6.   Metal leg trimming and drawer pull.

3. Holding the top and frame together with one or more clamps, fasten them together with screws.

K. FASTEN THE DRAWER PULL (FIG. 8).

L. REMOVE THE DRAWER PULL, AND GIVE THE TABLE A SUITABLE FINISH.

M. INSTALL HARDWARE, SUCH AS FEET AND DRAWER PULL.

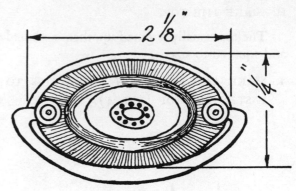

Fig. 8.   Detail of antique-finish brass drawer pull.

Serving Tray With Glued-on Turnings

THIS wooden serving tray is a bit out of the ordinary, and not too difficult to make. The tray shown above was made of mahogany, but other woods which turn well and take a nice finish also will do.

PROCEDURE

A. TRAY BOARD.

1. Plane and square the board to the sizes given in the bill of material.

2. Plane the bottom to shape, as shown by the outline of the front view in Figure 1.

3. Form the hollows for the handles, as shown by the dotted lines in Figure 1. This

BILL OF MATERIAL

Pieces	Use	Dimensions
1	Tray	⅞ x 8 x 15
	Turnings at ends	⅞ diam. x 6¾
	Turnings at sides	¾ diam. x 3⅞

NOTE: Wood for the turnings at each end should be 1 in. square. This 1-in. square should be made of two pieces of wood ½ in. thick by 1 in. wide and at least 1 in. longer than the turning is to be. The two ½-in. pieces should be glued together with a piece of brown wrapping paper between them. After turning, if they have been correctly centered in the lathe, they may be split apart to form the two half-turnings needed.

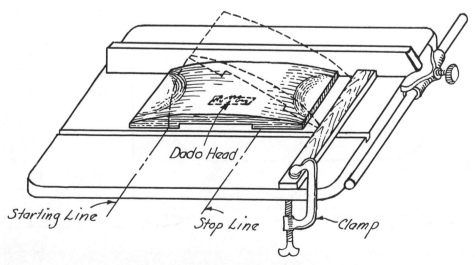

Fig. 2. Hollowing tray on circular saw.

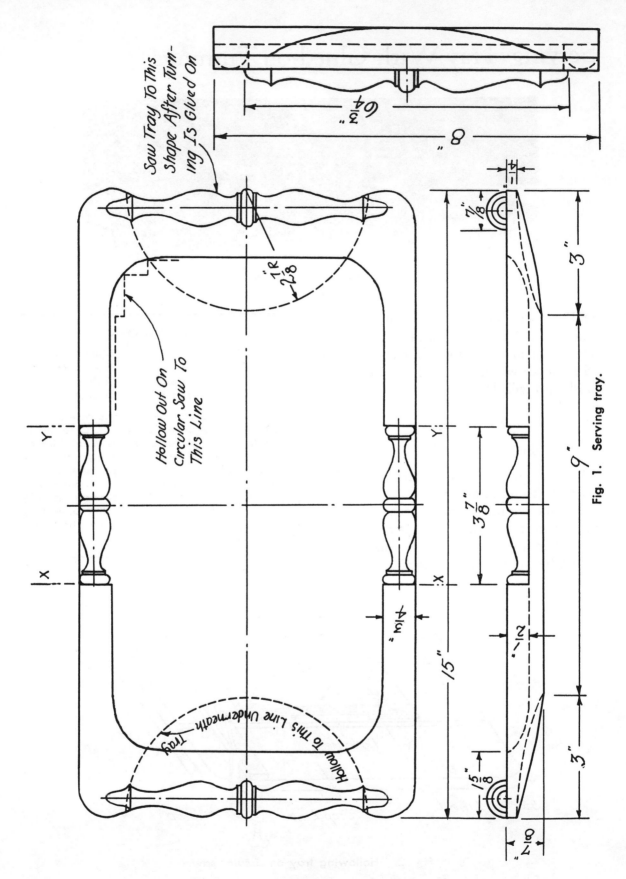

Saw Tray To This Shape After Turning Is Glued On

Hollow Out On Circular Saw To This Line

$2\frac{1}{8}$" R

Hollow To This Line Underneath Tray

$6\frac{3}{4}$"

8"

$\frac{7}{8}$"

$\frac{1}{4}$"

3"

$3\frac{7}{8}$"

9"

$\frac{3}{4}$"

15"

$\frac{1}{2}$"

$\frac{5}{8}$"

3"

$\frac{7}{8}$"

Fig. 1. Serving tray.

64

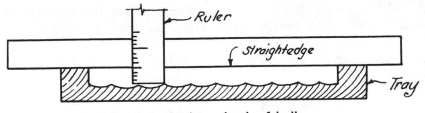

Fig. 3. Checking depth of hollow.

may be done with a shallow wood carver's gouge.

4. On the upper side, make a layout for the part to be hollowed out. This may be partly hollowed out on a circular saw with a dado head, and then finished with wood carver's gouges, scraping tools, and sandpaper; or it may be done entirely with gouges, by hand.

5. If hollowed on the circular saw, set the blades to cut ½ in. deep. Using the cross-cutting fence, hollow out across the middle of the board to a width of 3⅞ in. as shown from X to Y in Figure 1.

6. Hollow out the tray lengthwise by setting up the saw as shown in Figure 2. Clamp the board used as a backstop, in positions to make the cuts of various lengths as indicated by the dotted lines in Figure 1. First hold

the board in the position indicated by the dotted lines in Figure 2; then lower its elevated end until it rests flat upon the saw table. As you slowly lower it, the dado head will begin the cut at the starting line. Push the board forward until the end nearest the operator reaches the stop line. If a second stop-board has been clamped to the far end of the saw table to halt movement of the tray at the stop line, it may be more easily removed from the saw without danger of cutting too far.

7. If the tray is to be hollowed entirely by hand, the depth of the hollow may be gauged by the method shown in Figure 3. No matter which method is used, the hollowed-out part will have to be finished with scraping tools and sandpaper.

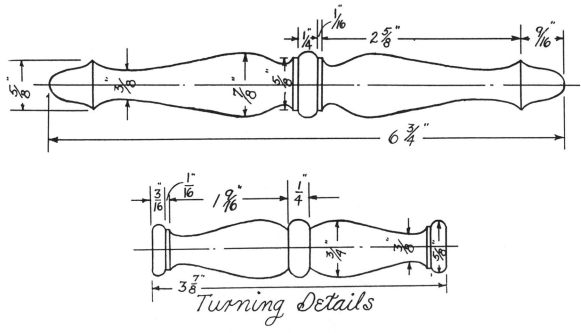

Fig. 4. Two turnings.

B. SPLIT TURNINGS.

Follow the directions given in the note under the bill of material. Turn those at the side to the exact length of the cut made for them (Fig. 4).

C. GLUE THE SPLIT TURNINGS TO THE TRAY.

The glue on the split turnings where they have been separated must be scraped off clean before regluing the turnings to the tray. If this is not done, the joint may fail to hold.

D. GIVE THE TRAY A SUITABLE FINISH.

Because a tray often has liquids spilled on it, and because it frequently needs washing, it should be finished with a good spar varnish which is not readily marred by the action of liquids. The final coat should be rubbed down with pumice stone and oil.

Carved and Scroll-Sawed Serving Tray

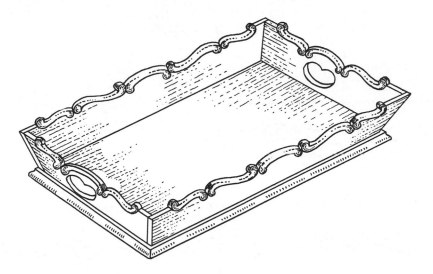

THIS tray in the Chippendale manner, with its simple carving around the upper edges of the sides, should be made of either mahogany or walnut. The tray, an attractive and useful object in itself, also is a good project for anyone who wants to do simple carving.

Though mitered corners would be nicer, the simpler butt joint has been substituted to make the project easier.

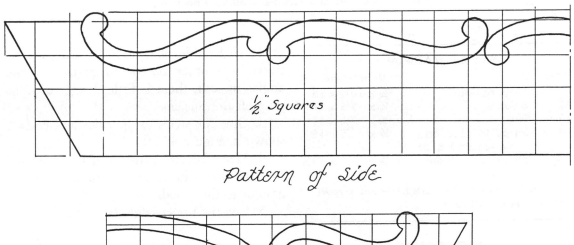

½" Squares

Pattern of Side

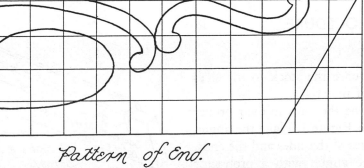

Pattern of End.

Fig. 4.   Patterns for sides and ends.

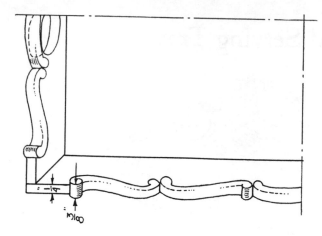

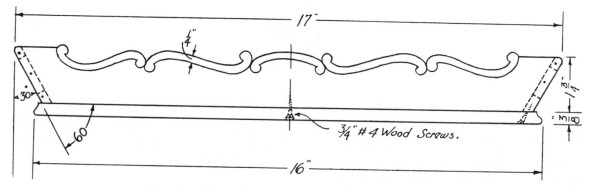

Fig. 1.   Carved and scroll-sawed serving tray.

BILL OF MATERIAL

Pieces	Use	Dimensions
1	Tray bottom	⅜ x 10¼ x 16
2	Sides	¼ x 2⅛ x 17
2	Ends	¼ x 2⅛ x 11
4	Strips to glue on sides (see Fig. 3)	⅛ x ⅞ x 15
4	Strips to glue on ends	⅛ x ⅞ x 9½

Ten ¾-in., No. 4 f.h. bright wood screws
1¼-in., No. 18 brads

PROCEDURE

A. SIDES AND ENDS.

1. Plane and square the stock to the sizes given in the bill of material.

2. Saw and plane the ends to their proper angles as shown in Figure 1. Plane the angles on the bottom edges of the sides and the ends.

a) Lay out the angles with a protractor and a sliding T bevel.

b) If the sides and ends are clamped between two other boards to plane the end angles smooth, there is little danger of chipping off the corners.

3. Glue the strips to the sides and ends as shown in Figure 3.

4. Make full-size patterns of the sides and ends as shown in Figure 4, and transfer the designs to the wood.

5. Saw the upper edges to shape.

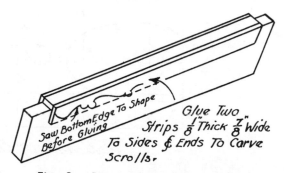

Fig. 3.   Preparing to carve scrolls.

6. Carve the scrolls.

a) Outline the scrolls with a V tool.

b) Round and shape the scrolls with a skew chisel.

7. Saw out the handles.

8. File the handles smooth.

9. Sandpaper the sides and ends.

10. Assemble the sides and ends.

B. MAKE THE BOTTOM.

1. Plane and square the bottom to the size given in the bill of material.

2. Cut a molding around the edges.

This may be done on a shaper, or it may be carved by hand with wood-carving chisels.

3. Sandpaper the bottom.

C. FASTEN THE BOTTOM TO THE SIDES AND ENDS WITH WOOD SCREWS.

D. GIVE THE TRAY A SUITABLE FINISH.

Because liquids are likely to be spilled on the tray, give the tray one or two final coats of a good spar varnish.

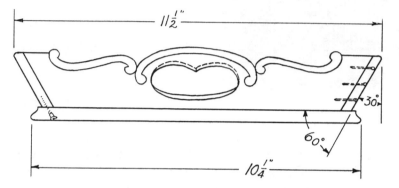

Fig. 2.   End view of tray.

Knotty-Pine Paneled Wastebasket

A LITTLE bit different from the conventional type of wastebasket, this Colonial basket is one which will be worth owning when it has been completed, and one which will try your skill while it is being built.

BILL OF MATERIAL		
Pieces	Use	Dimensions
4	Stiles	⅝ x 1¾ x 14⅞
4	Stiles	⅝ x 1⅛ x 14⅞
4	Upper rails	⅝ x 1¾ x 11½
4	Lower rails	⅝ x 2 x 6½
4	Panels	⅝ x 10⁵⁄₁₆ x 10¾
1	Bottom	⅝ x 9¼ x 9¼
4	Feet	⅝ x 2 x 9¼
	Corner strips	⅜ x ⅜ x 14⅜
	Hardwood pegs	¼ x ¼ x 1½
1-in., No. 8 f.h. bright wood screws		

PROCEDURE

A. FRAMES.

1. Plane and square the stock for all stiles and rails.

2. Lay out and cut the panel grooves on the rails and stiles. This is most satisfactorily done with a dado head on a variety saw.

3. Lay out and cut the mortises on the stiles, as shown in Figure 1, which is a jig used in cutting the mortises.

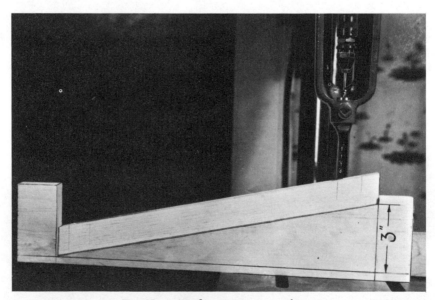

Fig. 1. Jig for mortising stiles.

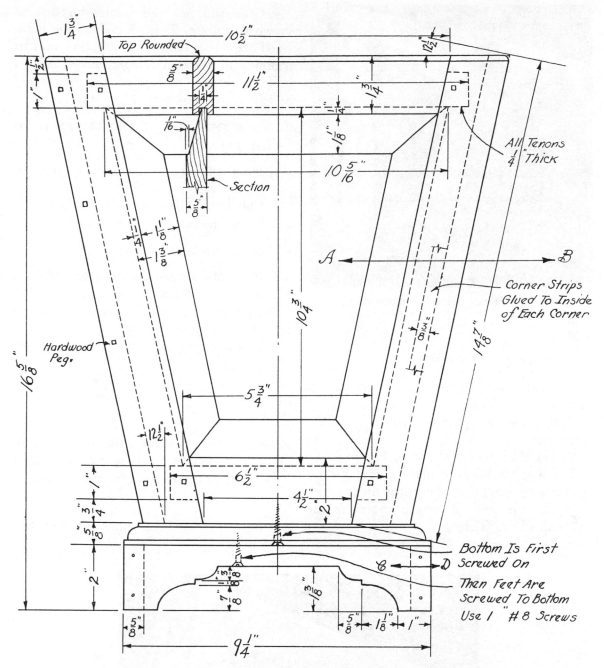

Fig. 3. Knotty-pine paneled wastebasket.

4. Lay out and cut the tenons on the rails.

5. Make a trial assembly of each frame, as shown in Figure 2.

B. PANELS.

1. Plane and square the stock to the size given in the bill of material.

2. Lay out and saw the angles at the sides as shown in Figure 3.

3. Raise the panels to the shape shown in Figure 5. The saw or the saw table is tilted to make an angle of 16 deg. The panel then is raised as shown in Figure 4.

4. Plane and sandpaper the sawed surfaces.

71

Fig. 2.   Pieces being fitted together.

6. Glue and peg the frames together as shown in Figures 3 and 5. Where the hardwood pegs enter the round hole, they may be trimmed to a rough octagon shape, with a knife or chisel. The tops of the pegs should be left square, however.

D. MAKE THE BOTTOM AND FASTEN IT TO THE FRAME.

1. Plane and square the board to the size given in the bill of material.

2. Cut the molding around the edges.

3. Screw the bottom to the frames.

E. MAKE AND FASTEN THE FEET.

1. Plane and square the stock to size.

2. Miter the corners.

3. Saw the feet to the shape shown in Figure 3. File all sawed edges.

4. Nail and glue the feet together as shown in Figure 6.

5. Drill and countersink holes in the feet for 1-in., No. 8 screws, and fasten the feet to the bottom.

F. MAKE AND FASTEN THE REINFORCING CORNER STRIPS SHOWN IN FIGURES 3 AND 5. GLUE AND BRAD THE STRIPS IN PLACE.

G. GIVE THE WASTEBASKET A SUITABLE FINISH.

C. ASSEMBLE THE FRAME.

1. Fit the panels to the frames, and glue all mortises and tenons.

NOTE: Do not glue the panels into the grooves.

2. Peg the joints as shown in Figure 3.

3. Plane the joints to make a level surface where necessary; then sandpaper them.

4. Lay out and plane the angles at the bottoms of the frames.

5. Round the tops of the frames.

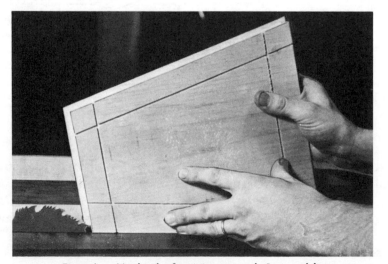

Fig. 4.   Method of raising panel. Saw table or saw is tilted.

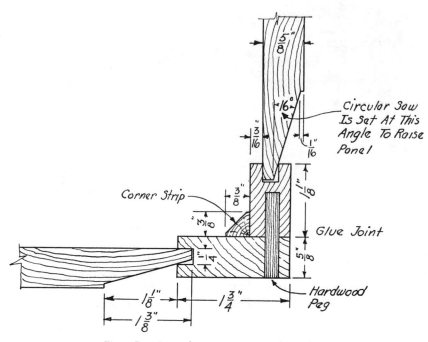

Fig. 5.   Detail cross-sectioned at A-B.

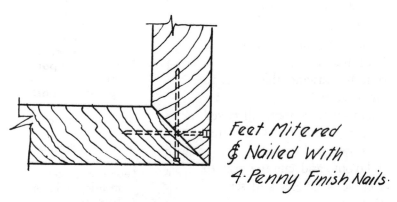

Fig. 6.   Section C-D.

Cobbler's-Bench Coffee Table

THE person who first hit upon the idea of using a cobbler's bench as a coffee table had a happy thought indeed. With this sidesaddle seat, the hostess has a comfortable place from which to serve guests. The quaintness of the design is its chief charm.

PROCEDURE

A. MAKE THE PLANK FOR THE TABLE SEAT.

1. Glue up planks to the size needed.
2. Plane and square the plank to the size given in the bill of material.
3. Make a layout for sawing the edges to shape, as shown in Figure 1.
4. Saw the edges to shape. Smooth all sawed edges with a file and sandpaper. Also soften all sharp edges as shown in Figure 1.
5. Make a seat layout, and cut the seat to shape. Use wood carver's gouges and scraper blades to shape the seat.

B. MAKE THE LEGS.

1. Make the legs octagon shaped, 1½ in. across the flats at the bottom, and 1¼ in. across the flats at the top.
2. Turn the legs at the top to fit a 1-in. hole.

C. FASTEN THE LEGS TO THE PLANK.

1. On top of the plank, locate centers for boring holes, as shown in Figure 1.

BILL OF MATERIAL

Pieces	Use	Dimensions
1	Plank for table seat	1½ x 16 x 36¼
1	Side	¾ x 5½ x 16½
1	Block against side	¾ x 2 x 8
1	End	¾ x 4 x 15¼
2	Drawer supports	1 x 2 x 15½
2	Drawer strips	½ x ½ x 15
2	Drawer ends	¾ x 5½ x 6
2	Drawer sides	½ x 5½ x 14½
1	Drawer bottom (plywood)	¼ x 5½ x 14
1	Strip for top compartments	¼ x ⅜ x 13⅝
1	Strip for compartments	¼ x ⅜ x 13½
1	Strip for compartments	¼ x ⅜ x 13¼
2	Strips for compartments	¼ x ⅜ x 4
2	Strips for compartments	¼ x ⅜ x 4⅞
4	Legs (hardwood: maple, oak, or hickory)	1½ x 1½ x 14½
2	Drawer pulls	1 diam. x 2¼

1¼-in., No. 10 wood screws to fasten side and end to table edge
2½-in., No. 10 wood screws to fasten drawer supports
3-penny finish nails to nail drawer sides after gluing
1-in., No. 18 brads to fasten compartment strips
4 hardwood wedges, 1 in. wide by 1½ in. long for tops of legs
Dowel rods to plug screwhead holes

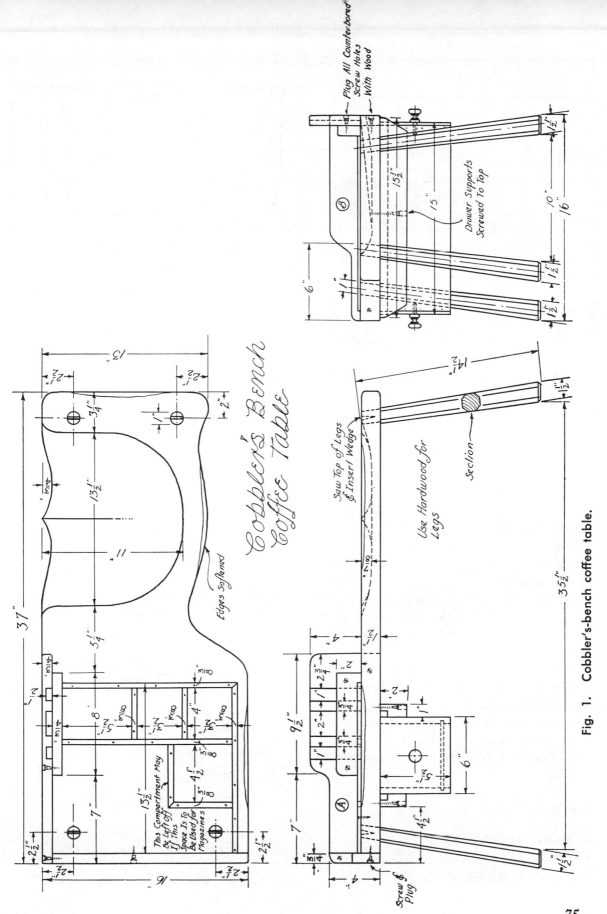

Cobbler's Bench Coffee Table

Plug All Counterbored Screw Holes With Wood

Drawer Supports Screwed To Top

Saw Top of Legs & Insert Wedge

Use Hardwood for Legs

Section

Edges Softened

This Compartment May Be Left Off If This Space Is To Be Used for Magazines

Screw & Plug

Fig. 1. Cobbler's-bench coffee table.

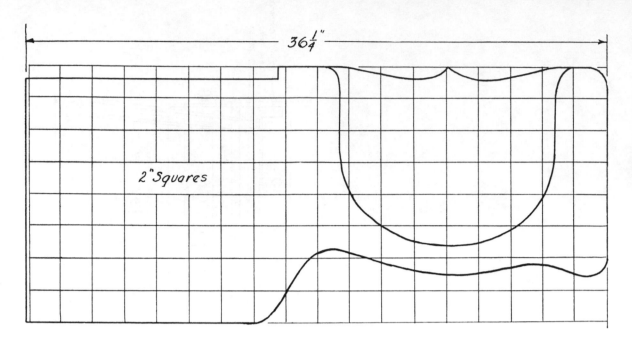

$36\frac{1}{4}''$

2" Squares

Fig. 2. Seat layout.

2. Set a sliding T bevel to the angle of 77 deg., as shown in Figure 3.

3. Bore the holes.

4. Fit the legs to the holes, and trim the shoulder angle.

a) The best way to mark the shoulder angle for trimming is to push the leg into the hole as far as it will go. Then, with a block of wood as thick as the highest point of the un-trimmed shoulder under the pencil point, mark a line clear around the leg, thus getting the proper angle.

b) Be sure that all of the legs have the flat sides turned facing the same way before trimming the shoulder angle.

5. Cut a saw kerf at the top of each leg for the wedges (front view, Fig. 1).

6. Glue the legs to the plank, and drive the wedges.

7. When the glue has set, trim the tops level with the surface of the plank.

D. MAKE THE DRAWER.

1. Plane and square all drawer stock to the sizes given in the bill of material.

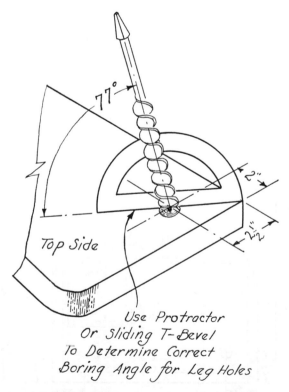

77°

2"

2½"

Top Side

Use Protractor
Or Sliding T-Bevel
To Determine Correct
Boring Angle for Leg Holes

Fig. 3. Determining boring angle.

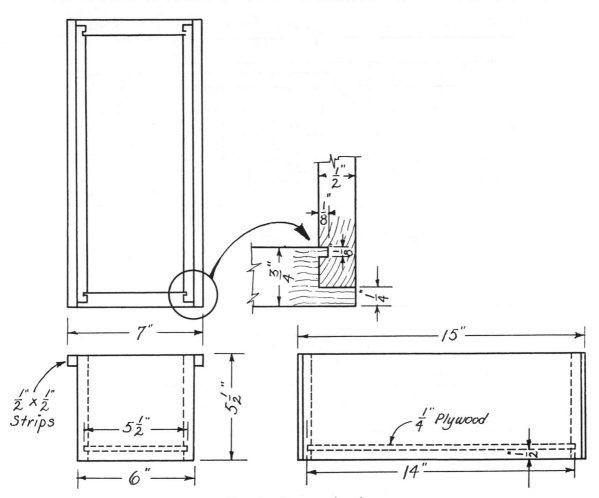

Fig. 4. Drawer details.

2. Make layouts for all joints as shown in Figure 4.

3. Make and fit all joints. These joints are best made with a dado head on a circular saw. The sides are glued and bradded to the ends.

4. Fasten the drawer-runner strips to the upper edges of the sides as shown in the front elevation of **Figure 4.**

5. Turn the drawer pulls, Figure 5. Bore holes, and fasten them to the drawer.

E. MAKE AND FASTEN THE DRAWER-SUP-PORTING STRIPS TO THE UNDERSIDE OF THE PLANK, AS SHOWN IN FIGURE I.

F. FIT THE DRAWER TO THE SUPPORTS, MAKING SURE THE DRAWER SLIDES FREELY.

G. MAKE AND FASTEN THE REMAINING PARTS, CONSISTING OF SIDE, END, AND BLOCK AGAINST SIDE.

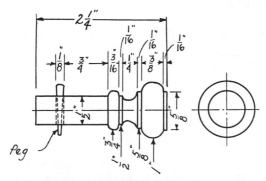

Fig. 5. Detail of wooden drawer pull.

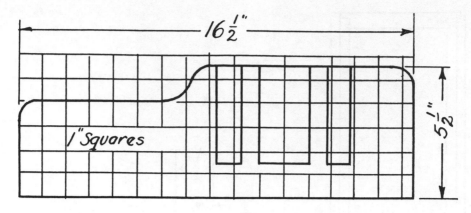

Pattern of A

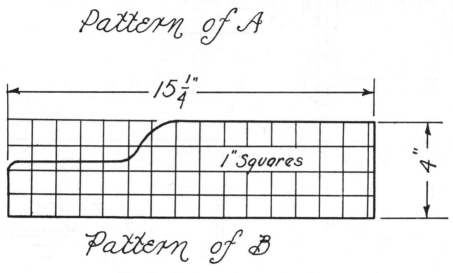

Pattern of B

Fig. 6.   Patterns of parts A and B.

1. Plane and square the pieces to the size given in the bill of material.

2. Locate and cut grooves across the side (Figs. 1 and 6).

3. Lay out the shape of the upper edges of the side and the end from Figure 6, and saw these to shape.

4. File all sawed edges, and sandpaper the pieces.

5. Fasten the side, end, and block to the plank.

H. MAKE AND FASTEN COMPARTMENT STRIPS AS SHOWN IN FIGURE I.

Some or all of these may be left off if so desired.

I. GIVE THE COFFEE TABLE A SUITABLE FINISH.

Wall Shelves With a Fall Drawer

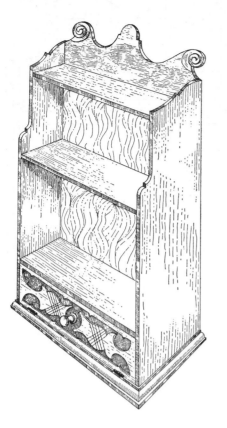

BILL OF MATERIAL		
Pieces	Use	Dimensions
2	Sides	½ x 6¼ x 23¾
1	Top	½ x 6 x 17½
1	Upper shelf	½ x 4¼ x 17½
1	Middle shelf	½ x 6 x 17½
1	Lower shelf	½ x 6 x 17½
1	Base	½ x 6¾ x 19
1	Back (plywood)	¼ x 17½ x 22¼
1	Drawer (piece A)	¾ x 4 x 17
1	Drawer (piece B)	¾ x 3¼ x 16
1	Drawer (piece C)	¼ x 2 x 16
2	Drawer (piece D)	¼ x 4 x 4
1	Pull	⅞ diam. x 1⅝

Two 1-in. middle brass butt hinges

Fig. 3. Using router plane.

A UNIQUE feature in this project is the **fall drawer** which is more practical than a regular drawer would be on a cabinet having little depth. It serves as a good place to keep pencils, erasers, and other small items.

The little bit of carving on the top and the drawer front makes it a good project for a beginner in wood carving.

This is a good project in hand woodwork. Besides the usual tool processes and the little wood carving, it also teaches a little bit of wood turning in the making of the drawer pull.

PROCEDURE

A. SIDES.

1. Plane and square two boards to the sizes given in the bill of material.

2. Lay out the mortises; then cut the mortises.

First cut along the lines with a knife or chisel; then cut to depth with a router plane (Fig. 3).

3. Make a full-size pattern of the side as shown in Figure 2. Lay out the pattern on the sides; then cut it to shape with a coping saw or on a jig saw.

4. File the sawed edges smooth, and sandpaper the pieces.

5. Lay out and cut rabbets on the back edges. Note that the rabbet is ½ in. wide where the top is joined to the sides, and only ¼ in. wide from there on down.

B. SHELVES.

1. Plane and square stock to size.

79

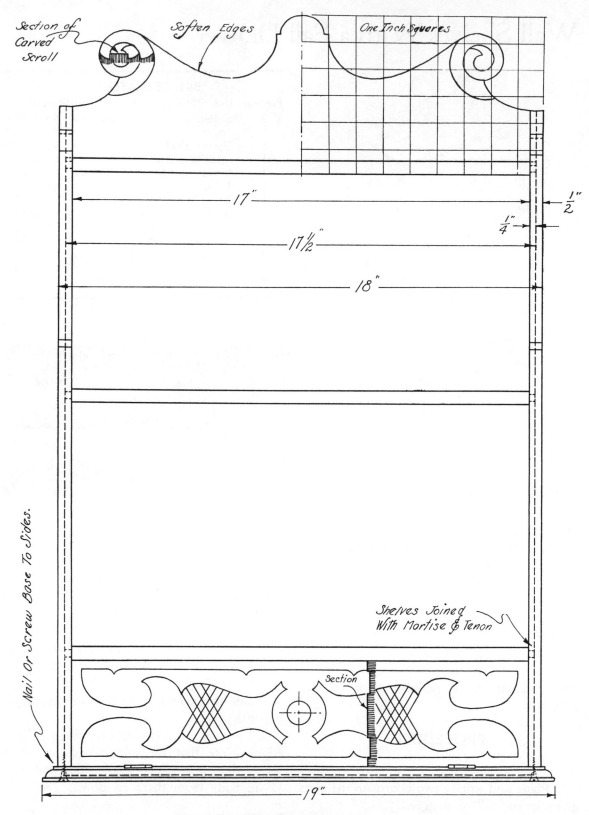

Section of Carved Scroll

Soften Edges

One Inch Squares

17"

17½"

18"

½"

¼"

Nail Or Screw Base To Sides.

Shelves Joined With Mortise & Tenon

Section

19"

Fig. 1.   Wall shelves with fall drawer.

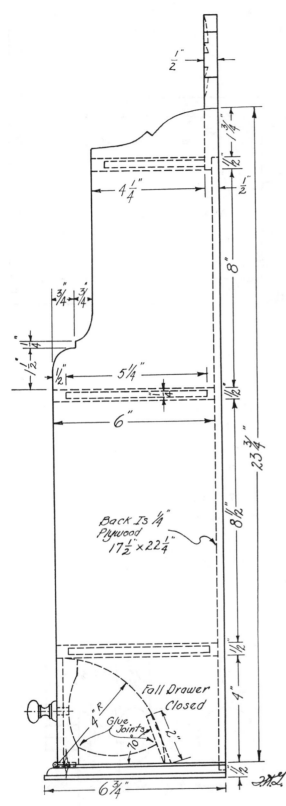

Fig. 2. Side view.

- Back Is ¼"
  Plywood
  17½" × 22¼"

- Fall Drawer
  Closed
- 4" R
- Glue Joints
- 10
- 2"

2. Make a layout for the tenons; then cut the tenons.

a) Clamp a straightedged block to the shoulders.

b) Saw the shoulder cuts with a backsaw.

c) Chisel the cheek cuts.

d) Fit the tenons to the mortises.

C. ASSEMBLE THE SIDES AND SHELVES.

First make a trial assembly; then glue and clamp the pieces together. Test to see if they are square.

D. BASE.

1. Square and plane the base.

2. Cut the molding. See Figure 3, page 101, for methods of cutting moldings. If a shaper with proper cutters is available, it should be used.*

3. Cut the rabbet on the back edge of the base. Notice that this does not go clear to the ends of the board.

E. FALL DRAWER.

1. Plane and square pieces *A*, *B*, *C*, and *D*, Figure 4, to size.

2. Hollow pieces *A* and *B* by first roughing

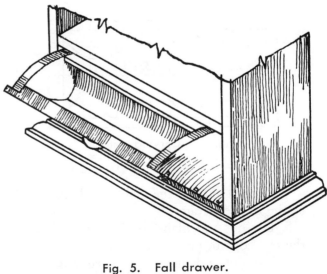

Fig. 5. Fall drawer.

*An inexperienced person should not use a shaper or a circular saw. It is too dangerous. Where hand tools alone are used to make this project, the edges of the base may be chamfered instead of cutting a molding.

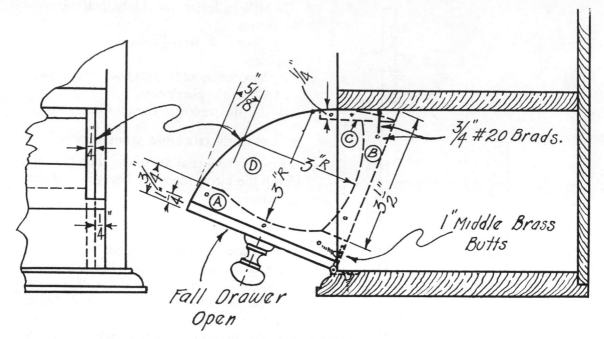

Fig. 4.   Detail of fall drawer.

them to shape on a circular saw. Then carve them with wood-carving gouges to finish the job.

3. Draw the design of the carving on the drawer face, and carve it (Fig. 6).

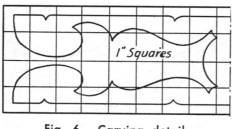

1" Squares

Fig. 6.   Carving detail.

4. Lay out and cut the rabbets on both ends of the drawer front.

5. Lay out and plane the 70-deg. angle on the one edge of piece *B* (Fig. 2).

6. Lay out and plane the 70-deg. angle on one edge of piece *C* (Fig. 4).

7. Lay out and saw the curves on the pieces *D*.

8. Assemble the drawer.

9. Turn and fasten the drawer pull (Fig. 7).

82

F. **FASTEN THE DRAWER TO THE BASE WITH HINGES.**

The fall-drawer hinges are fastened before the base is screwed or nailed to the sides.

G. **SCREW THE BASE TO THE BOTTOM OF THE WALL SHELVES.**

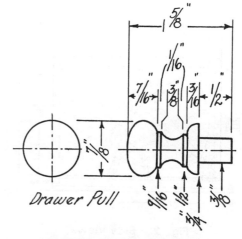

Drawer Pull

Fig. 7.   Detail of wooden drawer pull.

H. TOP.

1. Plane and square the board. Lay out and cut the rabbet on the lower edge.

2. Make a full-size pattern of the top (a half pattern will do).

3. Saw the top to shape.

4. File all sawed edges, and sandpaper them.

5. Carve the scrolls.

a) First outline the spiral with a V tool.

b) Then shape the background toward each V-tool cut using a shallow gouge. The cross section in Figure 1 will give you the shape.

I. FASTEN THE TOP TO THE WALL SHELVES.

Nail from the back.

J. NAIL THE BACK TO THE SHELVES.

K. GIVE THE WALL SHELVES A SUITABLE FINISH.

If the lowered portions of the carvings are painted gold, they will contrast beautifully with the other colors or color used. If painted, a contrasting color for the background will dress up the project.

Small Carved Frame for Photograph or Mirror

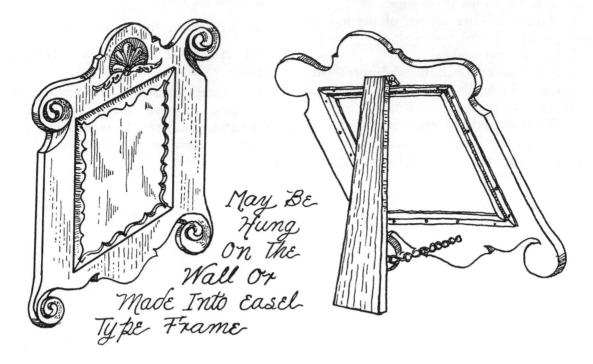

May Be Hung On The Wall Or Made Into Easel Type Frame

WHEN furnishing a home, the small decorative things, such as this little carved photograph frame, give it distinction, and reveal the true personality of the owner.

PROCEDURE

A. FRAME.

1. Plane and square a board for the frame to the size given in the bill of material.

2. On a piece of heavy drawing paper or cardboard, draw a full-size pattern of the frame design as shown in Figure 1. Include the designs of the carving on this pattern (Fig. 3).

3. From this pattern, trace the outlines of the outside of the frame and the outline of the inside of the frame surrounding the opening.

4. Saw these to shape on a jig saw. File and sandpaper all sawed edges.

5. From the pattern, transfer all layouts for the carving to the wood.

6. Glue the small block to the top of the frame as shown in Figure 1.

BILL OF MATERIAL

Pieces	Use	Dimensions
1	Frame (mahogany, walnut, or maple)	⅜ x 9¼ x 12⅛
1	Glue block for carving	¼ x ¾ x 3⅜
2	Tin cut from tin can	¾ x 7¾
2	Tin cut from tin can	¾ x 5¾

¼-in., No. 18 nails or escutcheon pins to tack strips of tin
5 x 7-in. glass or mirror
5 x 7-in. cardboard
2 small screw eyes, No. 213½
5-in., No. 18 single jack chain⎫ Needed only if
¼ x 1¼ x 9¼-in. easel strip ⎬ frame is easel
1-in. broad brass butt hinge⎭ type
About 2 ft. tinned-wire picture cord (needed only if frame is to be hung on wall)

B. CARVE THE FRAME.

This may be done with wood-carving chisels or with carving burrs on a high-speed rotary tool.

C. MAKE THE TIN ANGLE STRIPS AS SHOWN IN FIGURE 2.

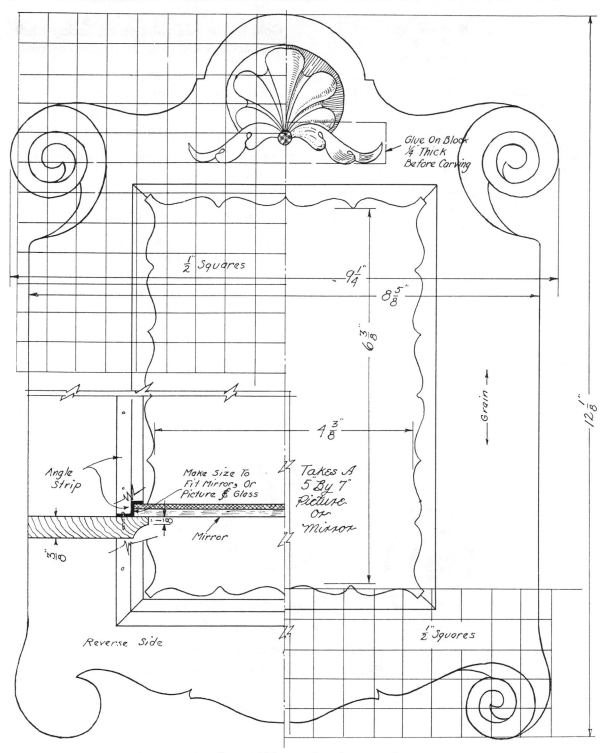

Glue On Block
¼ Thick
Before Carving

½" Squares

9¼"

8⅝"

6⅜"

Grain →

12⅛"

Angle
Strip

Make Size To
Fit Mirrors Or
Picture & Glass

4⅜"

Takes A
5" By 7"
Picture
Or
Mirror

Mirror

⅝"

Reverse Side

½" Squares

Fig. 1.   Small carved frame for photograph or mirror.

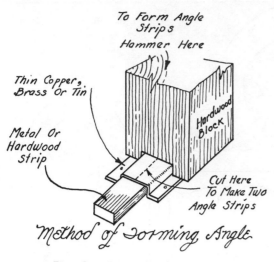

Fig. 2. Forming an angle.

Fit them to the frame but do not fasten them.

D. GIVE THE FRAME A SUITABLE FINISH.

Gold leaf or gold paint on the backgrounds of the carvings will make the frame attractive.

E. PLACE THE MIRROR, PICTURE, OR PORTRAIT IN ITS PROPER POSITION; THEN NAIL ON THE ANGLE STRIPS TO HOLD IT AND THE CARDBOARD BACKING IN PLACE.

F. MAKE THE EASEL STRIP, OR FASTEN PICTURE WIRE TO THE FRAME.

1. This strip should be 1 in. wide at the top and 1¼ in. wide at the bottom. It should be hinged to the top of the frame in the back as shown in the sketch at the beginning of the chapter. With two small screw eyes, fasten the jack chain, adjusting it to suit.

2. If the frame is to be hung on a wall, fasten picture wire to the frame so the wire will not show above the frame when it is hung on the wall.

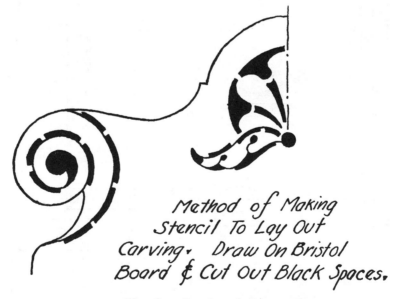

Fig. 3. Carving design.

Utility Chest

THIS minature chest of drawers provides a novel method of storing socks, handkerchiefs, neckties, collar and cuff buttons, jewelry, and countless other items. In a dining room it could be used for the storage of silver, although, to hold knives, it would have to be made deeper. In the kitchen it could become a spice cabinet or a place to store nails, screws, faucet washers, electric fuses, and the great number of odds and ends which are often so hard to find when needed. In a workshop, it could hold nails, screws, small pieces of hardware, sandpaper, and many other items. If used for purposes such as these, the inlaid banding could be omitted, and turned drawer pulls could be substituted. The simpler base, shown in Figure 1, could be substituted for the French bracket feet on this Hepplewhite design.

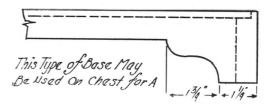

Fig. 1. Another type of base.

BILL OF MATERIAL

Pieces	Use	Dimensions
	Case:	
2	Ends	½ x 10 x 12½
1	Top	½ x 10 x 16
1	Back (plywood)	¼ x 12½ x 15½
4	Feet (the four feet should be made from one piece, 1¾ x 1¾ x 12 in., and should not be cut apart until all grooves have been cut for the joints)	1¾ x 1¾ x 2½
1	Front rail in base	⅞ x 1¾ x 15
2	End rails in base	¾ x 1¼ x 8¾
1	Rear rail in base	¾ x 2½ x 15
8	Drawer runs	⁷⁄₁₆ x ½ x 9½
	Drawers:	
1	Upper drawer front	⅝ x 1¹⁵⁄₁₆ x 14¹⁵⁄₁₆
2	Middle drawer fronts	⅝ x 2¹⁵⁄₁₆ x 14¹⁵⁄₁₆
1	Lower drawer front	⅝ x 3¹⁵⁄₁₆ x 14¹⁵⁄₁₆
2	Upper drawer sides	½ x 1¹⁵⁄₁₆ x 9½
4	Middle drawer sides	½ x 2¹⁵⁄₁₆ x 9½
2	Lower drawer sides	½ x 3¹⁵⁄₁₆ x 9½
1	Upper drawer back	⅜ x 1⁷⁄₁₆ x 14³⁄₁₆
2	Middle drawer backs	⅜ x 2¹⁵⁄₁₆ x 14³⁄₁₆
1	Lower drawer back	⅜ x 3¹⁵⁄₁₆ x 14³⁄₁₆
4	Drawer bottoms (plywood)	¼ x 9⅜ x 14⅜

NOTE: If the drawers will be partitioned, the sizes of the partitions will be determined directly from the drawing, since the sizes of the compartments in the respective drawers will determine the sizes of the partitions.
8 Drawer pulls — oval bail in antique finish
1-in., No. 18 brads
Four 1¼-in., No. 6 wood screws
⅛-in. inlay banding, approximately 36 in. per drawer
Sheet-metal curved bottoms for drawer compartments optional (see Fig. 5)
Use 24-gauge metal — brass, copper, or I-C bright tin

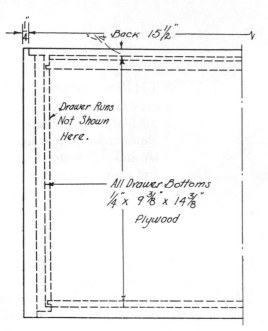

Back 15½"

Drawer Runs
Not Shown
Here.

All Drawer Bottoms
¼" x 9⅜" x 14⅜"
Plywood

If the Hepplewhite design is used, the chest should be made of mahogany, or possibly walnut. If used in the kitchen or workshop, cheaper woods, such as poplar or birch, could be substituted.

PROCEDURE

A. CASE OF THE CHEST.

1. Plane and square up stock for ends, top, and back.

2. Lay out and cut rabbets at the ends and the back edge of the top, and at the back edges of the ends (Figs. 2 and 3).

3. Lay out and cut grooves for all drawer runs in the ends.

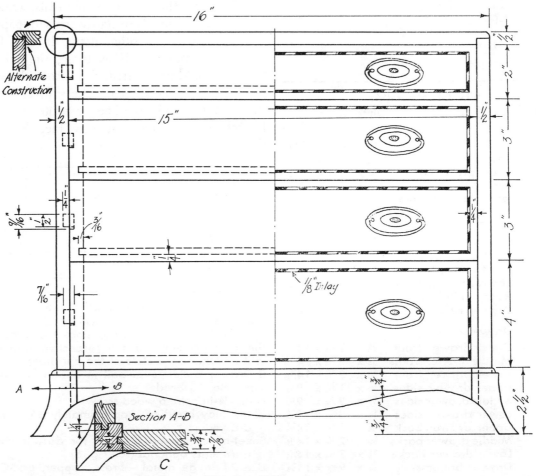

Alternate
Construction

16"

15"

⅛" Inlay

Section A-B

Fig. 2. Utility chest.

4. Make the drawer runs, and glue them into the grooves.

5. Assemble the case.

B. BASE.

1. Make the feet by first squaring a piece to 1¾ by 1¾ by 12 in., and cutting the grooves for the joints. Then bandsaw the legs to shape, but save the waste from the first cuts and tack them back on, to make a flat surface for the other saw cuts. If the legs are sawed to shape before they are cut off from the main piece, the first three legs may be sawed to shape without tacking on the waste since they may be easily held at the end without danger to the operator.

2. Square the stretchers, lay out and cut the tongues on both ends of each one, and fit them to the grooves in the legs. The face of the front stretcher must be sloped a bit to make it flush with the fronts of the legs. Allow for this when laying out the joint (C, Fig. 2).

3. Cut rabbets on the top edges of the stretchers, and saw and chisel out the corners at the tops of the legs. Use the method shown in Figures 3 and 4, page 50.

4. Assemble the base.

5. Shape the molding on the base. Use a shaper, or saw the fillet on a circular saw, and round it over with a wood carver's skew chisel.

6. Screw the base to the case.

C. DRAWERS.

1. The joint shown in Figure 4 is best, although, if only hand tools are available, a

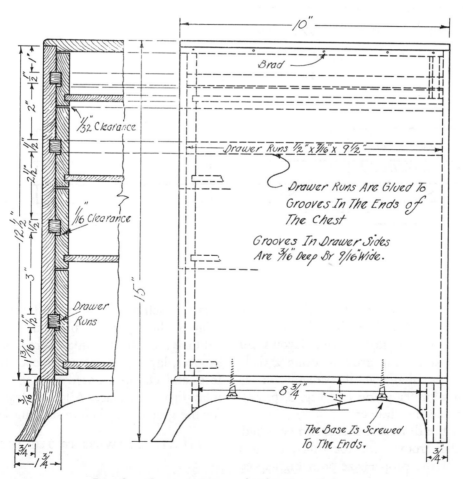

Fig. 3.   Cross section and side view of chest.

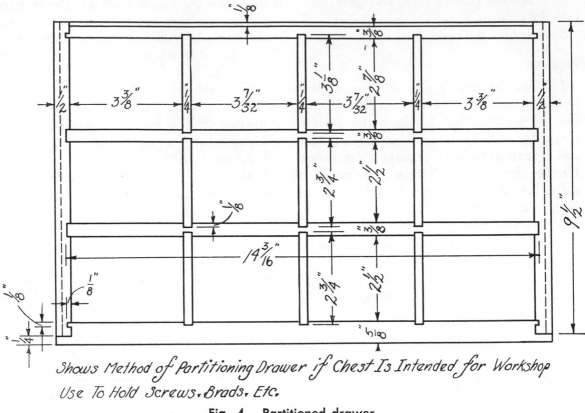

Shows Method of Partitioning Drawer if Chest Is Intended for Workshop Use To Hold Screws, Brads, Etc.

Fig. 4. Partitioned drawer.

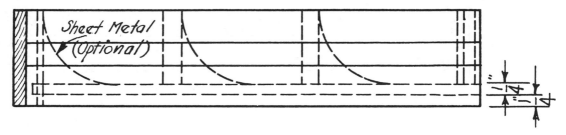

Fig. 5. Side view of drawer.

rabbet-and-butt joint should be substituted to join the front and back to the sides.

2. Square up the stock, make layouts for all joints, and cut the grooves, using a dado head on a circular saw, if available, or by hand with a router plane (see Fig. 3, p. 79).

3. Assemble the drawers.

NOTE: If the drawer fronts are to be inlaid, first cut the grooves for the inlay, using a router bit of the proper size on a high-speed

rotary machine or on a drill press. Fit the inlay to these grooves and glue it in place.

Put glue on the inlay, press it into the grooves, lay a piece of paper over the drawer face, and clamp a board over it to press the inlay firmly in place. Allow at least 12 hours for the glue to dry before sanding level.

D. FIT THE DRAWERS TO THE CASE.

90

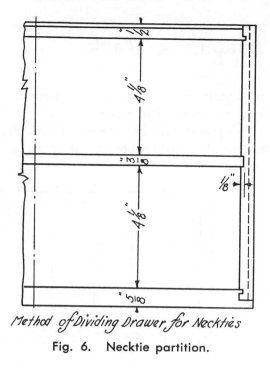

Method of Dividing Drawer for Neckties

Fig. 6.   Necktie partition.

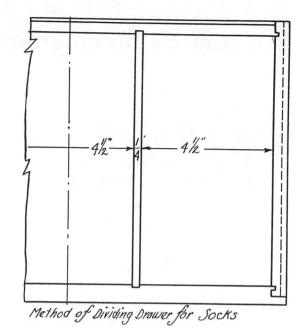

Method of Dividing Drawer for Socks

Fig. 7.   Sock partition.

E. GIVE THE CHEST A SUITABLE FINISH.

If inlaid, provided the drawer fronts are of mahogany, a beautiful color may be obtained by whitewashing the piece. The quicklime dissolved in water gives a rich red color to mahogany but does not color the inlay. All traces of the lime should be washed off with boiled linseed oil mixed with turpentine before proceeding with the subsequent finishing coats.

F. FASTEN THE DRAWER PULLS (FIG. 8).

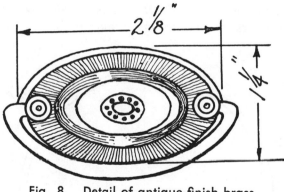

Fig. 8.   Detail of antique-finish brass drawer pull.

Blacksmith's Shoeing-Box Magazine Rack

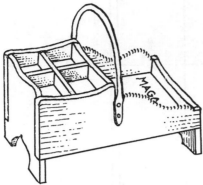

nice, quaint lines, and, almost without exception, constructed them sturdily.

This project falls into the above class. From blacksmith's shoeing box to parlor magazine

MANY lowly items of grandfather's and grandmother's day, which served them only in a strictly utilitarian capacity, as, for instance, the cobbler's bench and the spinning wheel, have now moved into the living room. This probably came about because somehow designers of these things fashioned them along

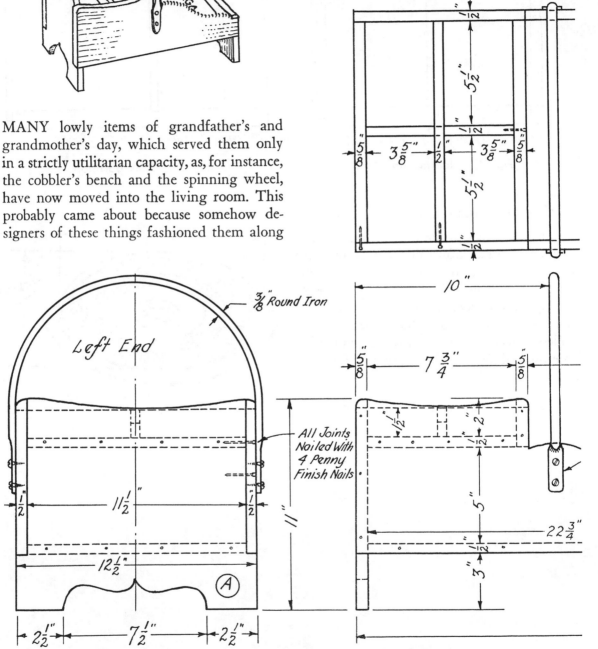

Fig. 1.   Blacksmith's shoeing-box magazine rack.

92

rack certainly is scaling the house furnishing's social ladder, if we may be permitted the simile, and yet it serves this new purpose well.

PROCEDURE

A. PLANE AND SQUARE THE STOCK TO THE SIZES GIVEN IN THE BILL OF MATERIAL.

BILL OF MATERIAL

Pieces	Use	Dimensions
1	A — end	⅝ x 12½ x 11
2	B — sides	½ x 8 x 24
1	C — end	⅝ x 5 x 12½
1	Floor	½ x 11½ x 22¾
1	Floor of partitioned upper section	½ x 7¾ x 11½
1	Front of partitioned section	⅝ x 2½ x 11½
1	Long partition	½ x 1½ x 11½
1	Short partition	½ x 1½ x 7¾
1	Handle (round bar iron)	⅜ diam. x 28

Four ⅝-in., No. 8 r.h. blued screws to fasten handle

4-penny finish nails

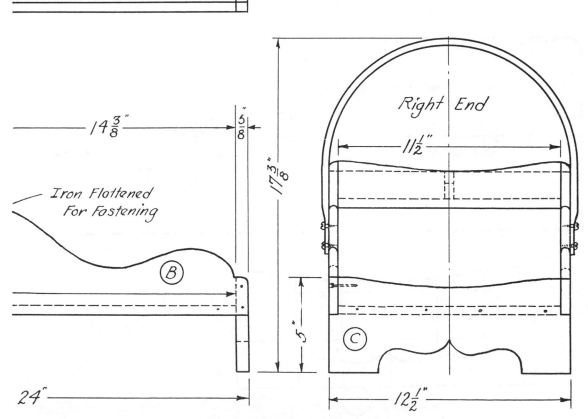

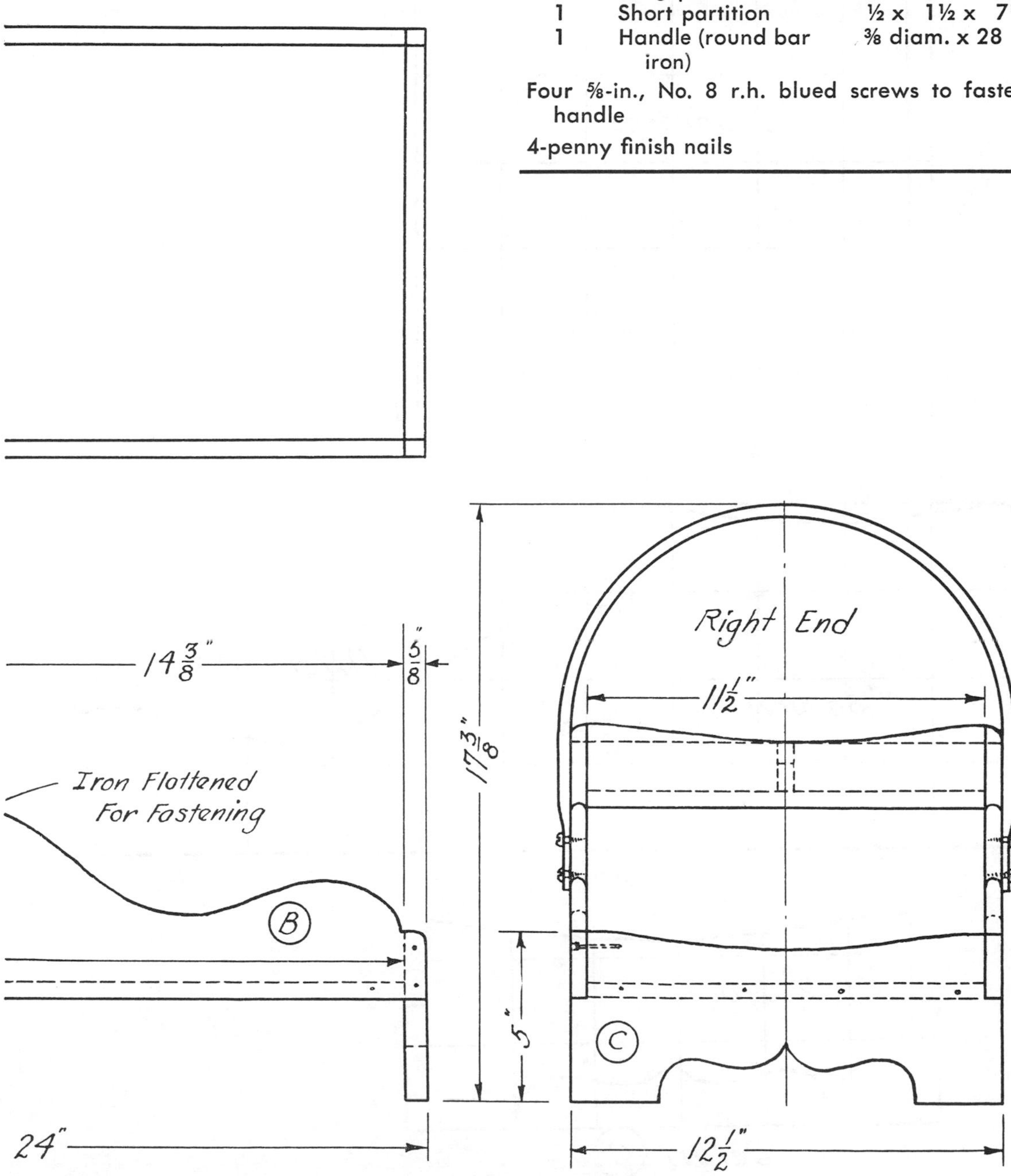

Fig. 1-A.   Blacksmith's shoeing-box magazine rack.

93

B. MAKE THE SIDES AND ENDS.

1. Make full-size patterns of *A*, *B*, and *C*, from Figure 2.

2. Transfer these to the wood, and saw the pieces to shape.

3. Trim, file, or otherwise true up all sawed edges.

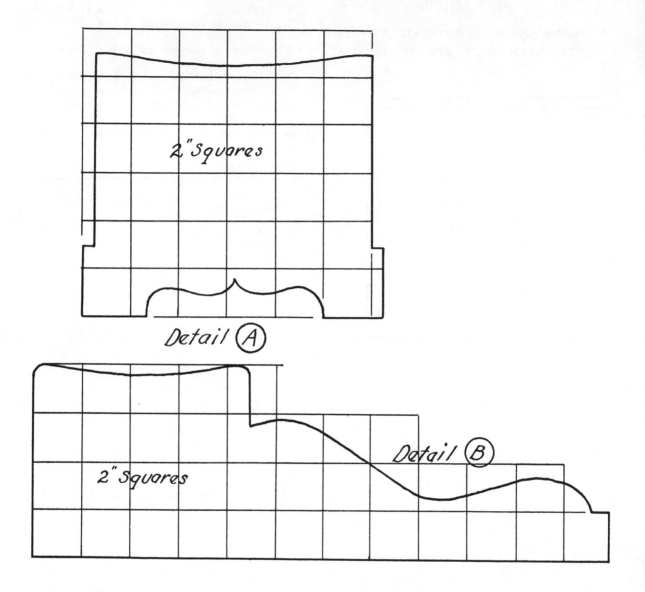

Detail Ⓐ

2" Squares

Detail Ⓑ

2" Squares

2" Squares

Detail Ⓒ

Fig. 2.   Details of parts A, B, and C.

C. ASSEMBLE THE FOLLOWING PARTS IN THIS ORDER.

1. Nail together the sides and ends.
2. Nail the floor in place.
3. Nail in the floor of the partitioned section.
4. Nail in the front of the partitioned section.

D. JOIN THE PARTITIONS TOGETHER.

Fasten these pieces together with a half-lap joint.

E. NAIL THE JOINED PARTITIONS TO THE BOX.

F. GIVE THE BOX A SUITABLE FINISH.

G. MAKE THE HANDLE.

1. Flatten about 2½ in. of each end of a ⅜-in. diameter (or ½ in.) round iron rod. (NOTE: It is best to work the iron red-hot, if facilities permit.)
2. Locate places for holes; then center-punch and drill holes for screws.
3. Bend the iron to shape for the handle.
4. Paint the handle with flat-black enamel.

H. FASTEN THE HANDLE TO THE BOX.

Lady's Handbag

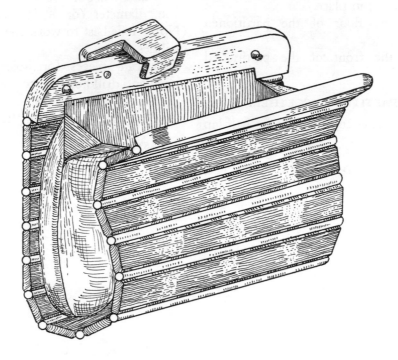

THIS bag is made of varicolored wooden strips. Usually these are alternately light and dark, such as walnut and maple, or mahogany and poplar, etc. The lining should be serviceable material, such as twill fabric or thin leather. If leather is used, the leather should be lined with cloth.

PROCEDURE

A. HANDLES.

1. Plane and square the well-seasoned hardwood to the sizes given in the bill of material.

2. On the inside lower edges, lay out rabbets as shown in Figure 1.

3. Cut the stopped rabbets, using the dado head or a router plane. The router plane is most easily used if both pieces are clamped between a vise dog and a bench stop, and both pieces are planed simultaneously.

4. Drill the small holes to which the lining is to be sewed.

5. Saw the handle to the shape shown in

BILL OF MATERIAL

Pieces	Use	Dimensions
2	Handles	½ x 1¾ x 12
13	Strips	¼ x ⅞ x 12
14	Dowel rods	¼ x 12
1	Catch	1 x 1⅜ x 2
		(Should be sawed from a longer piece)
2	Dowels to keep handles aligned	¼ x ½
2	Leather thongs (strong waxed linen twine may be substituted)	¹⁄₁₆ diam. x approx. 16 in.

2 No. 213½ screw eyes
⅛ x ¾-in. copper rivet
Cord or chain for handle — length to suit
Lining material for bag (see Fig. 3)

the front view in Figure 1. File and sandpaper all edges.

6. Locate and drill holes for the short aligning dowels.

7. Make and glue the aligning dowels to the one handle.

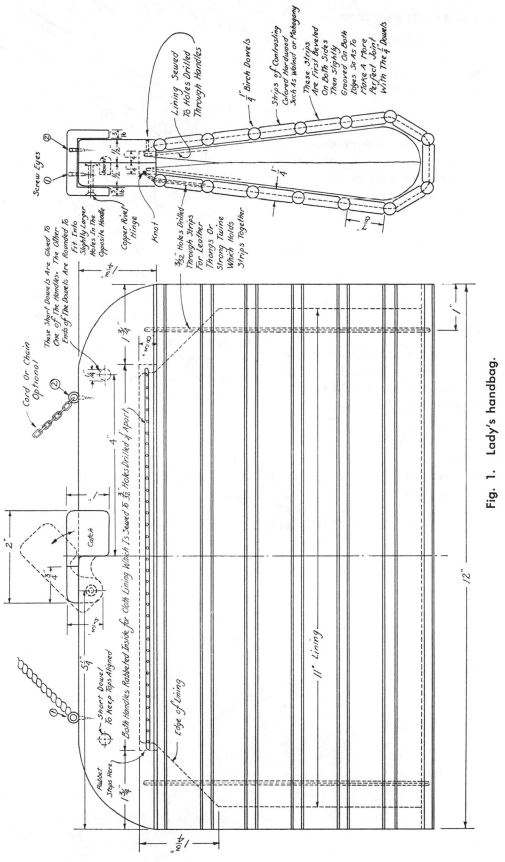

The following labels appear in the figure:

Screw Eyes

Lining Sewed To Holes Drilled Through Handles

$\frac{1}{4}''$ Birch Dowels

Strips of Contrasting Colored Hardwood Such As Walnut or Mahogany

These Strips Are First Beveled On Both Sides Then Slightly Grooved On Both Edges So As To Make A More Perfect Joint With The $\frac{1}{4}''$ Dowels

These Short Dowels Are Glued To One Of The Handles; The Other Ends Of The Dowels Are Rounded To Fit Into Slightly Larger Holes In The Opposite Handle

Copper Rivet Hinge

Knot

$\frac{3}{32}''$ Holes Drilled Through Strips For Leather Thongs Or Strong Twine Which Holds Strips Together

Cord Or Chain Optional

Catch

$\frac{3}{8}''$ Holes Drilled Through Strips Which Is Sewed To $\frac{3}{32}''$ Holes Drilled $\frac{1}{4}''$ Apart)

Both Handles Rabbeted Inside for Cloth Lining

Edge of Lining

11" Lining

Short Dowel To Keep Tops Aligned

Rabbet Stops Here

Fig. 1. Lady's handbag.

97

B. MAKE THE STRIPS AND DOWELS.

1. Cut and plane the strips to the size given in the bill of material.

2. Saw the dowels to length.

3. Cut grooves on both edges of each strip, and fit them to the shape of the dowel rods as shown in the end view in Figure 1.

The best way to make these grooves is with a curved shaper cutter having the proper radius. This work also may be done with a shaper attachment on a drill press. The grooves may be cut by hand if a gouge is used and a little patience is exercised.

4. Bevel all four edges of the strips as shown in Figure 1.

5. Locate and drill the holes for the thongs which hold the strips and dowels together.

C. MAKE THE CATCH.

1. The piece of wood should be long enough to handle easily and safely on a dado head. Square this piece to the thickness and width given in the bill of material.

2. Cut the groove as shown in Figure 2.

3. Saw out the catch. File and sandpaper the sawed edges.

4. Rivet the catch to the handle. The catch should not be too loose.

D. GIVE ALL WOODEN PARTS A SUITABLE FINISH.

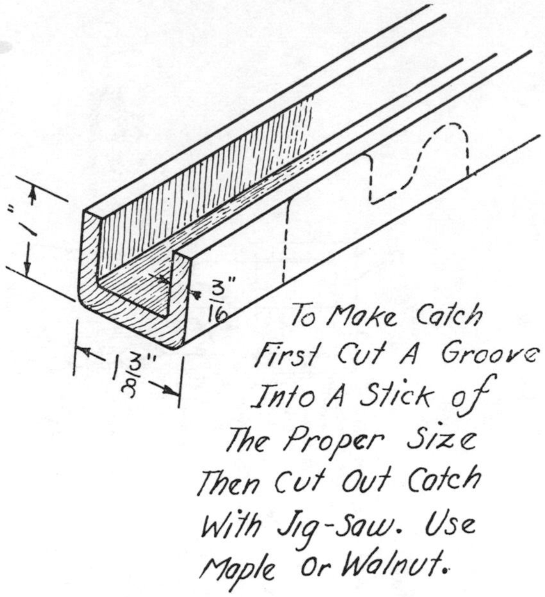

To Make Catch First Cut A Groove Into A Stick of The Proper Size Then Cut Out Catch With Jig-Saw. Use Maple Or Walnut.

Fig. 2. Making the catch.

E. ASSEMBLE THE WOODEN PARTS OF THE HANDBAG.

Thread the leather thongs or round lacing cord through the holes, and knot them inside the handles.

F. LINING.

Follow the directions given in Figure 3; then sew the lining to the holes drilled in the handles.

G. FASTEN THE CORD OR CHAIN TO THE HANDLES.

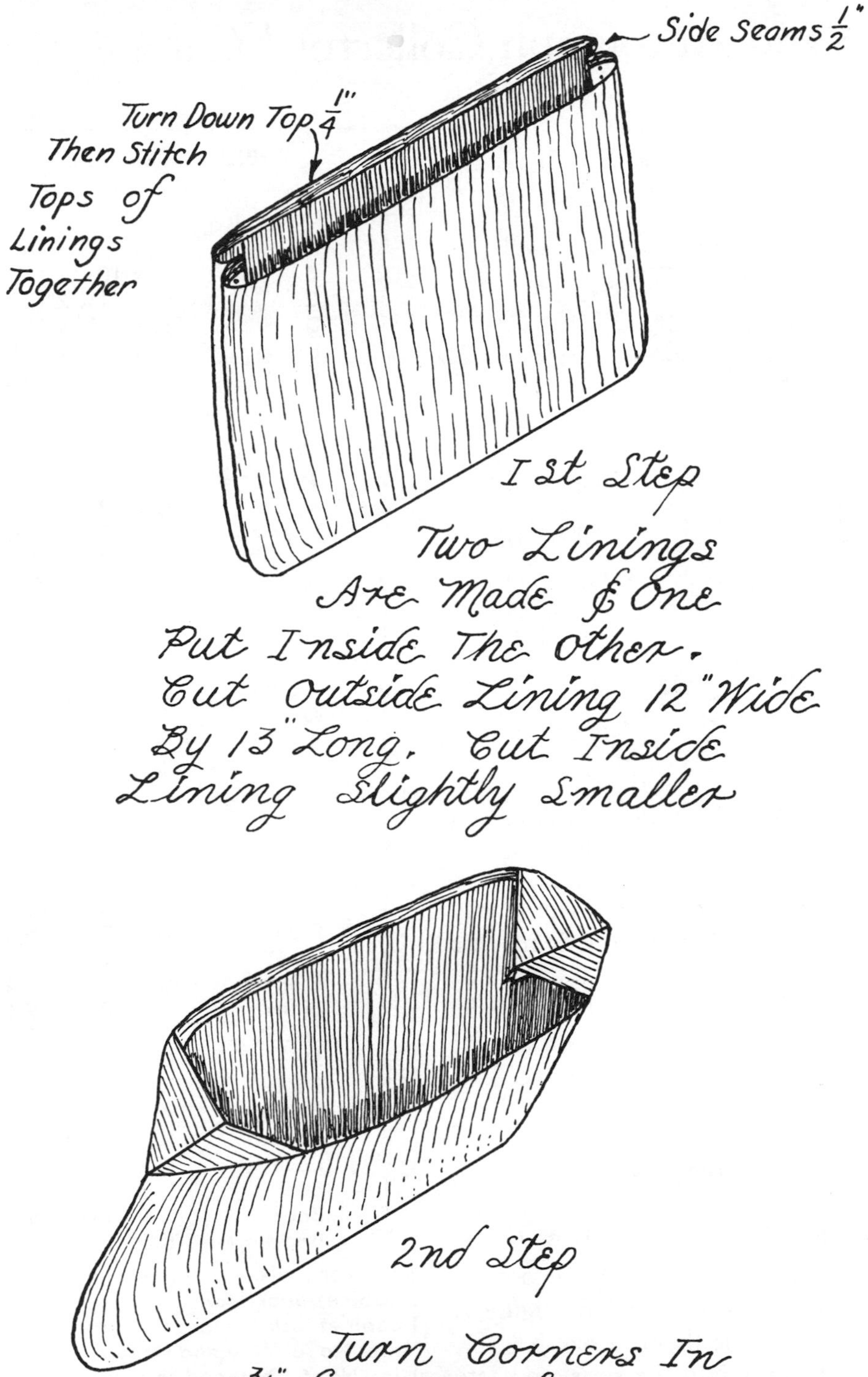

Side Seams $\frac{1}{2}$"

Turn Down Top $\frac{1}{4}$"
Then Stitch
Tops of
Linings
Together

1st Step

Two Linings
Are Made & One
Put Inside The Other.
Cut Outside Lining 12" Wide
By 13" Long. Cut Inside
Lining Slightly Smaller

2nd Step

Turn Corners In
1 $\frac{3}{4}$" from Top & Press
Before Sewing Lining
To Wooden Handles

Fig. 3. Making lining for handbag.

Stamp and Autograph Collectors' Cabinet

BILL OF MATERIAL

Pieces	Use	Dimensions
Fig. 1	Cabinet:	
1	A	¼ x 9⅝ x 6
2	B	½ x 10½ x 17
1	C	¾ x 11¼ x 12½
1	D	½ x 10½ x 10½
1	E	½ x 9⅝ x 10½
1	F	½ x 10½ x 10½
1	G	⅝ x 11⅛ x 12¼
2	H	⅜ x 9⅝ x 12¾
3	I	¼ x 9⅝ x 5½
2	J	½ x 2 x 12½
2	K	½ x 2 x 11¼
2	L	1 x 1 x 1½
1	M	¼ x 4½ x 9
2	N	1½ diam. x 4¹³⁄₁₆
2	O	¼ x 1⅜ x 9½
1	Back	¼ x 10½ x 16½ (plywood)
Fig. 7		
2	P	⅝ x 1½ x 16
1	Q	⅝ x 3 x 9
1	R	⅝ x 2 x 9
1	S	⁹⁄₁₆ x 7½ x 13½
Fig. 1		
1	T	¼ x 1 x 5¼
2	U	¼ x 1¼ x 1¼
Drawers:		
1	Front	½ x 3 x 10
1	Front	½ x 2½ x 5¼
1	Front	½ x 2 x 5¼
1	Front	½ x 1½ x 5¼
2	Sides	¼ x 3 x 9¼
2	Sides	¼ x 2½ x 9¼
2	Sides	¼ x 2 x 9¼
2	Sides	¼ x 1½ x 9¼
1	Bottom	¼ x 9¾ x 9 (plywood)
3	Bottoms	¼ x 5 x 9 (plywood)
1	Back	¼ x 2½ x 9¾ (plywood)
1	Back	¼ x 2 x 5 (plywood)
1	Back	¼ x 1½ x 5 (plywood)
1	Back	¼ x 1 x 5 (plywood)

5 drawer pulls — antique color brass
1 cabinet-door lock
1 cabinet lock for large drawer
¾-in., No. 6 f.h. wood screws
1-in., No. 6 f.h. wood screws

2 H hinges. If this size cannot be obtained, use butt hinges on the edge of the door. Cut the two halves of the H plate out of heavy sheet metal, such as brass, copper, or iron, and butt them against the barrel of the butt hinge to give the effect of a genuine H hinge.

WHILE this cabinet was designed primarily for stamp or autograph collectors, it may be used for many other purposes. It could be used to hold the family accounts, for example. It may be placed on a table or upon a shelf on the wall. If so desired, no door need be made.

PROCEDURE

A. MAKE THE CABINET (MAIN PART).

1. Get out stock for the sides B, the bottom and top D and F, and the shelf E, Figure 1. Square these and plane them to size.

2. Cut the grooves into the sides, and into F and E.

3. Plane and square pieces A, H, and I.

4. Lay out and cut grooves into H and into one of the pieces I.

5. Cut rabbets on the back edges of B, F, and D, for the back to fit into.

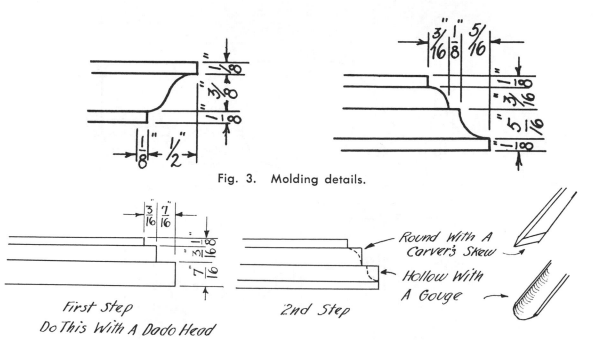

Fig. 3.   Molding details.

First Step
Do This With A Dado Head

2nd Step

Round With A Carver's Skew

Hollow With A Gouge

Fig. 4.   Shaping the molding.

NOTE: All grooves and rabbets may be cut with a dado head, or by hand with a router plane if they are first cut on the lines with a knife. But, they also may be done with a routing bit on a high-speed hand router or drill press.

6. Make a trial assembly of all the pieces thus far made; then assemble.

First, assemble pieces *H* and *I*. Next, glue together this assembled section and pieces *E*, *F*, and *A*. Finally, glue together the assembled section and sides *B* and bottom *D*.

7. Make piece *T*, and glue it in place.

B. **MAKE THE MOLDED BASE AND THE TOP** (FIG. 3).

Fasten them to the cabinet.

1. The molding on these should be cut on a shaper, if one is available, but they may be carved with wood-carving tools, by hand. The cuts may be roughed out on a circular saw before carving (see Fig. 4).

2. Screw *C* to the base of the assembled cabinet.

3. Screw or nail *G* to the top of the assembled cabinet.

C. **MAKE THE FEET, AND FASTEN THEM TO THE MOLDED BASE WITH WOOD SCREWS.**

Miter the corners of the pieces before sawing them to shape.

D. **MAKE THE SCROLLED TOP, AND FASTEN IT TO THE CABINET WITH GLUE BLOCKS AND BRADS** (FIG. 5).

The finials may be turned of wood (Fig. 6, or finials made of brass similar to these may

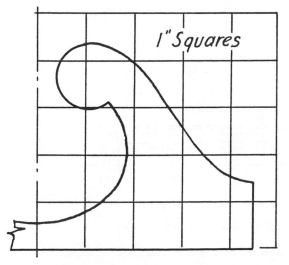

1" Squares

Fig. 5.   Top detail.

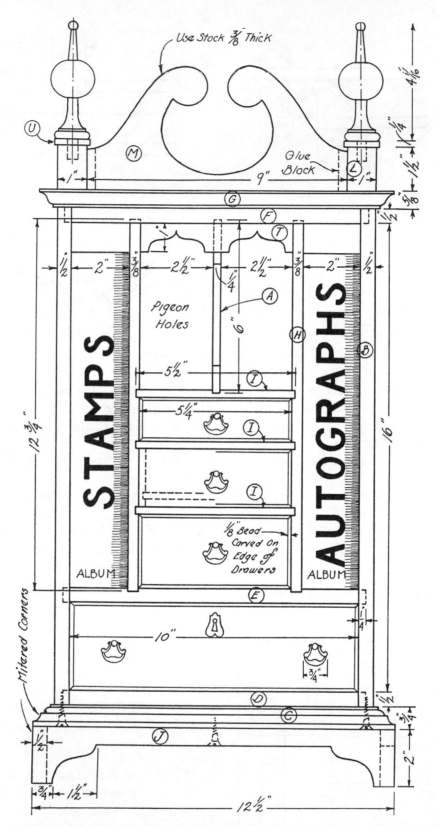

Use Stock ⅜" Thick

Glue
Block

9"

STAMPS

AUTOGRAPHS

Pigeon
Holes

ALBUM

ALBUM

⅛" Bead
Carved On
Edge of
Drawers

Mitered Corners

5½"

5¼"

10"

12½"

Fig. 1. Stamp and autograph collector's cabinet.

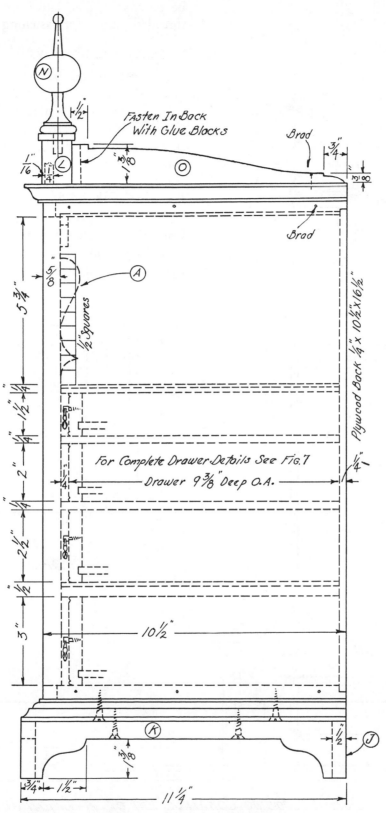

Fasten In Back
With Glue Blocks

Brad

Brad

Plywood Back ¼" x 10½" x 16½"

½ Squares

For Complete Drawer Details See Fig. 7
Drawer 9⅜" Deep O.A.

Fig. 2. Side view of cabinet.

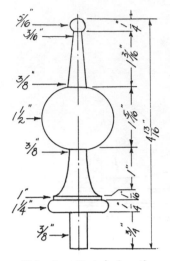

Fig. 6.   Finial detail.

be purchased. The latter are equipped with threaded screws for fastening.

E. MAKE THE DRAWERS.

1. These should be assembled and fitted before the back of the cabinet is nailed on.

2. Dovetailed drawer joints as shown in *A*, Figure 7, are the best, but they require more skill to make than the machine-made type shown in *B*, Figure 7.

F. MAKE THE DOOR.

The raised panel of this door is a nice feature. The arched top of the panel must be carved by hand. This is not so difficult after the other raising has been done.

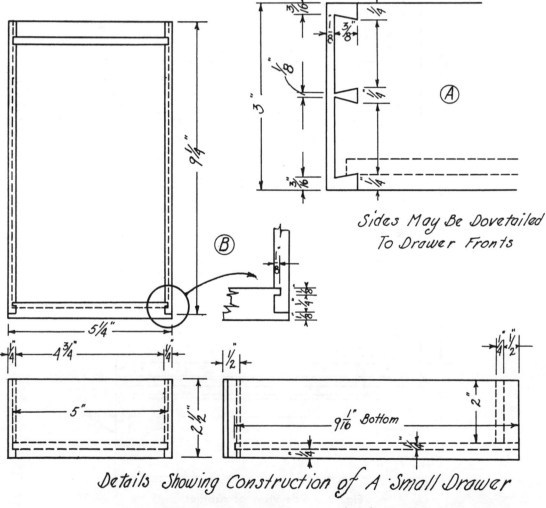

Sides May Be Dovetailed To Drawer Fronts

Details Showing Construction of A Small Drawer

Fig. 7.   Drawer-construction details.

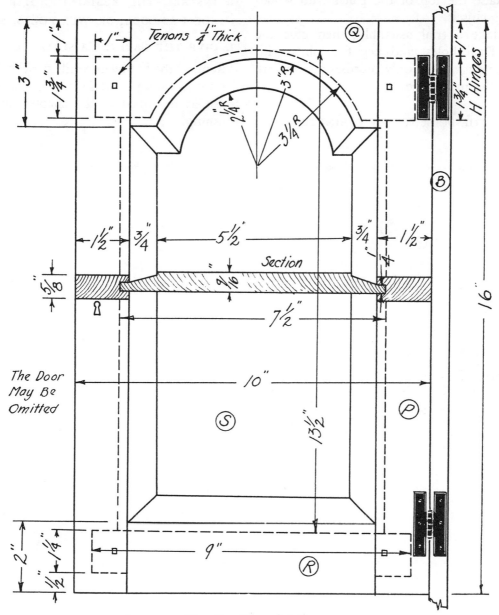

Fig. 8. Door detail.

1. Square up the stiles *P* and the rails *Q* and *R*, Figure 8.

2. Make the mortises in the stiles.

3. Make the tenons on the rails.

4. Cut grooves, ¼ in. wide and deep, into the inside edges of the rails and stiles, including the lower and as yet unarched edge of rail *Q*. The grooves in the stiles should be cut only between the two mortises, and should not continue to the ends of the stiles.

5. Arch rail *Q* on the band saw.

6. Cut the arched part of the groove in *Q*. This may be done on a mortising machine or by hand with a chisel.

7. Raise the panel by tilting the saw table to an angle of about 13 deg. to cut the angles. Be sure the panel is ¼ in. thick at the edge of the rail or stile when assembled.

See Figure 4, page 72, for the method of raising panels.

8. Raise the top of the panel with wood-carving chisels.

9. Make a trial assembly; then glue the door. Drill holes, and peg the joints with wooden pegs. Glue only mortises and tenons. Leave the panel free.

G. FIT THE DOOR TO THE CABINET.

H. INSTALL THE REMAINING HARDWARE, SUCH AS LOCK, DRAWER PULLS, ETC.

I. GIVE THE CABINET A SUITABLE FINISH.

Remove the hardware while performing the various finishing operations. Apply a suitable finish as described in the chapter on wood finishing.

Small Folding Desk Box

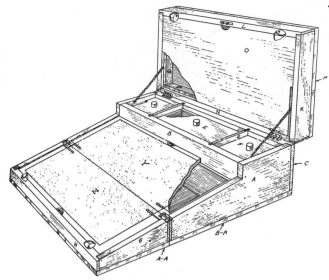

BILL OF MATERIAL

Pieces	Use	Dimensions
2	A	⅝ x 4⅛ x 11½
1	B	½ x 4⅛ x 14¾
1	C	⅝ x 4⅛ x 16
2	D	¼ x 4⅛ x 3⅜
1	E	¼ x 2⅞ x 8½
2	F	¼ x 2⅞ x 2⅞
2	G	⅝ x 1⅞ (approx.) x 7½
1	H	⅝ x 1¼ (approx.) x 16
2	K	⅝ x 1½ x 11½
1	L	⅝ x 1½ x 16
1	M	½ x 12 x 16
1	N	⅝ x 1½ x 16
1	O	½ x 10¾ x 14¾
2	P	¼ x 1 x 14¾
2	Q	¼ x 1 x 10¼
1	Y	⅜ x 7⅜ x 14¾
1	Z	⅜ x 6¾ x 14¾
1	A-A	⅜ x 8 x 16
1	B-B	⅜ x 12 x 16

The following pieces are shown in Figure 1:

1	I	⅝ x 2 (approx.) x 16
1	J	⅝ x 1¹⁵⁄₁₆ (approx.) x 16
2	R	¼ x 3½ x 8½
6	S	¼ x 3½ x 2⅜
4	T	¼ x 3½ x 2⅞
1	U	¼ x 2³⁄₁₆ x 14¾
1	U-U	¼ x 1³⁄₁₆ x 14¾
2	V	¼ x 2³⁄₁₆ x 6⅞
1	W	¼ x 1⅞₆ x 14¾
1	W-W	¼ x ¹¹⁄₁₆ x 14¾
2	X	¼ x 1⅜ (approx.) x 6¼
1	Calfskin	13¾ x 14½

Glue to glue leather

3 Dowels, ⅜-in. diameter by ⅜ in. long for lid handles

2 pr. narrow (⅞-in. open) or middle (1-in. open) x 1½-in. brass butt hinges

3 pr. narrow (¾-in. open) or middle (¹³⁄₁₆-in. open) x 1-in. brass butt hinges

Four 16-gauge x ½ x 1-in. brass lid catches

Small brass chest lock

Chain, single jack, brass or steel, Nos. 18 or 16. (Use enough to allow the lid to tilt slightly backward, about 6 in. to a side.)

DURING Civil War days and earlier, it was not uncommon for travelers to carry a small desk like the above when they went on a trip. Many of these desks were made of the finest material, such as walnut, mahogany, or rosewood. Some of them were decorated with ivory inlay or mother-of-pearl. Some had hardware and mounts of silver or gold. The author has repaired one made of rosewood, inlaid with ivory. One belonging to Benjamin Franklin is on display at the Franklin Institute in Philadelphia.

This box could be fitted with a handle to be carried like a valise. It is undecorated, and its construction is very simple so as not to discourage the amateur cabinetmaker. If so desired, it can be embellished with attractive inlays, marquetry, or simple carving.

All pieces in the following bill of material are designated by letter instead of by name, shown in the above illustration.

PROCEDURE

A. MAKE THE MAIN PART OF THE BOX.

1. Get out stock for the following parts: *A, B, B-B, C, D, E, F, U, U-U, V, R, S, T, I,* and *Y.*

Since the three parts of the box should fit snugly together when folded it is essential to make each part exactly the correct size. This is especially true of parts *A* and *G.*

2. Lay out and cut the grooves in *B* and *C,* and fit pieces *D* to these grooves.

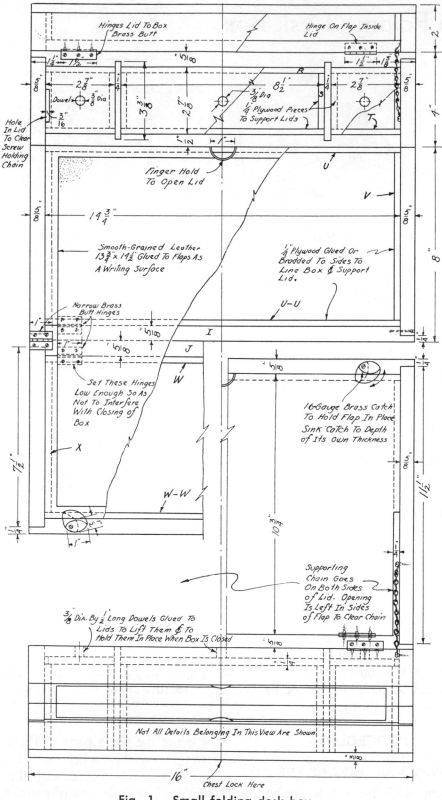

Fig. 1. Small folding desk box.

108

3. Cut the rabbets on the ends of *C* and *I*.

4. Assemble pieces *A*, *B*, *C*, *I*, *D*, and *B-B*. Use brads, and glue on the rabbeted and grooved joints. The use of glue on the other joints is optional.

5. Glue pieces *R*, *S*, *T*, *U*, *V*, and *U-U* to the insides of their respective compartments.

6. Fit and fasten lid *Y* to the box with hinges.

B. MAKE THE FOLDING FRONT PART OF THE BOX.

1. Get out stock for the following parts: *G*, *H*, *J*, *W*, *X*, *W-W*, *A-A*, and *Z*.

2. Cut rabbets on the ends of *H* and *J*.

3. Assemble parts *G*, *H*, *J*, and *A-A*. Use glue and brads on the rabbeted joints.

4. Glue pieces *W*, *X*, and *W-W* to the inside of this compartment.

5. Fit and fasten lid *Z* to this part with hinges.

The barrels of these hinges must not protrude above the upper edges of pieces *G*. They and the hinges which fasten lid *Y* must remain level with, or below the slanting upper edges of *A* and *G*, in order not to touch each other when these two parts rest upon each other in their folded position. For this reason

the surfaces of lids *Y* and *Z* have been lowered ¹⁄₁₆ in. below the level of these edges. If ¹⁄₁₆ in. is not enough to bring the barrels of these hinges below or even with the level of these slanted edges, then the surfaces of these lids may have to be lowered slightly more than this. Assure yourself that these parts are properly adjusted to fit together in their folded position before actually joining them together with hinges.

C. FASTEN THE FOLDING PART TO THE BOX WITH HINGES.

1. Another type of hinge, known as a box hinge (Fig. 3), with long narrow leaves which could be fitted to the slanted edges of *A* and

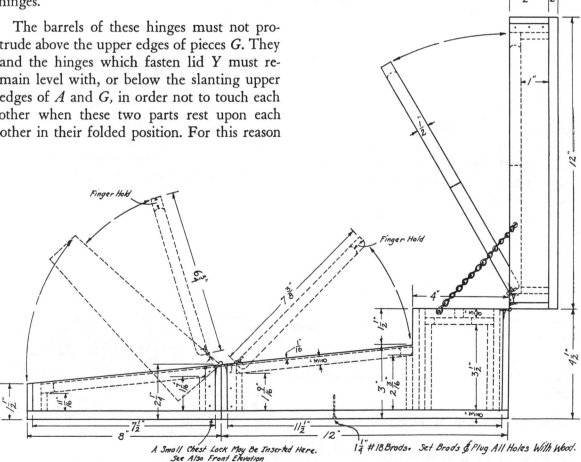

A Small Chest Lock May Be Inserted Here.
See Also Front Elevation

1¼" #18 Brads. Set Brads & Plug All Holes With Wood.

Fig. 2.   Side view of desk box.

G, could be substituted for the butt hinges which fasten the folding part to the box proper. These could also be used to fasten the lid to the box.

2. Still another type of hinge, known as the dolphin hinge, may be substituted for hinging the parts as shown in Figure 3.

2. Cut rabbets on the ends of pieces *N* and *L*.

3. Assemble the lid, glue the rabbeted joints, and fasten the others with brads or glue, or both.

4. Glue pieces *P* and *Q* to the inside of the lid.

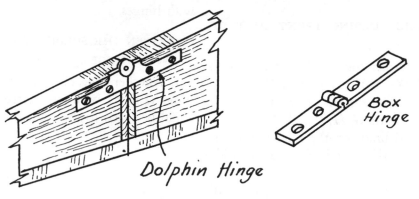

Fig. 3.   Hinges.

D. GLUE A PIECE OF TOOLING CALF TO LIDS Y AND Z.

Calfskin is good leather to use because it does not stretch much. It may be purchased dyed in various colors.

1. Coat the surfaces to which the leather is to be glued with woodworker's glue. Rubber cement cannot be used since it does not adhere well to wood.

2. Allow the glue to become tacky; then, working from the center toward the edges, press the leather firmly down on the lids.

3. Hold the leather down by first covering it with waxed paper, followed by several layers of newspaper, and then clamp a board to the top of these until the glue has thoroughly dried.

4. Trim off the edges of the leather, if necessary, to make them straight after the glue has dried.

E. MAKE THE LID OF THE BOX.

1. Get out stock for the following parts: *K, L, N, M, O, P, Q*.

5. Cut away the parts on the ends of lid *O* for the chain or the quadrant stays.

Quadrant stays, shown in Figure 4, may be used instead of the chain to keep the lid from tilting back too far. The stays are nicer than the chain, but more expensive.

6. Hinge lid *O* to the other part of the lid.

7. Hinge the main lid to the box.

8. Fasten the chain or quadrant stays.

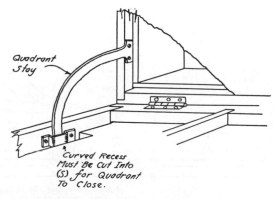

Fig. 4.   Placing quadrant stay.

F. MAKE THE BRASS CATCHES TO HOLD LIDS O AND Z IN PLACE.

Use 16-gauge brass. Drill and countersink for ½-in., No. 4 f.h. brass wood screws.

G. MAKE LAYOUTS FOR RECESSES INTO WHICH THESE CATCHES FIT, AND ROUT THEM OUT.

H. FASTEN THE CATCHES.

I. MAKE THE HANDLES FOR LIFTING THE COMPARTMENT COVERS E AND F.

Make these handles of ⅜-in. dowels. They serve to hold the covers down when the lid is closed, as well as to lift them.

J. IF A LOCK IS DESIRED, IT SHOULD BE MORTISED INTO THE OUTSIDE COVER OF THE FRONT COMPARTMENT.

Various types of brass catches are available, which can be fastened to the outside of the box. They are easier to install than a chest lock, and in most cases are not as expensive.

K. GIVE THE BOX A SUITABLE FINISH.

Make-up Box

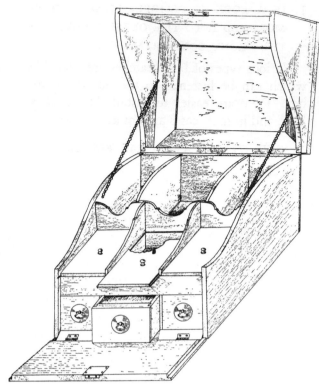

BILL OF MATERIAL

Because it is best to make the corner joints of the box and lid simultaneously, pieces **D** and **E** should be left in one piece until the joints have been made and fitted. The same holds true with pieces **A** and **I**.

Pieces	Use	Dimensions
1	A	3/8 x 7 3/8 x 15
2	B	1/4 x 3 x 6 7/16
1	C	1/4 x 5 7/8 x 14 1/2
2	D	3/8 x 3 1/4 x 11 7/8
2	E	3/8 x 7 3/8 x 11 7/8
1	F	1/4 x 11 x 14 1/2
2	G	1/4 x 7 1/8 x 11 7/16
1	H	3/8 x 3 1/4 x 15
1	I	3/8 x 3/4 x 15
2	J	1/2 x 1 1/4 x 11 3/8
2	K	1/2 x 1 1/4 x 14 1/4
2	L	1/4 x 4 5/8 x 6 7/16
1	M	1/4 x 4 7/8 x 6 7/16
1	N	3/8 x 11 7/8 x 14 1/2
1	O	3/8 x 4 7/8 x 15
1	P	3/8 x 12 1/8 x 15
1	Q	3/8 x 1 1/2 x 14 1/2

Side drawers:

2	Fronts	5/8 x 2 1/2 x	3 1/2
4	Sides	1/4 x 2 1/2 x	6 1/4
2	Backs	1/4 x 2 1/2 x	3 1/4
2	Bottoms	1/4 x 3 1/4 x	5 3/4

Middle drawer:

1	Front	5/8 x 2 1/2 x	6 3/4
2	Sides	1/4 x 2 1/2 x	11 1/4
1	Back	1/4 x 2 1/2 x	6 1/2
1	Bottom	1/4 x 6 1/2 x	10 3/4

Three 1/2-in. brass knobs for sliding covers
Three brass drawer pulls
Three narrow 1-in. brass butts to fasten lid to box
Three broad 1-in. brass butts to fasten flap to box
One 8 7/8 x 12 1/2-in. mirror
Approximately 11-in. single jack chain for each side. Quadrant stays may be substituted for chain if so desired (see Fig. 4, Folding Desk Box)
One small chest lock

THE make-up box shown above can be used as a substitute for a dressing table. It also can be used on a dressing table, or it may be fitted with a handle and a lock to be carried along on trips, like a suitcase or overnight bag.

It has been designed with compartments deep enough to hold bottles containing various toilet preparations, as well as compartments with sliding covers to hold face powders, etc. It has three drawers to hold comb and brush set and other toilet articles. The inside of the lid has a framed mirror.

This is one of the most difficult projects in the book, and will require considerable skill and care in the making.

PROCEDURE

A. BUILD THE BOX.

1. Get out stock for the two sides of the box and the lid, *E* and *D*, for the back of the box and lid *A* and *I*, and for the front of the lid, *H*. But first:

To the sides *D* and *E* and to the backs *A* and *I* add enough width to saw them apart after the corner joints have been made.

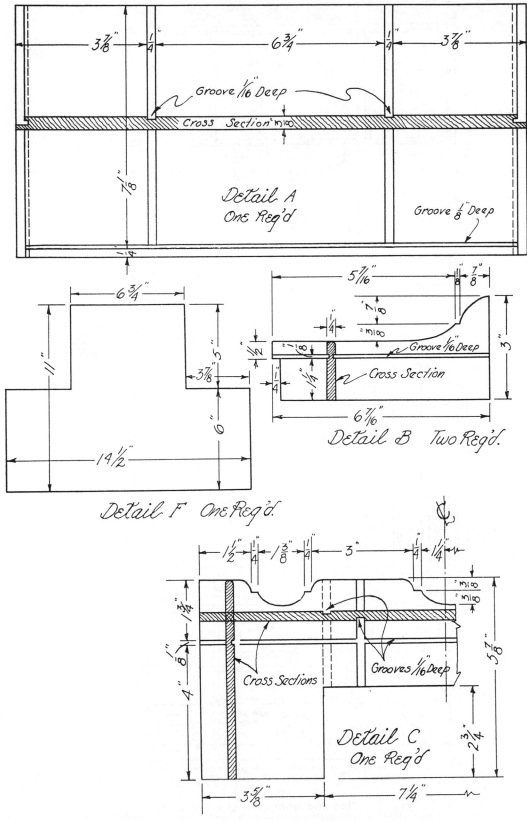

Fig. 3.   Details of parts A, B, C, and F.

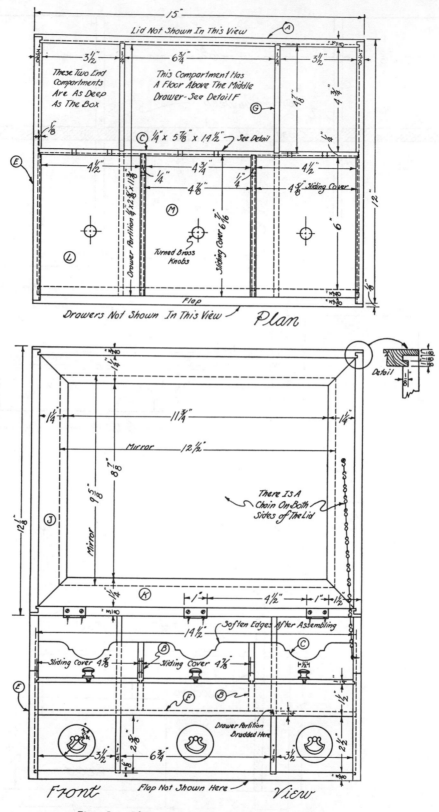

Fig. 1.   Plan and front view of make-up box.

114

2. Make a full-size pattern of *E*, as shown in Figure 4.

3. Lay out the grooves and joints on *A* and *E*, as shown in Figures 3 and 4.

4. With a ⅛-in. dado blade, cut the tongue-and-groove corner joints on a circular saw.

5. Cut all other grooves with a router bit mounted on a high-speed motor, drill press, or rotary tool.

6. Cut the pieces for the lid from those intended for the box.

7. Make the floors *F* and *N*, the partitions *C*, *B*, and *G*, and the front *Q*. No separate detail of the floor *N* is shown, but it has two grooves for partitions *G*. These may be laid out from the details given in Figures 1 and 2. These grooves are stopped just short of the slanted front edge, Figure 2.

8. Make a trial assembly of all the pieces comprising the box which have thus far been completed.

9. Glue them together. Use brads only where absolutely necessary.

10. Make the sliding covers.

The tongues on these may be made with a dado head on a circular saw.

B. BUILD THE DRAWERS.

1. Get out all the stock.

2. Cut the tongue-and-groove joints with a dado saw.

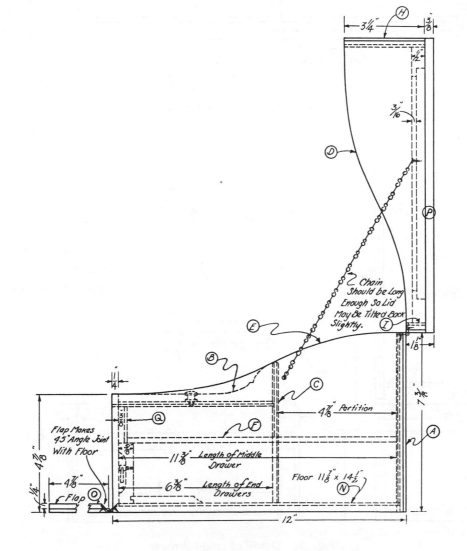

Fig. 2.   End view of make-up box.

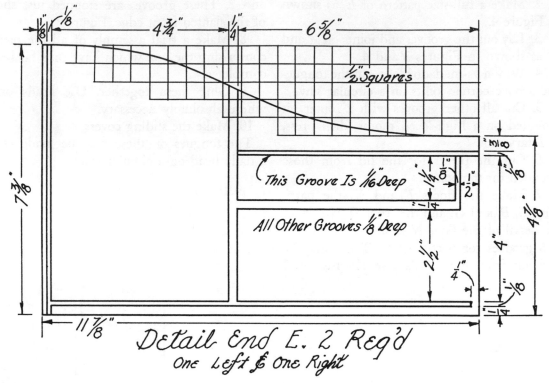

½" Squares

This Groove Is ¹⁄₁₆ Deep

All Other Grooves ⅛ Deep

Detail End E. 2 Req'd
One Left & One Right

Fig. 4. Detail of end E.

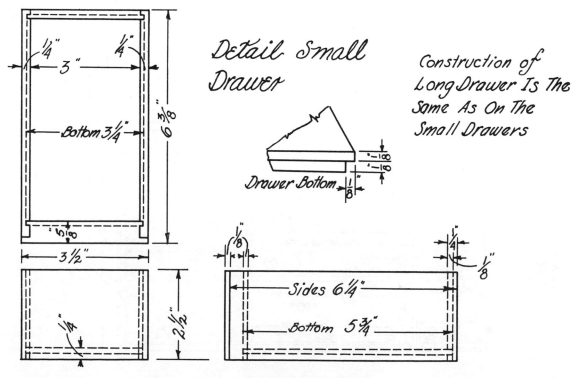

Detail Small Drawer

Construction of Long Drawer Is The Same As On The Small Drawers

Bottom 3¼

Drawer Bottom

Sides 6¼"

Bottom 5¾"

Fig. 5. Detail of small drawer.

3. Mount the drawer fronts on a faceplate to turn the handle depressions for the drawer pulls.

4. Assemble the drawers, using glue and brads.

5. Fit the drawers to their places.

C. MAKE THE FRONT FLAP, AS SHOWN IN FIGURE 2.

D. FASTEN THE FLAP TO THE BOX WITH HINGES.

E. LID.

1. Make a trial assembly of the sides, front, and back; then glue them together.

2. Make the mirror frame. The rabbets may be cut on a dado head. To make a frame like this, see instructions *D* and Figures 3 and 4, in the Tilting Photo Frame, pages 54 and 55.

3. Fasten the mirror into the frame.

4. With glue and a few brads, fasten the frame to the sides, front, and back, which have just been assembled.

5. Fasten the top of the lid.

F. FASTEN THE LID TO THE BOX WITH HINGES.

G. FIT THE LOCK TO THE FLAP.

H. FIT THE CHAIN OR THE QUADRANT STAYS TO THE BOX AND LID.

I. FIT THE OTHER HARDWARE TO THE BOX.

J. GIVE THE BOX A SUITABLE FINISH.

Remove the hardware while performing the finishing operations.

Carved Jewelry Box

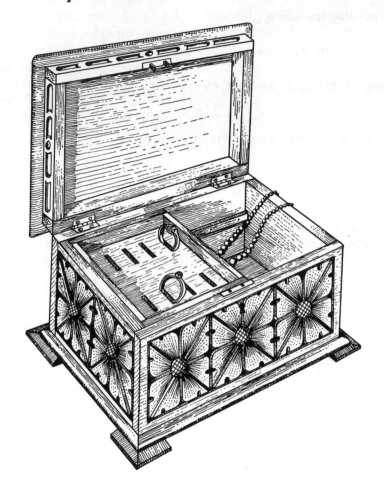

BILL OF MATERIAL

Pieces	Use	Dimensions
2	Sides	¼ x 2¼ x 6½
2	Ends	¼ x 2¼ x 3
1	Bottom	⁵⁄₁₆ x 4 x 7
2	Sides of lid	¼ x ⅜ x 6½
2	Ends of lid	¼ x ⅜ x 3
1	Top	⅜ x 4 x 7
4	Feet	¼ x 1 x 1
2	Sides of ring tray	³⁄₁₆ x 1 x 3
2	Ends of ring tray	³⁄₁₆ x 1 x 2⅝
2	Bottom of ring tray	⅛ x 2⅝ x 2⅝
2	Small strips to support ring tray	⅛ x ¼ x 6

Two ¾-in. narrow brass butt hinges
One small chest lock or box catch
½-in., No. 20, ⅝-in., No. 20, and 1-in., No. 18 brads
Brass lid support
Velvet to line box and ring tray
Green felt for bottoms of feet

HAND-CARVED things are interesting. Simple as the carving on this box is, the design is unique and quite appropriate for a jewelry box, and should be a good project to teach the art of wood carving. The construction of the box also is simple.

PROCEDURE

A. BOX.

1. Plane and square up the sides and ends to the sizes given in the bill of material.

2. Trace full-size patterns of the carving designs from Figure 3.

3. Transfer these patterns to the wood, and carve, following the directions in Figure 1.

Fig. 3. Carving details of front and end of box (full size).

119

Sandpaper the carving with 2/0 flint paper or 4/0 garnet paper.

Carving often has more character if it is not sandpapered, provided it is carefully finished off with chisels.

4. Assemble the sides and ends.
5. Make the bottom.
6. Nail the bottom to the assembled part.
7. Make the feet. Fasten them to the box.

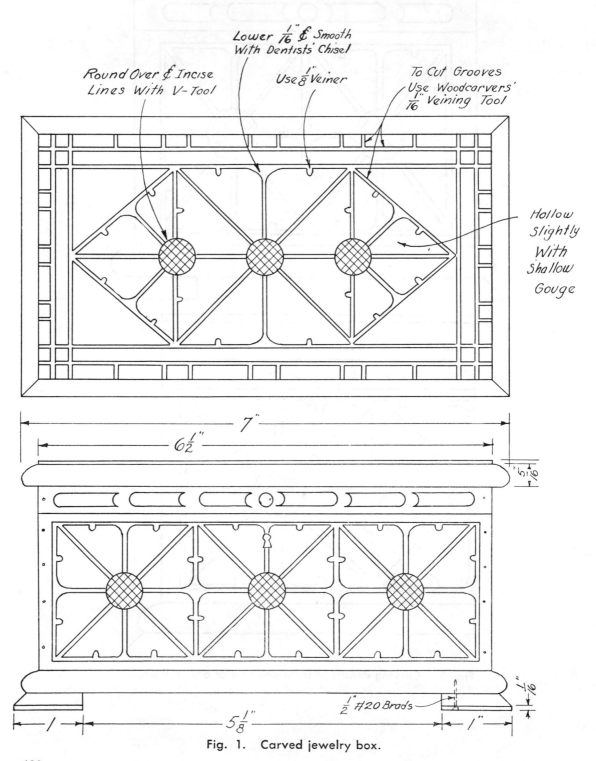

Fig. 1. Carved jewelry box.

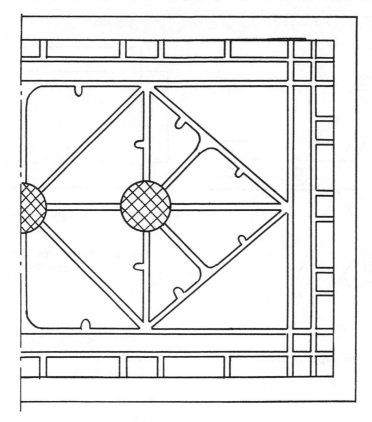

Fig. 4. Carving detail of cover (full size).

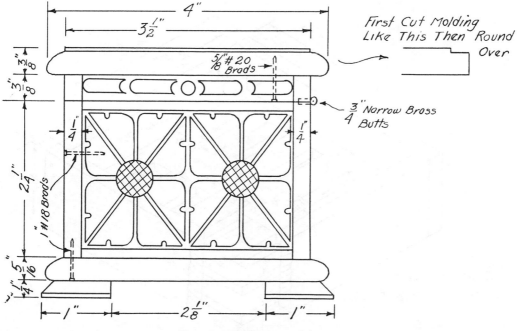

First Cut Molding
Like This Then Round
Over

4"

3½"

⅜" 3"/8

3"/8

5/8"# 20 Brads

¾" Narrow Brass Butts

¼"

¼"

2¼"

1 # 18 Brads

5/16"

¼"

1"

2⅛"

1"

Fig. 2. End view of box.

121

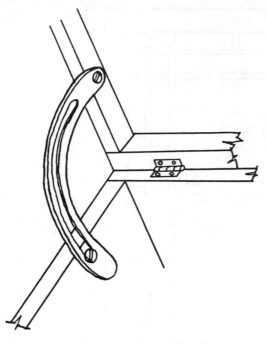

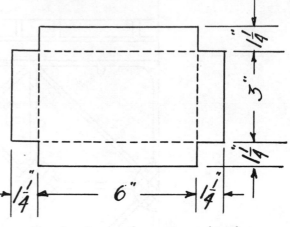

Fig. 6.   Pattern for cutting velvet for box lining.

Fig. 5.   Lid support detail.

3. Carve the sides, ends, and top of the lid. Get design from Figures 3 and 4.

4. Assemble the lid.

B. MAKE THE LID.

1. Plane and square the sides, ends, and top of the lid.

2. Cut the molding on the edges of the top.

C. FASTEN THE LID TO THE BOX WITH HINGES.

D. INSTALL THE LOCK OR A BRASS BOX CATCH.

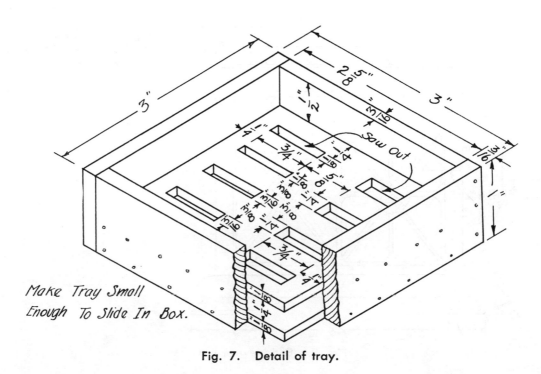

Make Tray Small Enough To Slide In Box.

Fig. 7.   Detail of tray.

E. INSTALL A LID SUPPORT AS SHOWN IN FIGURE 5.

F. CUT THE VELVET FOR THE BOX LINING, AND GLUE IT IN PLACE (FIG. 6).

G. MAKE AND FASTEN THE TWO STRIPS TO SUPPORT THE RING TRAY.

H. MAKE THE RING TRAY (FIG. 7).

1. Plane and square all of the pieces.

2. Locate all the ring slots, and saw them out with a coping saw or on the jig saw. Only the upper deck of the ring-tray bottom has the slots.

3. Assemble the ring tray.

4. Cut out the lining for the ring tray, and glue it in place (Fig. 8).

With a sharp knife, cut slits through the lining at each ring slot, and glue the ends down into the slots.

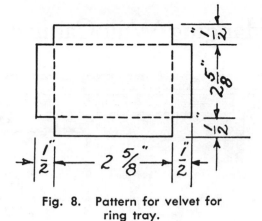

Fig. 8. Pattern for velvet for ring tray.

5. Sandpaper the ring tray on the outside until it slides freely on the strips in the jewelry box.

I. GLUE THE PIECES OF FELT TO THE BOTTOMS OF THE FEET.

J. GIVE THE BOX A SUITABLE FINISH.

Hanging Wall Cabinet

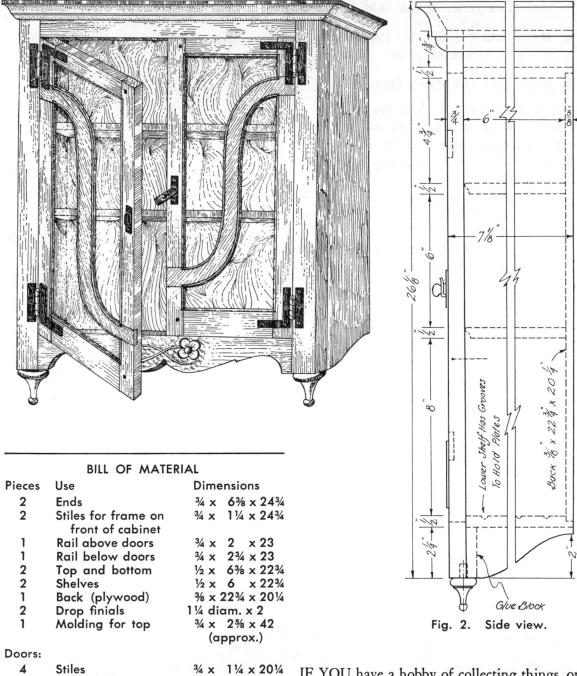

BILL OF MATERIAL

Pieces	Use	Dimensions
2	Ends	¾ x 6⅜ x 24¾
2	Stiles for frame on front of cabinet	¾ x 1¼ x 24¾
1	Rail above doors	¾ x 2 x 23
1	Rail below doors	¾ x 2¾ x 23
2	Top and bottom	½ x 6⅜ x 22¾
2	Shelves	½ x 6 x 22¾
1	Back (plywood)	⅜ x 22¾ x 20¼
2	Drop finials	1¼ diam. x 2
1	Molding for top	¾ x 2⅝ x 42 (approx.)

Doors:

4	Stiles	¾ x 1¼ x 20¼
2	Upper rails	¾ x 1¼ x 9¾
2	Lower rails	¾ x 1¾ x 9¾
2	Curved pieces	¼ x 3¼ x 18¼
2	Glass	8½ x 17¾

2 sets black-iron, dull-finish H-L hinges

Black-iron, dull-finish latch

Fig. 2. Side view.

IF YOU have a hobby of collecting things, or if you make small objects, this cabinet can be used to display these articles. It also can be used to hold a small set of dishes or as a spice cabinet for the kitchen. Spacing of shelves may be changed.

124

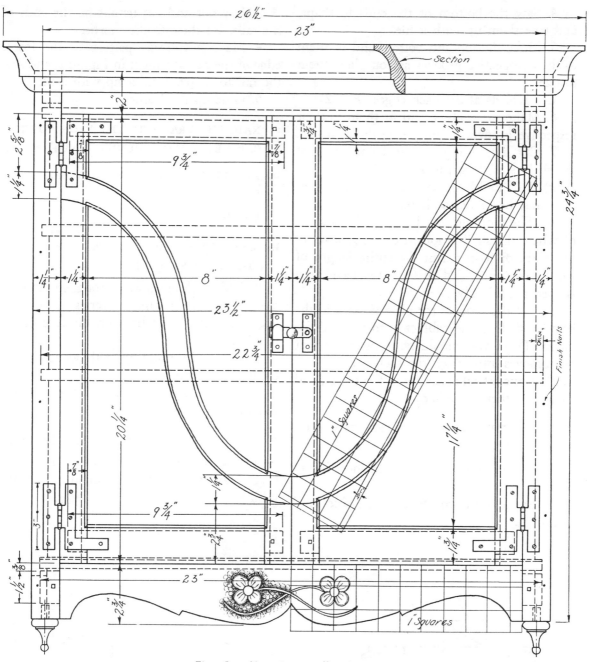

Fig. 1. Hanging wall cabinet.

While this is the largest project in the book, it is not the most difficult to build. Except for the doors, the construction of the project is quite simple.

PROCEDURE

A. MAKE AND ASSEMBLE THE CABINET,
THE SHELVES, AND THE BACK.

1. Plane and square the ends to size.
2. Make layouts for the grooves and rabbets on the ends (Fig. 2).
3. Cut these out with a router plane or on a circular saw with a dado head, or with a power router using suitable bits.

125

4. Saw the bottom of the ends to shape, and true them up with a file.

5. Make the top and bottom and fit them to their respective grooves as you plane them to size.

Cut rabbets at the back edges (Fig. 2).

6. Make the shelves, and fit them to their respective grooves as you plane them to size.

7. Cut a molding on the front edges of the shelves as shown in Figure 2.

a) This molding may be cut on a shaper, or it may be carved by hand.

b) The molding may be stopped just short of where the shelf is joined to the grooves in the ends, or it may run the entire length of the shelves, provided the grooves have been shaped accordingly.

8. Cut the grooves for plate holders in the bottom shelf if the cabinet is to be used for china. These also should be stopped short of the grooves into which the shelves fit.

9. Make a trial assembly of the pieces, and then glue them together.

B. MAKE THE FRAME FOR THE FRONT OF THE CABINET.

1. Square and plane the rails and stiles to size.

2. Lay out the mortises in the stiles and cut them.

3. Lay out and cut tenons on the ends of the rails. Fit these to the mortises.

4. Make a full-size pattern of the lower edge of the rail as shown in Figure 1, and saw the rail to shape. True it up with a file.

5. Glue up the frame.

C. NAIL THE FRAME TO THE FRONT OF THE CABINET WITH 6-PENNY FINISH NAILS.

D. SQUARE UP THE BACK, AND NAIL IT IN PLACE.

Use 2-penny common nails.

E. MAKE THE MOLDING FOR THE TOP OF THE CABINET (FIG. 3).

1. This molding may be roughed out on a circular saw, by running a series of saw cuts nearly to the curved lines on the face of the molding.

2. Carve the molding with wood-carving chisels.

3. With curved blocks, sandpaper the molding.

F. FASTEN THE MOLDING TO THE CABINET.

1. Saw the mitered corners on a miter box.

2. Nail and glue the molding to the cabinet.

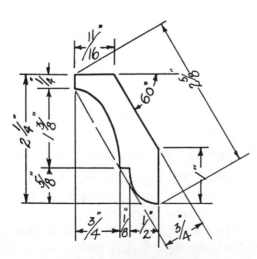

Fig. 3.   Molding detail.

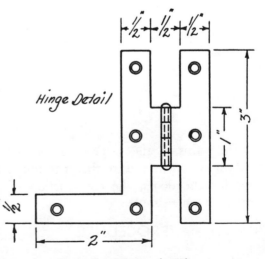

Fig. 5.   Hinge detail.

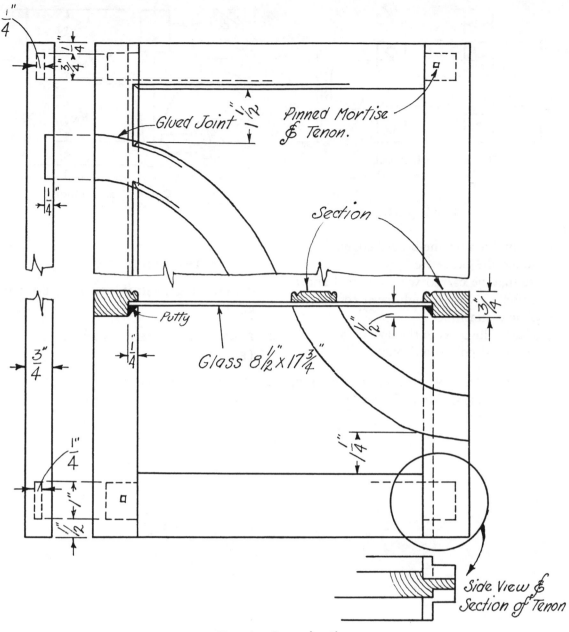

Fig. 4.   Door details.

G. **MAKE THE DOORS.**

1. Plane and square the rails and stiles to size.

2. Lay out and cut the rabbets on the inside edges of the rails and stiles. This may be done on a dado head.

3. Lay out and cut the mortises on the stiles.

4. Lay out and cut the haunched tenons on the rails. See Figure 4 for a side view and a section of the tenon.

5. Glue up the door frames.

6. Lay out a pattern, and make the curved pieces.

7. Lay the curved pieces on the door frames in their proper position, and mark for the joint with a sharp knife.

8. Rout out for these joints on the door stiles.

127

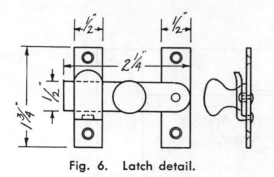

Fig. 6.   Latch detail.

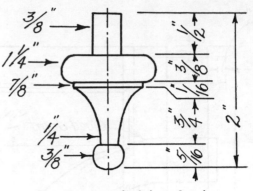

Fig. 7.   Detail of drop finial.

9. Glue the curved pieces to the door frames.

10. Draw lines for the beaded edges.

11. Make the beaded edges.

These may be carved with a V tool and a skew chisel, or with a high-speed rotary tool and suitable attachments.

12. Fasten the glass to the doors.

Use glaziers' points and putty.

H. FIT AND FASTEN THE DOORS TO THE CABINET WITH HINGES (FIG. 5).

I. FASTEN THE LATCH (FIG. 6).

J. CARVE THE DESIGN ON THE BOTTOM RAIL.

K. TURN AND FASTEN THE DROP FINIALS (FIG. 7).

L. REMOVE THE HARDWARE, AND GIVE THE CABINET A SUITABLE FINISH.

Colonial Dollhouse

A DOLLHOUSE for the kiddies, especially at Christmas time, is a worth-while project. When properly painted, this house is a thing of beauty, which youngsters can use for many years as a toy, and which they always will treasure as a keepsake.

The front, including the porch as high up as the frieze, is removable, and is secured to the sides with small brass hooks. The back wall also is removable and is fastened in the same manner.

PROCEDURE

A. MAKE THE FRONT, BACK, AND BOTH ENDS.

1. Square up the four pieces of ⅜-in. plywood; then lay out the window and door openings and the joints at the ends.

2. Cut out the window and door openings with a jig saw or a coping saw. File all edges smooth.

B. MAKE OR BUY SMALL BRASS HOOKS, AND FIT THESE TO THE ENDS AND SIDES AS SHOWN IN FIGURE 2.

The brass hooks may be sawed out of some 18-gauge sheet brass with a jeweler's saw.

C. MAKE THE FIRST AND SECOND FLOORS, THE SECOND-FLOOR CEILING, THE LANDING FLOOR, AND THE DOWNSTAIRS AND UPSTAIRS PARTITIONS.

1. Get these sizes from the bill of material.
2. Examine the layout of the second floor and of the landing floor (Fig. 6).
3. Make the inside doorway openings 6½ in. high.
4. Make the molded door trim and the inside window trim like that shown for the outside of the house, or more simply by using flat strips of wood ⅛ in. thick by ½ in. wide. Miter them at each corner; then glue and brad them in place.

BILL OF MATERIAL

Pieces	Use	Dimensions
2 plywood	Front and back	⅜ x 19 x 32¼
2 plywood	Ends	⅜ x 19 x 25
1 plywood	First floor	⅜ x 24¼ x 31½
1 plywood	Second floor	⅜ x 24¼ x 31½
1 solid stock	Ceiling of second floor and roof of porch	⅝ x 34 x 33¼
1 plywood	Landing floor	⅜ x 5½ x 8
2 plywood	Gable ends	⅜ x 7½ x 23¾
2	Porch floor and ceiling	¾ x 8 x 32¼
2 solid stock	Roof	⅝ x 15½ x 33¼
2 plywood	Downstairs hall partitions	¼ x 9 x 24¼
1 plywood	Kitchen-dining-room partition	¼ x 9 x 11½
1 plywood	Hall-entry partition	¼ x 9 x 8
2 plywood	Upstairs hall partitions	¼ x 8½ x 24¼
1 plywood	Upstairs bedroom partition	¼ x 8½ x 11½
1 plywood	Upstairs bathroom partition	¼ x 8½ x 8
2 solid stock	Chimneys	2 x 5 x 31⅝

(They are 2 in. thick at the top only, and may be made of a piece of stock ¾ in. thick. The extra 1¼-in. piece may be glued on. See Fig. 12.)

4	Turned columns	2 diam. x 17
8	Bases and caps of columns	¼ x 2¼ x 2¼
1 glued-up stock	Stairs	3 x 8¼ x 9⅝

Two Fireplaces:

2	Brickwork	¾ x 3⅝ x 5½
2	Frieze	⅜ x ⅞ x 5¾
2	Shelf	¼ x 1⅛ x 6¼
4	Pilasters	³⁄₁₆ x ½ x 2¹⁵⁄₁₆
4	Caps of pilasters	¼ x ¼ x ¾
4	Bases of pilasters	⅜ x ⁵⁄₁₆ x ¾
	Dentils	¹⁄₁₆ x ⅛ x ¼

For sizes of doors, windows, shutters, railing above porch, and stair railing, consult the drawings.

Fig. 1.   Dollhouse — front elevation.

5. The upstairs ceiling also is the porch roof, and is molded around the edges. This molding may be made on a shaper, or it may be bought and tacked on (Fig. 7). It also may be carved with wood-carving tools.

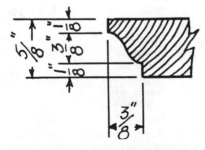

Fig. 7.   Cornice molding.

D. FASTEN FIRST-FLOOR AND DOWNSTAIRS PARTITIONS.

1. Fasten the floor with 1-in., No. 18 brads to the ends of the house only.

2. Nail the partitions to the floor and to the ends of the house.

E. MAKE THE STAIRWAY.

1. Glue up a piece of stock to the sizes given in the bill of material.

2. Saw out the steps as shown in Figure 8.

3. Make and glue on the end of the bottom step (Figs. 3 and 8).

4. Make and glue on the small pieces of molding around each step (Fig. 8).

5. Make the stair railing and posts, and

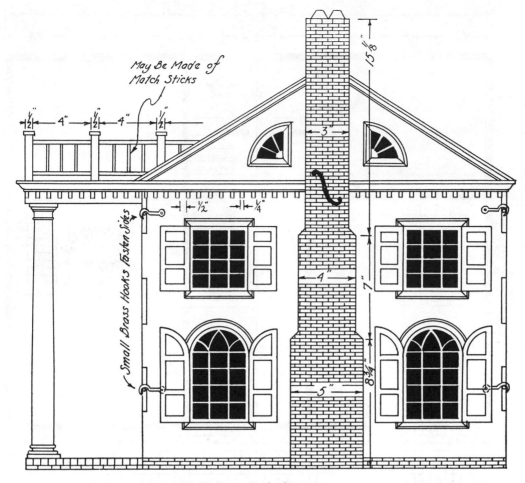

Fig. 2. End elevation.

fasten them to the stairway, as shown in Figure 8.

F. BRAD AND GLUE THE ASSEMBLED STAIRWAY TO THE WALLS AND FLOOR OF THE HOUSE.

G. PAINT THE DOWNSTAIRS.

1. Paint all walls light ivory. Wallpaper of small-scale pattern may be used instead of paint for the walls, if so desired.

Use two coats of enamel undercoat or flat inside paint, and two coats of enamel. Sandpaper each coat when dry before applying the next coat.

2. Paint the tile at the fireplace a brick-red color.

a) Mix brick-red stain by using yellow ocher as a base, and add Venetian red to suit. For very light shades, add white paint. Mahogany wood closely resembles brick in color, and veneer may be used for this part without painting.

b) When the red has dried, draw white lines, using white ink and a ruling pen.

3. Chartreuse (a pastel tint of yellow green) is a good color for inside trim.

H. VARNISH THE FLOOR AND STAIRWAY TREADS WITH TWO COATS OF CLEAR VARNISH.

I. MAKE THE FIREPLACES.

1. Make and paint the brick section. Lay off mortar lines with white ink and a ruling pen.

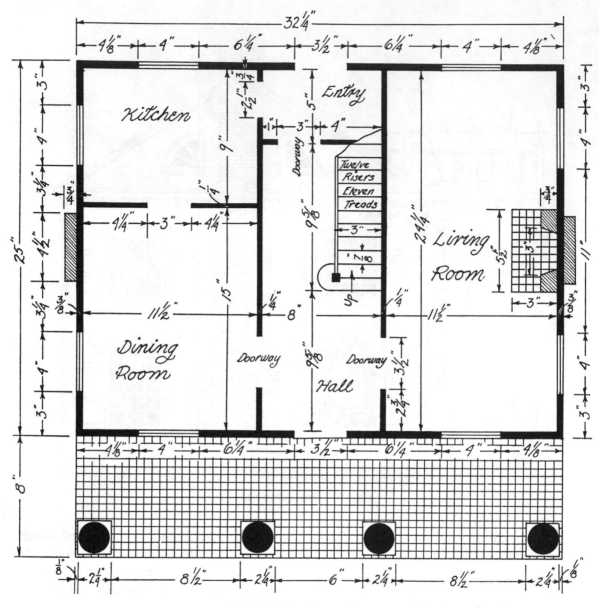

Fig. 3. First-floor plan.

2. Make and paint the pilasters and the other wood trim. Paint the wood trim chartreuse.

3. Brad the wood trim to the brick part.

J. FASTEN THE DOWNSTAIRS FIREPLACE TO THE WALL.

K. PAINT THE CEILING SIDE OF THE SECOND FLOOR AND THE LANDING FLOOR, AND VARNISH THE FLOOR SIDE.

L. MAKE AND FASTEN ANY OTHER FIRST-FLOOR FIXTURES YOU DESIRE TO ADD, SUCH AS CURTAINS, WALL LIGHTS, ETC.

M. FASTEN THE LANDING FLOOR AND THEN THE SECOND FLOOR TO THE DOWNSTAIRS PARTITIONS AND TO THE ENDS OF THE HOUSE.

Use 1-in. No. 18 brads, and drill holes where necessary.

132

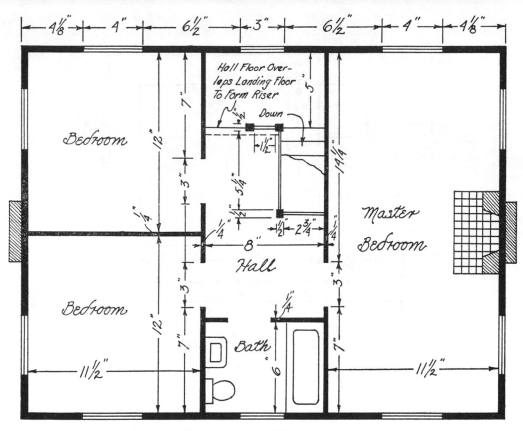

Fig. 4. Second-floor plan.

N. PAINT THE UPSTAIRS PARTITIONS, AND FASTEN THEM TO THE FLOOR AND THE ENDS OF THE HOUSE.

Since the long partitions are placed directly over the ones downstairs, the best way to fasten them to the floor is to first cut the heads off some brads. Then, by drilling and using pliers, this end of the brads can be pushed into the bottom of the partitions. Press the sharp points of the brads into the floor sufficiently to locate places to drill holes. Then, with glue applied to the edge, the partitions may be securely fastened to the floor.

Make and fasten the door trim to the partitions before painting.

O. COMPLETE AND FASTEN THE UPSTAIRS RAILING.

P. MAKE THE BATHROOM FIXTURES, AND FASTEN THESE IN PLACE (FIGS. 8 AND 9, P. 150).

Q. MAKE AND INSTALL WINDOW TRIM, CURTAINS, AND OTHER UPSTAIRS FIXTURES.

R. PAINT THE CEILING OF THE UPSTAIRS, AND NAIL IT TO THE TOPS OF THE ENDS OF THE HOUSE AND TO THE PARTITIONS.

Trim enough off the sides of the house at their upper edges so that they may be easily removed without binding.

S. MAKE THE GABLE ENDS, AND NAIL AND GLUE THEM TO THE TOP OF THE CEILING (FIG. 10).

T. MAKE AND PAINT THE CHIMNEYS (FIG. 12).

1. Glue and brad them to the ends of the house.

2. Paint the chimneys brick red and make plaster lines with white ink and a ruling pen.

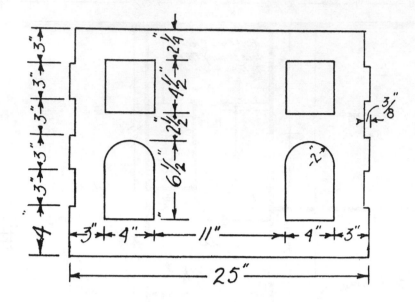

Layout of Ends Showing Window
Openings — Two Required

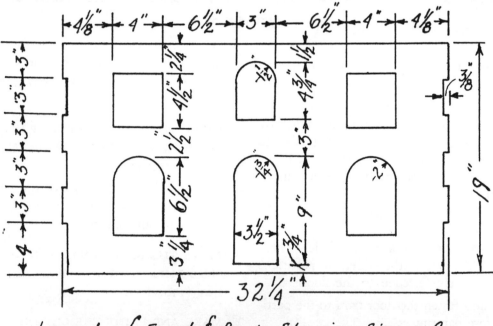

Layout of Front & Back Showing Sizes of
Door & Window Openings — Two Required

Fig. 5. Door and window openings.

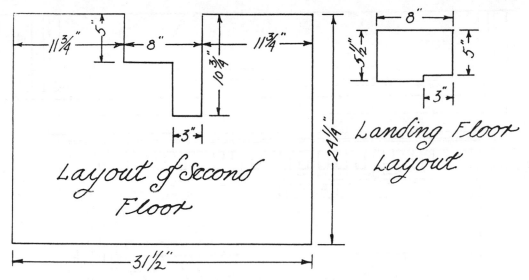

Fig. 6.   Layouts for second and landing floors.

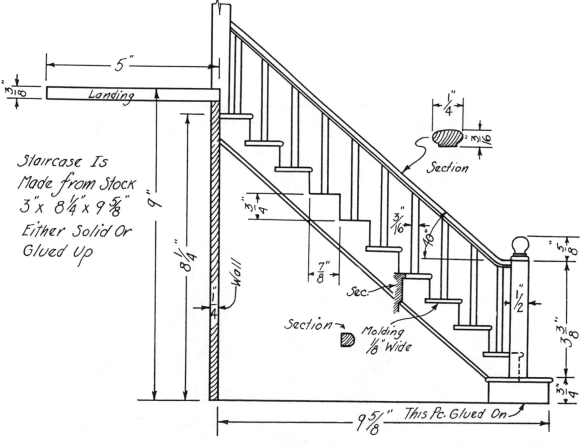

Staircase Is
Made from Stock
3" x 8¼" x 9⅝"
Either Solid Or
Glued Up

Section

Section →   Molding
⅛" Wide

This Pc. Glued On

Fig. 8.   Stairway detail.

135

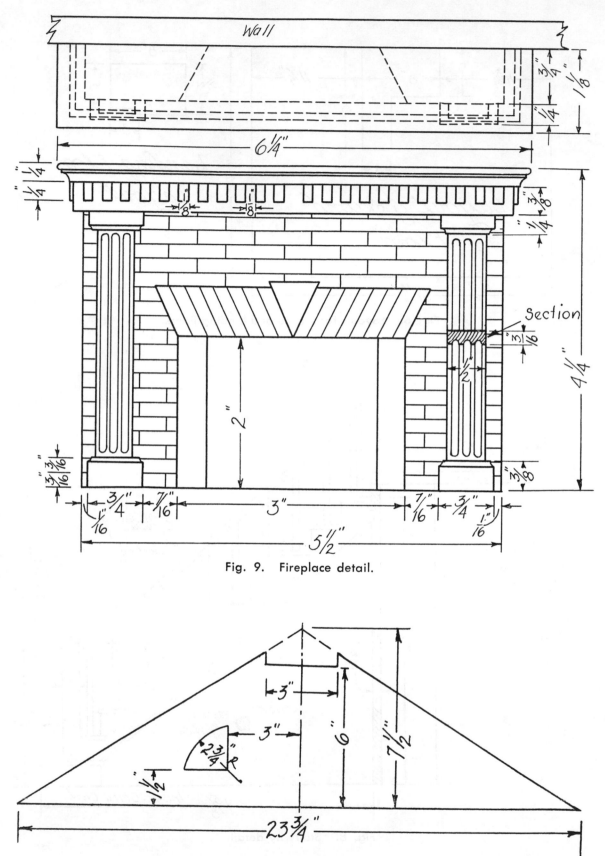

Fig. 9.   Fireplace detail.

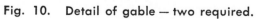

Fig. 10.   Detail of gable — two required.

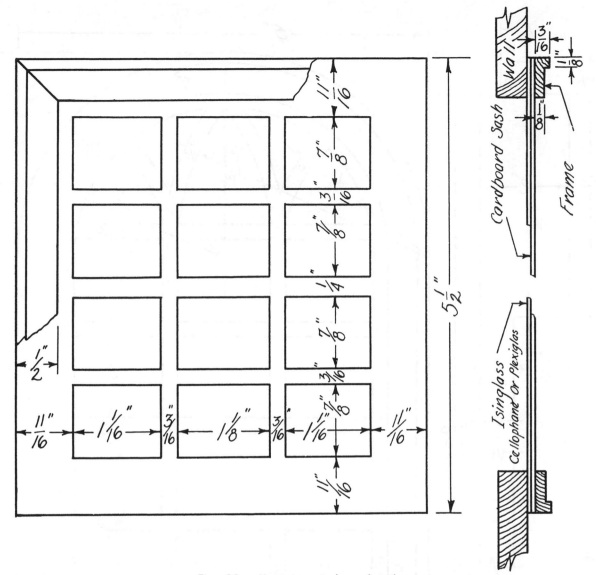

Fig. 11. Upstairs-window detail.

U. MAKE AND PAINT THE ROOF, AND NAIL
IT ON.

Paint the roof a light green or a tile red.

V. MAKE THE WINDOWS AND SASH, AND
NAIL THEM TO THE OPENINGS (FIGS.
11, 13, AND 14).

1. Cut the sash from Bristolboard or heavy
white-surfaced artist's board.

2. Use isinglass, Cellophane, or Plexiglas
for windows. Blue or clear, transparent Plexiglas of standard .069 (approx. ¹⁄₁₆ in.) thickness makes nice windows. NOTE: If Plexiglas

is used, holes for nails must be drilled to prevent cracking of the plastic.

W. MAKE DOORS AND SHUTTERS.

1. Obtain ⅛-in. plywood or solid stock of
white pine.

2. Cut these to shapes as shown in Figures
15 and 16.

3. Obtain some pieces of artist's Bristolboard, and cut out the panels of doors and
shutters as shown in Figures 15 and 16.

4. Glue these to both sides of the doors and
to one or both sides of the shutters.

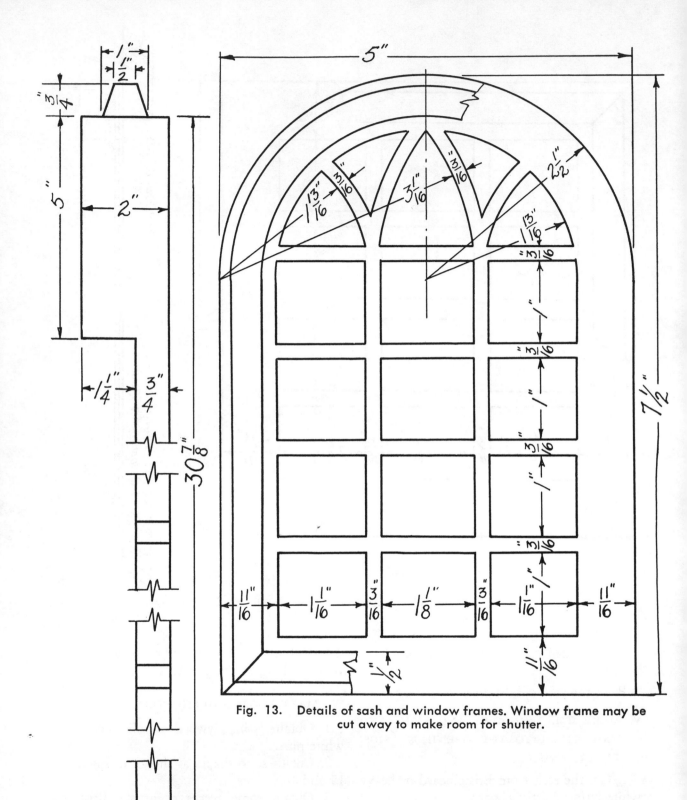

Fig. 13. Details of sash and window frames. Window frame may be
cut away to make room for shutter.

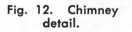

Fig. 12. Chimney
detail.

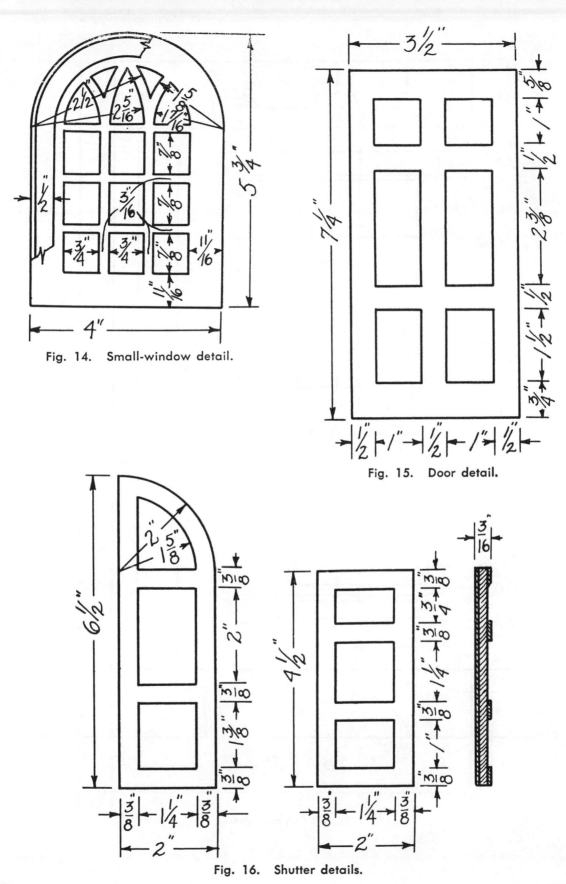

Fig. 14.   Small-window detail.

Fig. 15.   Door detail.

Fig. 16.   Shutter details.

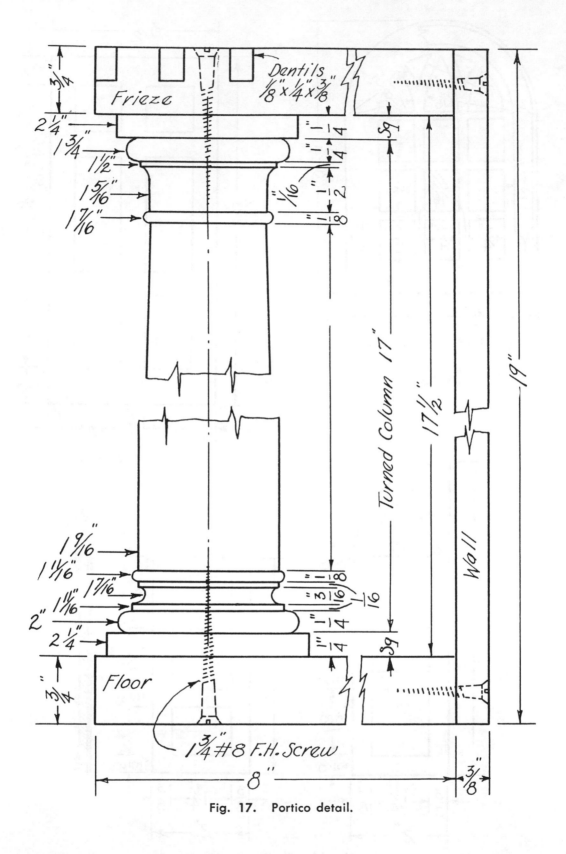

Dentils
1/8" × 1/4" × 3/8"

Frieze

3/4"

2 1/4"

1 3/4"

1 1/2"

1 5/16"

1 7/16"

1/16"

1"/4

1"/4

1"/2

1"/8

sg

Turned Column 17"

17 1/2"

19"

Wall

1 9/16"

1 11/16"

1 7/16"

1 11/16"

2"

2 1/4"

1"/8

3"/16

1/16

1"/4

1"/4

sg

Floor

3/4"

1 3/4" #8 F.H. Screw

8"

3/8"

Fig. 17. Portico detail.

Apply pressure with blocks and clamps when gluing the Bristolboard to the wood.

5. Brad and glue the shutters and doors to the house.

X. MAKE AND FASTEN THE OUTSIDE DOOR AND WINDOW TRIM.

Fit the trim around the shutters, as shown in Figures 1 and 2.

Y. TURN THE PORCH COLUMNS, MAKE THE COLUMN CAPS AND BASES, AND MAKE THE PORCH FLOOR AND CEILING.

The ceiling is the part with the frieze under the cornice molding.

Z. PAINT THESE PARTS, ASSEMBLE THEM, AND FASTEN THEM TO THE FRONT WALL WITH SCREWS (FIG. 17).

Z-Z. MAKE AND ASSEMBLE THE PARTS FOR THE RAILING ON THE TOP OF THE PORCH ROOF.

1. Drill small holes into the railing and glue matchsticks into the holes.

2. Cut off the heads of ¾-in., No. 20 brads and, with pliers, push the one end into the end of the rail. The other end may then be pushed into the soft white-pine posts after glue has been applied. Use quick-setting model-airplane glue, or household cement, which comes in a tube.

3. Paint the fence white.

Z-Z-Z. PAINT THE OUTSIDE OF THE HOUSE WHITE AND THE SHUTTERS AND DOORS DARK GREEN.

Dollhouse Furniture

ANYONE who has built the Colonial doll-house also will want a complete set of furniture for it. All of this furniture has been designed to scale, so that it will properly fit into the house. When completed, it may be finished like actual pieces of furniture, or it could be made of soft pine and painted in many colors. Indeed, one piece, the Welsh dresser, has been designed with this purpose in mind. Some of the pieces, such as the Hepplewhite dining chair and the Duncan Phyfe sofa, could be made of colored plastics.

Dining Table

BILL OF MATERIAL

Pieces	Use	Dimensions
10	Legs	¼ x ¼ x 2⅜
1	Apron section	½ x 3¼ x 7½
1	Top	⅛ x 3½ x 7¾

PROCEDURE

1. Cut the ten legs from a piece of stock 25 in. long.

DINING-ROOM FURNITURE

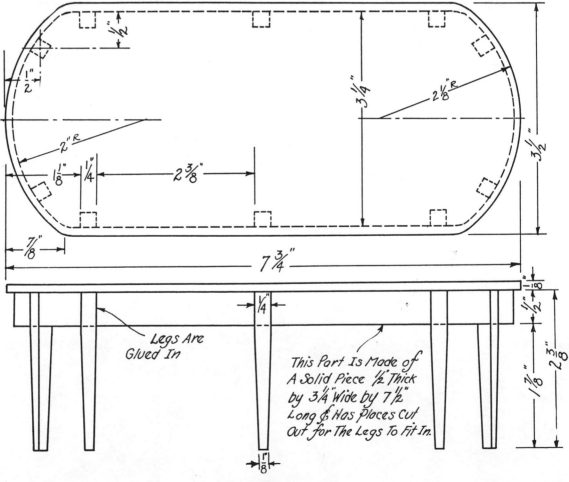

Fig. 1. Dining table.

142

2. Cut the legs to exact length after planing to width and thickness.

3. Taper the legs for a length of 1¾ in. only.

4. Saw out the part to which the legs are to be glued (apron section) on a band saw, a jig saw, or a coping saw.

5. Fit the legs to this piece, and glue them in place with quick-setting model-airplane glue.

6. Make the top and glue it to the part already assembled. Hold it in place with clamps while the glue dries.

7. Sandpaper all parts with 1/0 sandpaper, and give it a suitable finish.

BILL OF MATERIAL

Pieces	Use	Dimensions
1	Back	⅝ x 1½ x 3¼
1	Seat	¼ x 1⅝ x 1¾
2	Front legs	³⁄₁₆ x ³⁄₁₆ x 1½
	Stretchers	¹⁄₁₆ x ⅛ x length to fit

PROCEDURE

A. SAW OUT THE BACK.

1. If several chairs are being made, lay out the shape of the back, as shown in *A*, Figure 2, on the edge of a long strip of wood ⅝ in. thick by 1½ in. wide. Then saw along these lines.

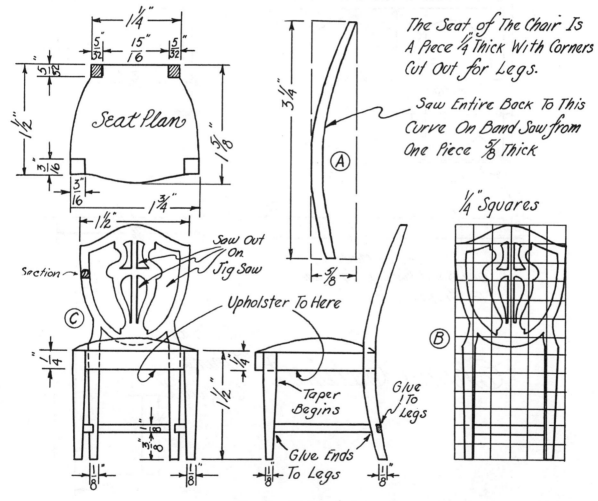

The Seat of The Chair Is A Piece ¼ Thick With Corners Cut Out for Legs.

Saw Entire Back To This Curve On Band Saw from One Piece ⅝ Thick

¼" Squares

Fig. 2.   Dining chair.

143

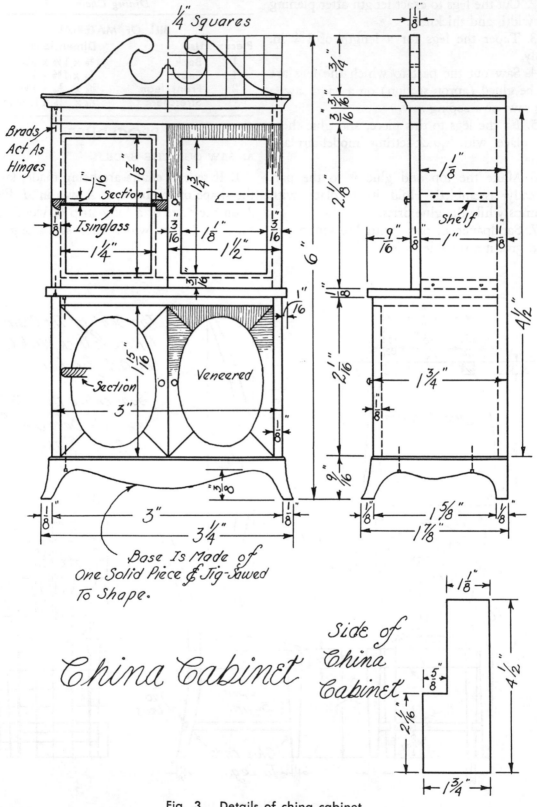

¼ Squares

Brads Act As Hinges

Section

Isinglass

Veneered

Section

Base Is Made of One Solid Piece & Jig-Sawed To Shape.

Shelf

China Cabinet

Side of China Cabinet

Fig. 3. Details of china cabinet.

2. Make a stencil pattern from *B,* Figure 2, and lay it out on the sides of the backs. Saw the backs apart, and with a fine blade in a jig saw, cut out the back as shown in *C,* Figure 2.

B. SMOOTH ALL EDGES.

1. Use needle files and fine sandpaper, or a high-speed rotary tool with cutting and sanding attachments. The members of the shield shape in the chair back should be rounded in the back as shown in the cross section in *C,* Figure 2.

C. SAW OUT THE SEAT.

D. MAKE THE FRONT LEGS.

E. GLUE THE FRONT LEGS AND THE BACK TO THE SEAT.

F. MAKE A CUTOUT FOR THE BACK STRETCHER JOINT WITH THE LEGS, AND GLUE THE STRETCHERS TO THE CHAIR.

G. PUT A SUITABLE FINISH ON THE CHAIR.

H. PAD THE SEAT WITH COTTON, AND UP-HOLSTER THE CHAIR SEAT.

1. Make a paper pattern of the seat cover before cutting it out.

2. Make the seat cover large enough to glue it underneath the seat of the chair.

China Cabinet

BILL OF MATERIAL

Pieces	Use	Dimensions
1	Base	$\frac{3}{16}$ x $1\frac{7}{8}$ x $3\frac{1}{4}$
2	Ends	$\frac{1}{8}$ x $1\frac{3}{4}$ x $4\frac{1}{2}$
1	Top	$\frac{3}{16}$ x $1\frac{3}{8}$ x $3\frac{1}{4}$
1	Back	$\frac{1}{8}$ x $2\frac{3}{4}$ x $4\frac{1}{2}$
2	Inside shelves	$\frac{1}{8}$ x 1 x $2\frac{3}{4}$
1	Outside shelf	$\frac{1}{8}$ x $\frac{11}{16}$ x $3\frac{1}{8}$
2	Veneered doors	$\frac{1}{8}$ x $1\frac{3}{8}$ x $1\frac{13}{16}$
2	Glazed doors	$\frac{1}{8}$ x $1\frac{1}{2}$ x $2\frac{1}{8}$
1	Rail above glazed doors	$\frac{1}{8}$ x $\frac{3}{16}$ x 3
1	Piece below outside shelf	$\frac{1}{8}$ x $1\frac{5}{8}$ x $2\frac{3}{4}$
1	Scrolled top	$\frac{1}{8}$ x $\frac{3}{4}$ x 3

$\frac{1}{2}$-in., No. 20 brads

$\frac{1}{4}$-in., No. 20 brass escutcheon pins for door pulls

Isinglass, Plexiglas (.060 thick for glass doors $1\frac{1}{4}$ x $1\frac{7}{8}$)

Mahogany and other veneers as needed

PROCEDURE

A. SAW OUT BOTH ENDS OF THE CHINA CABINET AS SHOWN IN THE SMALL SIDE DETAIL IN FIGURE 3, SMOOTHING AND SQUARING ALL EDGES.

B. SAW OUT THE BASE.

The best way to saw the base to shape is to take a block of wood $1\frac{7}{8}$ in. thick by $3\frac{1}{4}$ in. wide, and a length sufficient so that a band-saw operator may hold it with perfect safety (about 6 or 8 in. long). Then make repeated saw cuts from the end of the block to the curved lines of the base until the desired shape has been obtained (Fig. 4).

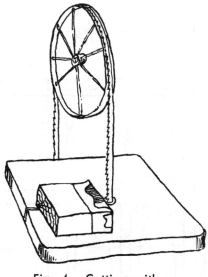

Fig. 4. Cutting with a band saw.

C. FILE AND SANDPAPER THE BASE.

D. MAKE THE TOP, BACK, SHELVES, RAIL ABOVE GLAZED DOORS, PIECE BELOW OUTSIDE SHELF, AND SCROLLED TOP.

Shape all moldings with a high-speed rotary grinder and suitable attachments, or with wood-carving chisels.

E. MAKE THE LOWER DOORS.

1. Cut the lower doors to size. They should be about $\frac{3}{32}$ in. thick.

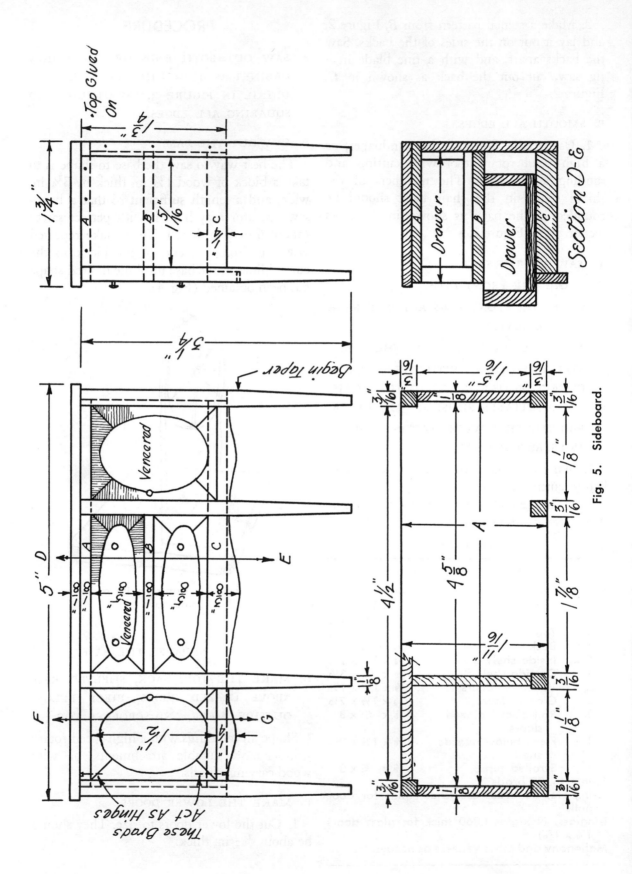

Fig. 5. Sideboard.

2. Get mahogany veneer for the border, and a veneer of contrasting color, such as satinwood, maple, or even poplar, for the oval center parts.

3. Cut and fit these pieces of veneer together carefully; then glue them to a piece of paper.

4. Cut a second piece of veneer for the back of the door.

Good veneering practice requires both sides of a door, such as this, to be veneered to prevent warping.

5. Glue the matched veneer to the front of the door with the paper side out. Glue the plain veneer to the back of the door, and clamp the door until the glue has dried.

6. Sandpaper the door to thickness, sanding off the paper during the process.

F. MAKE THE UPPER DOORS.

1. Cut the doors to size, and round the outside edges as shown in the front view in Figure 3.

2. In the middle of each door, saw out waste pieces 1⅛ by 1¾ in.

3. Cut a rabbet for the glazing material using a routing bit on a drill press, or a high-speed rotary grinder with suitable cutters and attachments. It is best to glue these doors to stiff cardboard, large enough to handle easily while performing this operation.

4. Use isinglass or Plexiglas for glazing.

G. ASSEMBLE THE CHINA CABINET, AND USE ½-IN., NO. 20 BRADS TO HINGE THE DOORS.

H. PUT A SUITABLE FINISH ON THE CABINET.

See the text on wood finishing.

Sideboard

BILL OF MATERIAL

Pieces	Use	Dimensions
6	Legs	3/16 x 3/16 x 3¼
2	Ends	⅛ x 1 5/16 x 1¾
2	Partitions	⅛ x 1⅜ x 1⅜
1	A	⅛ x 1 11/16 x 4⅝
1	B	⅛ x 1 9/16 x 1 15/16
1	C	¼ x 1 7/16 x 4⅝
1	Top	⅛ x 1¾ x 5
1	Back	⅛ x 1⅝ x 4½
2	Doors (veneered)	⅛ x 1⅛ x 1½
2	Aprons under doors	⅛ x ¼ x 1⅛
1	Apron under drawers	⅛ x ⅜ x 1⅞
2 Drawers:		
2	Fronts	3/16 x ⅝ x 1⅞
4	Sides	⅛ x ⅝ x 1½
2	Bottoms	⅛ x 1⅜ x 1⅝
2	Backs	⅛ x ½ x 1⅝

½-in., No. 20 brads
¼-in., No. 20 brass escutcheon pins for drawer pulls

PROCEDURE

A. MAKE THE LEGS.

B. MAKE PIECES A, B, C, THE TOP, THE ENDS, THE PARTITIONS, AND THE BACK. (SEE FIG. 6.)

C. ASSEMBLE THESE PARTS, USING ½-IN., NO. 20 BRADS AND GLUE.

D. MAKE THE APRONS UNDER THE DOORS AND THE LOWER DRAWER, AND FASTEN THEM IN PLACE.

E. MAKE THE DOORS.

These are cut to size (about 3/32 in. thick before veneering) and are then veneered.

To veneer the doors and drawer fronts, read the instructions given under *E* in the directions for making the china cabinet.

F. MAKE THE DRAWERS.

1. Veneer the fronts, and then rabbet the ends as shown in Figure 7.

2. Get out the rest of the drawer stock, and brad and glue the parts together, using ½-in., No. 20 brads. Keep the drawers square to make them slide easily.

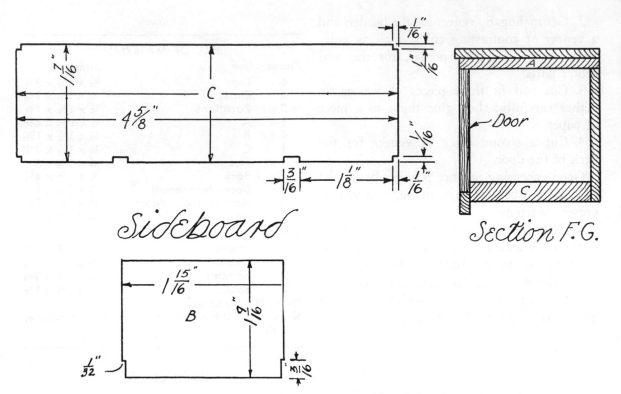

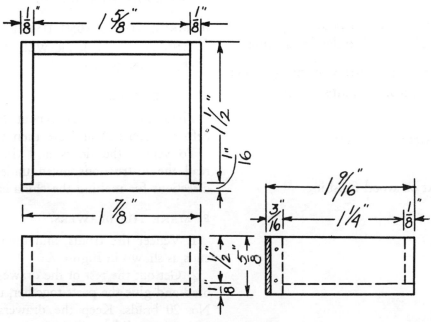

Fig. 6. Bottom, center partition, and end details.

G. GIVE THE SIDEBOARD A SUITABLE FINISH.

The oval-shaped veneer should be masked with scotch tape when staining the rest of the piece. This veneer should be shellacked or varnished when the rest of the finish has been put on, thus providing a handsome contrast in color.

H. FASTEN THE ESCUTCHEON-PIN DOOR AND DRAWER HANDLES.

Fig. 7. Drawer details.

BATHROOM FIXTURES
Bathtub

BILL OF MATERIAL

Pieces	Use	Dimensions
1	Bathtub	1½ x 2½ x 6

PROCEDURE

A. FROM A PIECE OF SOFT WHITE PINE, CUT A BLOCK AND SQUARE IT TO THE SIZE GIVEN.

B. HOLLOW OUT THE TUB WITH SUITABLE BALL-SHAPED BURRS FASTENED TO A HIGH-SPEED ROTARY GRINDER, OR WITH A FLEXIBLE SHAFT; OR USE CARVER'S GOUGES.

Lavatory

BILL OF MATERIAL

Pieces	Use	Dimensions
1	Lavatory	1½ x 2 x 2½

½-in., No. 18 brass escutcheon pins, solder, and wire for faucets

PROCEDURE

A. CUT AND SQUARE A BLOCK OF WHITE PINE TO THE GREATEST OVER-ALL SIZE OF THE LAVATORY.

B. SAW OUT THE SIDES ON A JIG SAW, AS SHOWN IN THE LOWER VIEW OF FIGURE 8.

Save one of the waste pieces.

C. BRAD THE WASTE PIECE JUST SAWED BACK ONTO THE BLOCK.

Saw out the shape of the front, taking off about the same amount as you did on the sides.

D. HOLLOW OUT THE BASIN WITH A SUITABLE CUTTER ON A ROTARY GRINDER.

E. SANDPAPER AND ENAMEL THE LAVATORY.

F. SOLDER A PIECE OF COPPER WIRE TO EACH ESCUTCHEON PIN FOR THE FAUCETS.

G. FILE THE SOLDERED JOINT AS NEARLY TO THE SHAPE SHOWN IN FIGURE 8 AS POSSIBLE.

H. DRILL TINY HOLES, AND FASTEN THE FAUCETS TO THE LAVATORY.

Toilet

BILL OF MATERIAL

Pieces	Use	Dimensions
1	Stool	1¼ x 1⅝ x 1¾
1	Tank	¾ x 1¼ x 1¾
1	Short pipe	¼ diam. x ½

PROCEDURE

A. SQUARE A BLOCK OF WHITE PINE TO THE OVER-ALL SIZE OF THE STOOL.

B. MAKE PAPER PATTERNS OF THE FRONT, SIDE, AND TOP VIEWS.

C. CUT THE STOOL TO SHAPE AS SHOWN IN THE FRONT VIEW FIRST.

Save one piece of waste.

D. BRAD THE PIECE OF WASTE BACK ONTO THE BLOCK, AND SAW THE STOOL TO SHAPE AS SHOWN IN THE SIDE VIEW.

E. WITH CHISELS, POCKETKNIFE, FILES, OR WITH A ROTARY TOOL AND CUTTERS, FINISH SHAPING THE STOOL.

F. SANDPAPER THE STOOL.

G. SQUARE A BLOCK OF PINE TO THE LARGEST OVER-ALL SIZES OF THE TANK.

H. FINISH SHAPING THE TANK AS SHOWN IN FIGURE 9.

I. GLUE THE SHORT ¼-IN. DOWEL TO THE STOOL AND TANK TO COMPLETE THE UNIT.

1. Cut the head off a ½-in., No. 20 brad,

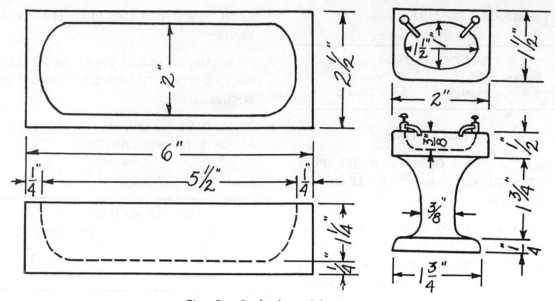

Fig. 8. Bathtub and lavatory.

and push it part of the way into one end of the dowel. Then drill a small hole for the other end to go into the tank or the stool, as the case may be. The glue joint thus will be greatly strengthened.

J. ENAMEL THE TOILET.

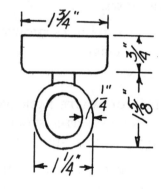

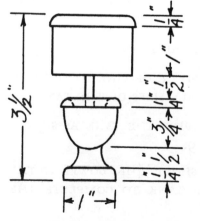

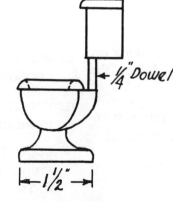

Fig. 9. Toilet details.

Carve All
Pieces from
Solid White
Pine, &
Enamel

Writing Desk

BILL OF MATERIAL

Pieces	Use	Dimensions
4	Legs	3/4 x 3/4 x 2 3/8
2	Ends (lower part)	1/4 x 15/16 x 1 3/8
1	Scrolled rail	1/8 x 7/16 x 3
1	Board with molded edges above legs	1/8 x 1 7/8 x 3 1/2
1	Table board	1/8 x 3 1/8 x 3
2	Drawer runs	1/8 x 1/8 x 1 5/8
2	Ends (upper section)	1/8 x 1 3/4 x 1 3/8
1	Top	1/8 x 7/8 x 3 1/4
1	Drawer front	3/16 x 5/8 x 3
2	Drawer sides	1/8 x 5/8 x 1 11/16
1	Drawer bottom	1/8 x 1 9/16 x 2 3/4
1	Drawer back	1/8 x 1/2 x 2 3/4
2	Shelves	1/16 x 5/8 x 3
2	Small partitions	1/16 x 3/16 x 5/8
6	Large partitions	1/16 x 5/8 x 11/16
2	Scrolled brackets	1/16 x 1/4 x 3/8
1	Scrolled pigeonhole rail	1/16 x 3/16 x 3
1	Desk back	1/8 x 2 7/16 x 3

1/2-in., No. 20 brads

2 3/8-in., No. 20 escutcheon pins for drawer pulls

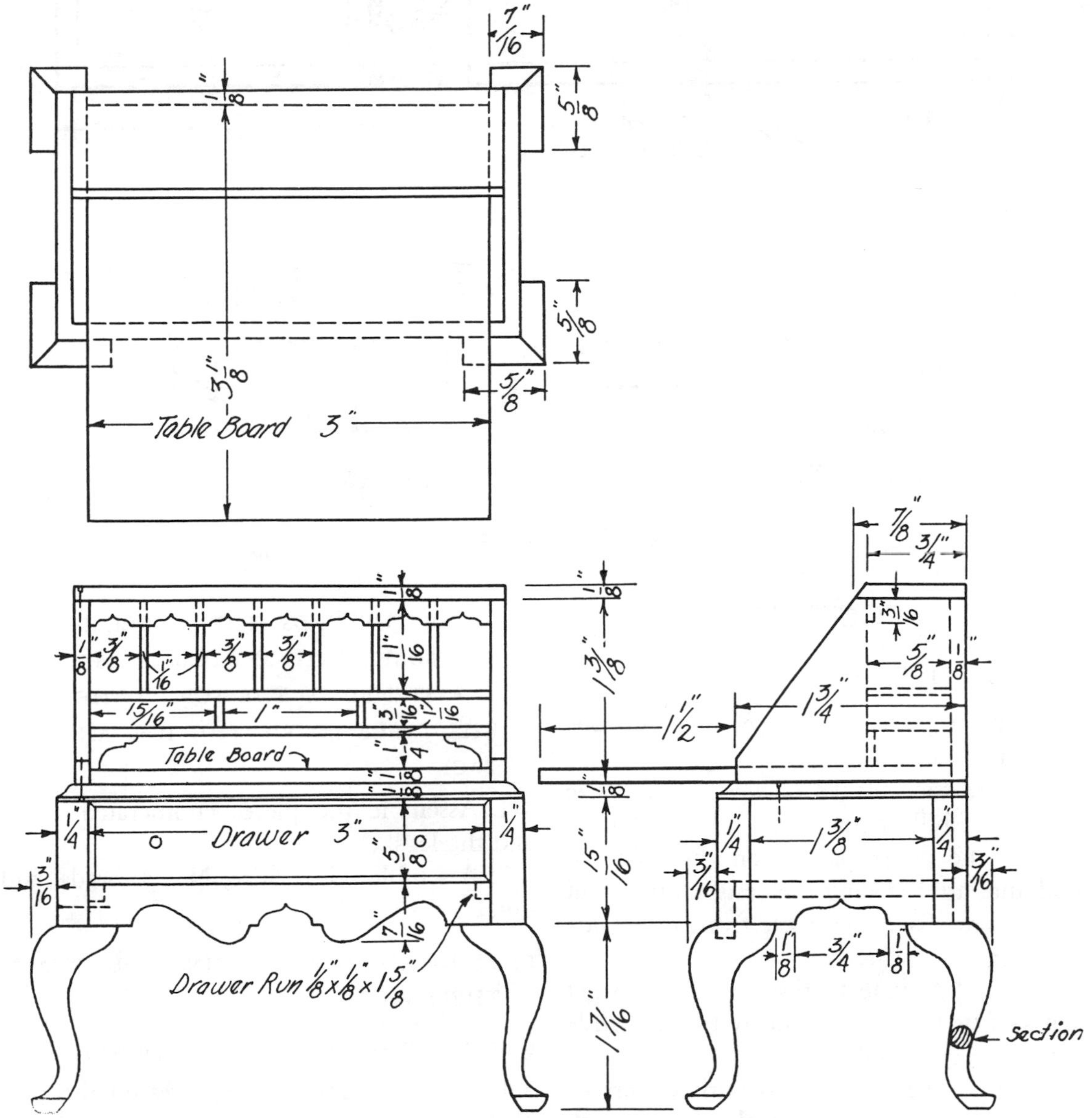

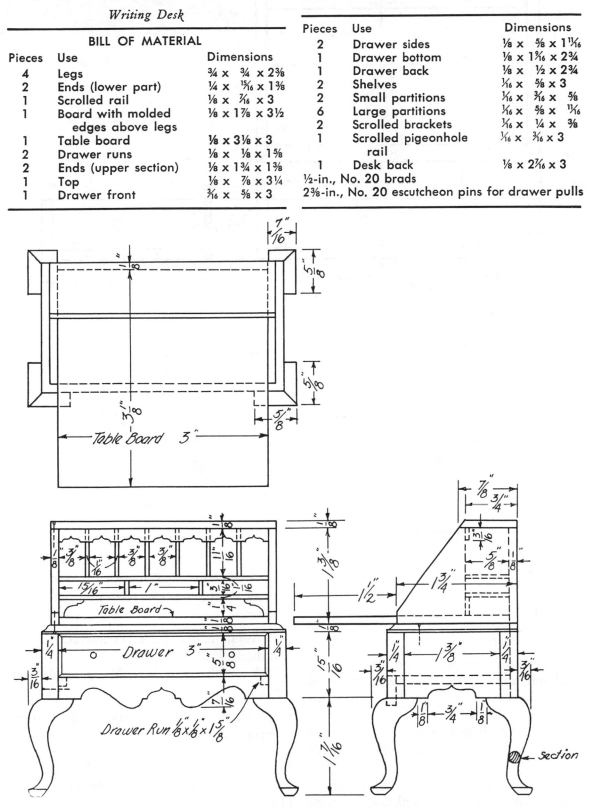

Fig. 10. Writing desk.

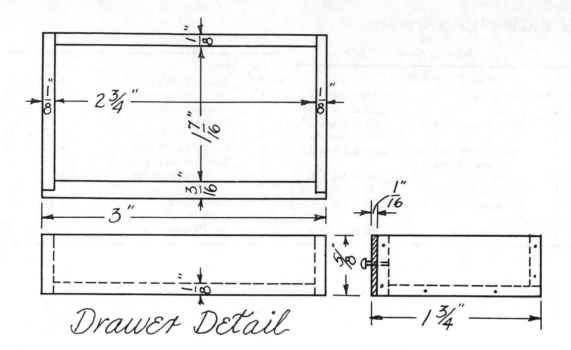

Drawer Detail

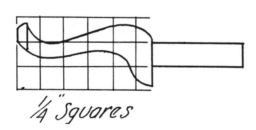

¼" Squares

Front Apron

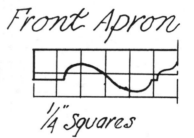

¼" Squares

Fig. 11. Desk details.

PROCEDURE

A. MAKE THE LEGS.

1. Make a pattern of paper like the one shown in Figure 11.

2. Square four blocks of wood to the size given in the bill of material.

3. Lay the paper pattern on the block of wood and, after tracing the design, saw it out on a jig saw. Save the waste from the inside of the leg.

4. Tack the waste to the leg again, to get a flat surface upon which to lay the leg while sawing the other side.

5. Finish shaping the legs with cutters of a rotary tool, with a pocketknife, or with small files.

B. MAKE THE ENDS, THE SCROLLED RAIL, THE BOARD WITH MOLDED EDGES WHICH IS FASTENED TO THE TOP OF THE LEGS, THE TABLE BOARD, THE TOP, AND THE BACK.

1. Assemble the pieces enumerated above and the legs.

2. Assemble with ½-in., No. 20 brads, and glue.

C. MAKE THE DRAWER RUNS, AND ATTACH THEM WITH GLUE.

D. MAKE THE PIGEONHOLE CABINET.

1. Cut and shape all the pieces for this part of the desk.

152

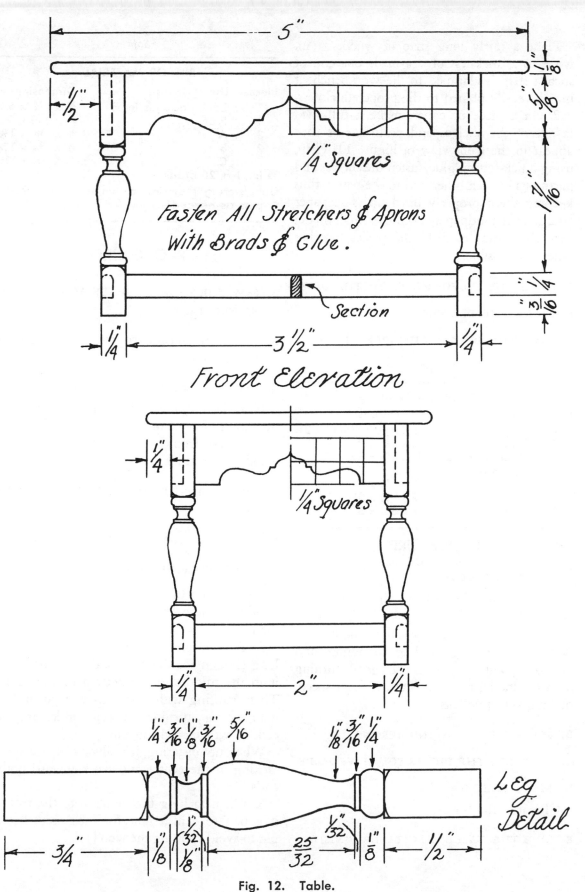

5"

1/2"

1/8"

5/8"

1/4 Squares

1 7/16"

Fasten All Stretchers & Aprons
With Brads & Glue.

Section

1/4"

3/16"

1/4"   3 1/2"   1/4"

Front Elevation

1/4"

1/4 Squares

1/4"   2"   1/4"

1/4" 3/16" 1/8" 3/16" 5/16"   1/8" 3/16" 1/4"

Leg
Detail

3/4"   1/8" 3/32"   25/32 1/32" 1/8"   1/2"
1/8"

Fig. 12. Table.

153

Plane a fairly long strip of wood, ⅝ in. wide, to a thickness of 1⁄16 in. If one end of such a strip is clamped to the workbench, it may be easily planed to the proper thickness.

2. On a piece of paper, make a full-sized layout of the shelves and partitions as they appear in the front view of Figure 10. Then, using quick-setting glue, fasten the shelves and partitions to each other and to the paper, thus keeping them properly lined up. The paper later may be sandpapered off. Use small model maker's clamps to hold the pieces together wherever possible.

E. GLUE THE PIGEONHOLES TO THE DESK.

F. MAKE THE DRAWER.

G. GIVE THE DESK A SUITABLE FINISH.

Table

BILL OF MATERIAL

Pieces	Use	Dimensions
4	Legs	⅜ (largest diam.) x 2½
2	End aprons	⅛ x ⅝ x 2
2	Front and back aprons	⅛ x ⅝ x 3½
2	End rails	⅛ x ¼ x 2
2	Side rails	⅛ x ¼ x 3½
1	Top	⅛ x 3 x 5

PROCEDURE

A. MAKE THE LEGS.

First, square the legs to the size of the largest diameter. Then square both ends to the proper size, and turn the middle section. Small files, ground to roundnose and diamond-point shapes, make good turning tools for model making. Turn at high speed, making very fine cuts.

B. MAKE THE RAILS AND APRONS.

C. ASSEMBLE THE PIECES YOU HAVE MADE.

D. MAKE THE TOP.

Glue it to the frame.

E. GIVE THE TABLE A SUITABLE FINISH.

Sofa

BILL OF MATERIAL

Pieces	Use	Dimensions
1	Back (includes legs)	3⁄16 x 2¾ x 6
1	Front	3⁄16 x 1 15⁄16 x 6
3	A	5⁄16 x 5⁄16 x 1⅜
2	B	3⁄16 x 5⁄16 x 1⅜
2	C	¼ x ⅜ x 1⅜

½-in., No. 20 brads
Upholstering material, cotton, and escutcheon pins as needed

PROCEDURE

A. SAW THE BACK TO SHAPE AS SHOWN IN FIGURE 13.

B. SAW THE FRONT TO SHAPE AS SHOWN IN FIGURE 13.

C. SAW AND SHAPE PIECES A, B, AND C.

If so desired, these pieces may be replaced by a solid piece of material sawed to the same shape as the front but sawed from a block of wood 1⅜ in. thick.

D. ASSEMBLE THE SOFA WITH BRADS AND GLUE.

E. GIVE THE SOFA A SUITABLE FINISH.

F. UPHOLSTER THE SOFA.

1. Upholster the sofa underneath first. Tack or glue a piece of cardboard to the bottom; then cover it with upholstering material.

2. Take a piece of upholstering material long enough for the back and the seat. Tack it in the middle to the bottom of the back. Then, stuffing with cotton as you go, fasten it to the top, turning the edge under as you tack it with escutcheon pins.

When upholstering, it is always best to start tacking in the center and work toward both ends.

3. When tacking the material to the front, it is best to drill a hole for each escutcheon pin to avoid splitting the wood.

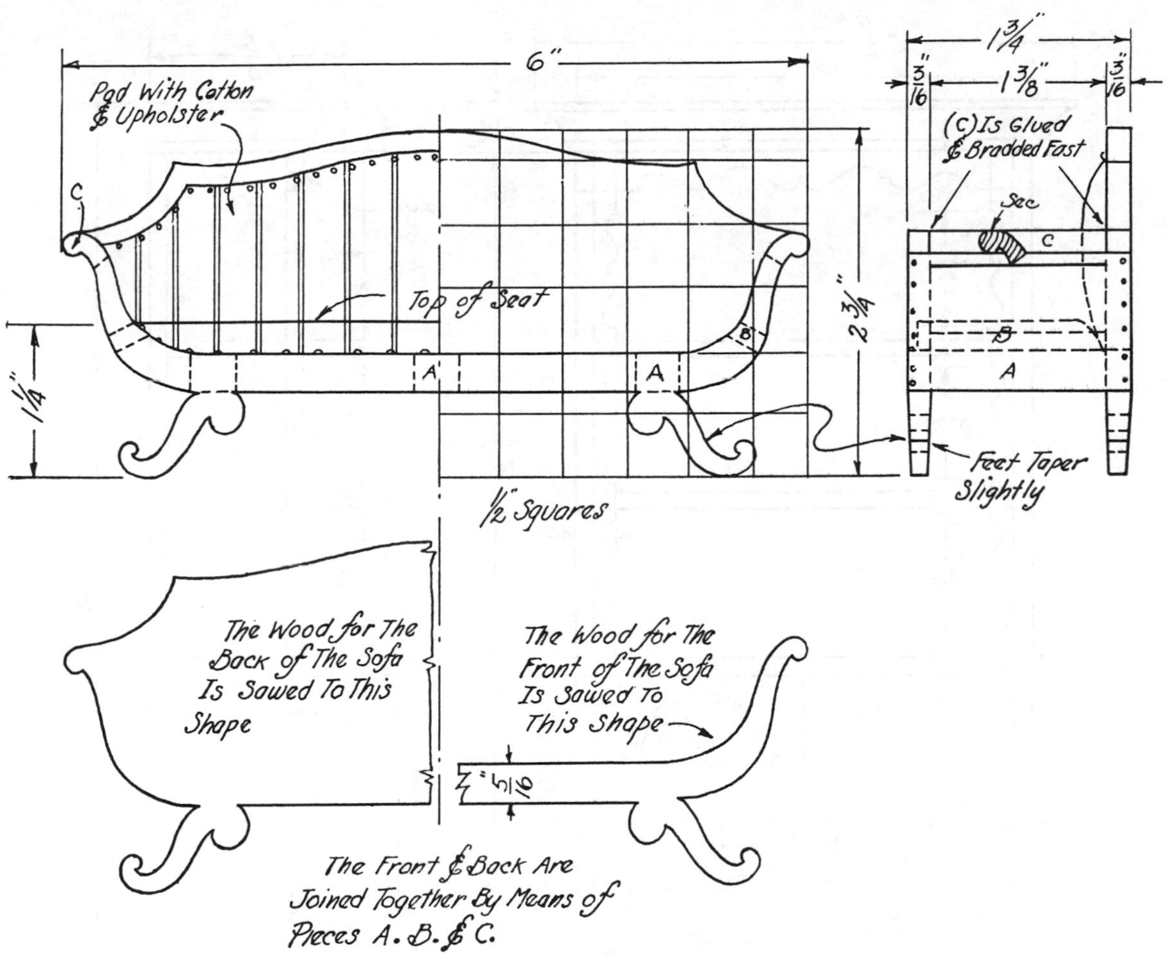

Fig. 13. Sofa.

Welsh-Dresser Bookcase

BILL OF MATERIAL

Pieces	Use	Dimensions
2	Ends	⅛ x 1¾ x 5½
1	Top	5⁄16 x 1 5⁄16 x 3½
1	Table board	⅛ x 1 11⁄16 x 3⅛
1	Floor	⅛ x 1⅞ x 3 3⁄16
4	Feet	⅝ x ⅝ x ½
1	Back	⅛ x 2¾ x 5½
2	Shelves	⅛ x ¾ x 2¾
2	Scrolled stiles	⅛ x ¼ x 3¼
1	Scrolled rail	⅛ x ¼ x 3
2	Doors	⅛ x 1⅜ x 2⅛

½-in., No. 20 brads
¼-in., No. 20 escutcheon pins for door pulls

PROCEDURE

A. SAW OUT BOTH ENDS.

These are ⅞ in. wide at the top, and 1¾ in. wide at the bottom.

B. MAKE THE TOP, TABLE BOARD, FLOOR, BACK, SHELVES, SCROLLED RAIL, AND SCROLLED STILES.

C. ASSEMBLE THESE PARTS, USING BRADS AND GLUE.

D. MAKE THE DOORS.

1. Cut the doors to size, and sandpaper them well.
2. Draw the design on each door.
3. Paint the design using whatever colors you choose.

The color scheme for the whole cabinet should be worked out before painting the doors. Water colors may be used.

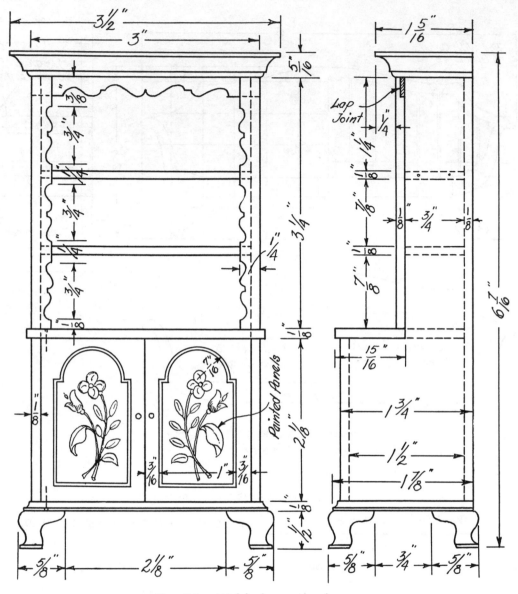

Fig. 14. Welsh dresser bookcase.

E. FASTEN THE DOORS TO THE CABINET, HINGING THEM BY MEANS OF ½-IN. BRADS DRIVEN THROUGH THE TABLE BOARD AND THE BASE.

F. MAKE THE FEET.

1. The grain runs vertically.
2. Cut a long stick of wood ⅝ in. square.

Saw each foot to shape before sawing it loose from the rest of the stick.

This is done by first sawing one side of the foot to the shape shown, and then the adjacent side.

G. GLUE THE FEET TO THE BASE.

H. PAINT THE CABINET.

Water colors may be used.

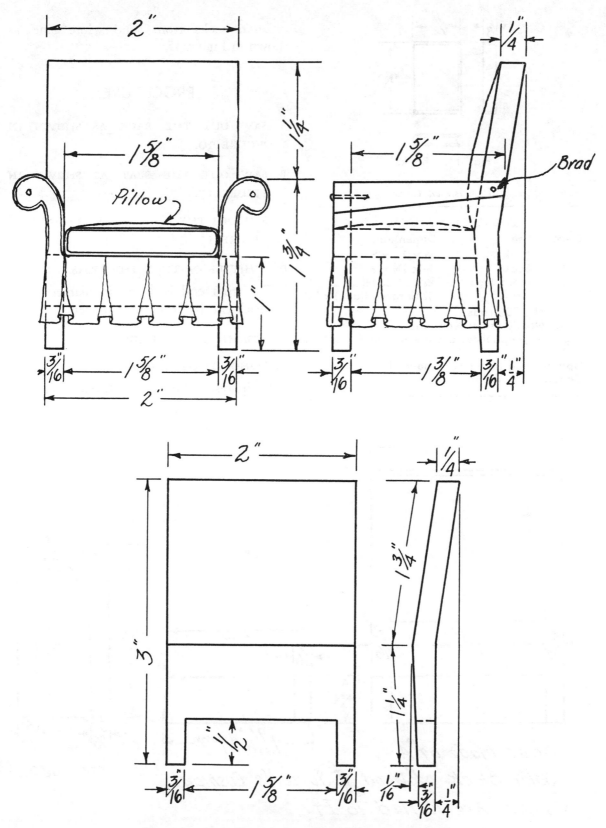

Fig. 16. Upholstered chair. The back is made of one
solid piece and a part is cut out to form feet.

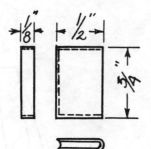

Fig. 15. Book.

Upholstered Chair

BILL OF MATERIAL

Pieces	Use	Dimensions
1	Back	½ x 2 x 3
1	Seat	½ x 1 9/16 x 2
2	Front legs	3/16 x ½ x 1¾
2	Arms	3/8 (largest diam.) x 1 5/8

½-in., No. 20 brads
½-in., No. 20 escutcheon pins
1 pillow — upholster a piece of wood ¼ x 1 7/16 x 1 5/8
Upholstering material as needed
Cotton for padding

Book

Carve books from solid white pine, as shown in Figure 15.

PROCEDURE

A. SAW OUT THE BACK AS SHOWN IN FIGURE 16.

B. SAW OUT THE SEAT AS SHOWN IN FIGURE 17.

C. SAW OUT THE FRONT LEGS AS SHOWN IN FIGURE 17.

D. WHITTLE OR TURN THE ARMS.

The front end is 3/8 in. in diameter, and the back end is 3/16 in. in diameter.

E. ASSEMBLE THE CHAIR.

F. UPHOLSTER THE CHAIR.

1. Upholster the back first, both front and

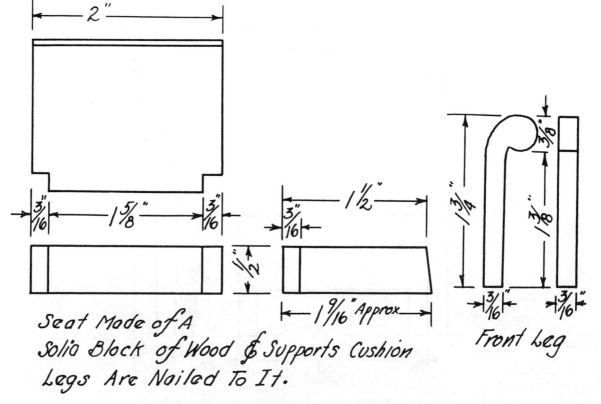

Seat Made of A Solid Block of Wood & Supports Cushion Legs Are Nailed To It.

Front Leg

Fig. 17. Seat and arms of chair.

158

rear, by bringing the cloth around the edges and sewing it at the rear edge.

2. The skirt at the bottom is ruffled, and must be made separately. It is then sewed to the rest of the cloth, after all other upholstering has been done.

3. Upholster the arms next. First tack the cloth to the seat. Then bring it up over the arms, and down the outside, tacking it at the bottom of the seat. Before tacking the cloth to the outside of the arms, it is a good idea to glue a piece of cardboard to this surface. If this is done, pad the arm as you pull the cloth up over the inside of the arm. Use a separate piece of cloth for the front of the arm, and sew it to the sides.

G. MAKE THE PILLOW, AND UPHOLSTER IT.

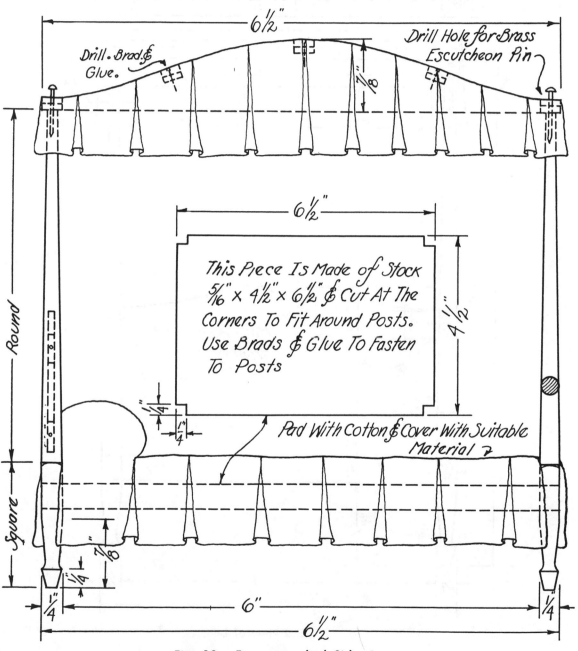

Fig. 18. Four-poster bed. Side view.

BILL OF MATERIAL

Pieces	Use	Dimensions
4	Posts	¼ x ¼ x 6
1	Mattress	5⁄16 x 4½ x 6½
1	Headboard	⅛ x 1¾ x 4 1⁄16
2	Sidepieces for tester frame	¼ x ⅞ x 6½

Pieces	Use	Dimensions
5	Crossrails for tester frame	3⁄16 x ¼ x 4½

Four ¾-in., No. 16 escutcheon pins for finials on each post

Upholstering material for bedspread and tester

Cotton for padding

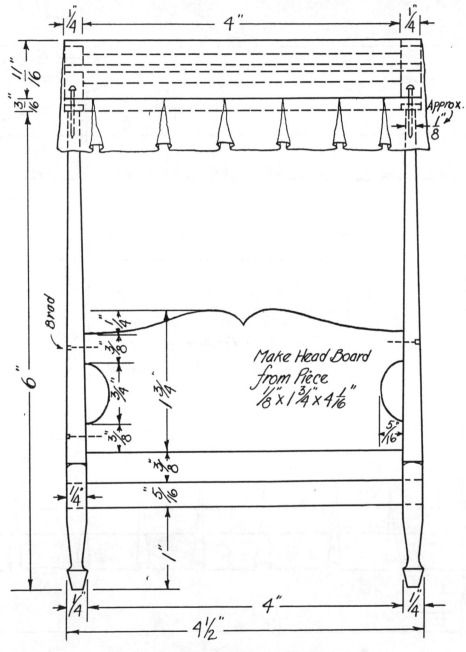

Make Head Board from Piece ⅛" x 1¾" x 4 1⁄16"

Fig. 19. End view of bed.

PROCEDURE

A. SAW AND TURN THE POSTS TO SHAPE.

1. The posts may be rounded with files and sandpaper instead of on a lathe.

B. SAW THE "MATTRESS" PIECE TO SHAPE.

This corresponds to what would be the rails in a real bed.

C. MAKE THE HEADBOARD.

D. ASSEMBLE THE POSTS, MATTRESS, AND HEADBOARD.

E. MAKE THE TESTER FRAME (THE TESTER IS THE FRAME WHICH SUPPORTS THE CANOPY).

1. The sides of these frames have the camel-backed shape shown at the top of Figure 18. This is notched out to depths of ⅛ in. for the cross rails.

2. Make a lap joint at the ends of each cross rail, and assemble the tester frame.

F. FASTEN THE TESTER FRAME TO THE TOPS OF THE BEDPOSTS WITH ¾-IN., NO. 16 ESCUTCHEON PINS.

Drill holes into the tops of the bedposts for the purpose.

G. GIVE THE BED A SUITABLE FINISH.

H. MAKE THE BEDSPREAD, AND FIT IT TO THE BED.

It is best to pad the mattress with cotton, and tack a muslin cover over it before putting on a spread.

I. MAKE THE CANOPY, AND PLACE IT OVER THE TESTER FRAME.

Mirror

BILL OF MATERIAL

Pieces	Use	Dimensions
1	Frame	³⁄₁₆ x 2⅛ x 3¼
1	Mirror	1⅜ x 2¼

PROCEDURE

A. PLANE AND SAW THE MIRROR FRAME TO SIZE, ³⁄₁₆ BY 2⅛ BY 3¼ IN., AND LEAVE THE EDGES STRAIGHT.

B. SAW OUT THE WASTE MIDDLE SECTION ON A JIG SAW.

C. CUT A RABBET FOR THE MIRROR.

This may be done with a small router bit on a drill press, or with a suitable cutter and accessories on a high-speed rotary cutter, or it may be done with a pocketknife.

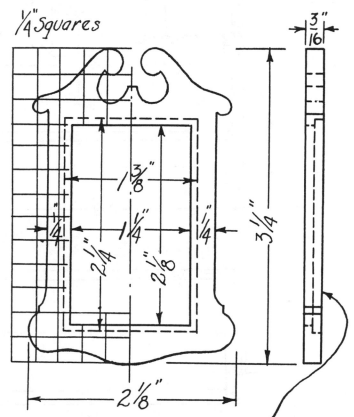

Cut Mirror To Size · Place In Frame & Glue Heavy Paper To Back of Frame To Hold It In Place.

Fig. 20. Mirror.

Clamp a guide to the drill-press table if you use a router bit.

D. SAW THE OUTSIDE EDGES OF THE FRAME TO SHAPE AS SHOWN IN FIGURE 20.

E. FILE AND SANDPAPER THE EDGES.

F. GIVE THE FRAME A SUITABLE FINISH.

G. GET A SMALL MIRROR AND, IF NECESSARY, CUT IT TO SIZE.

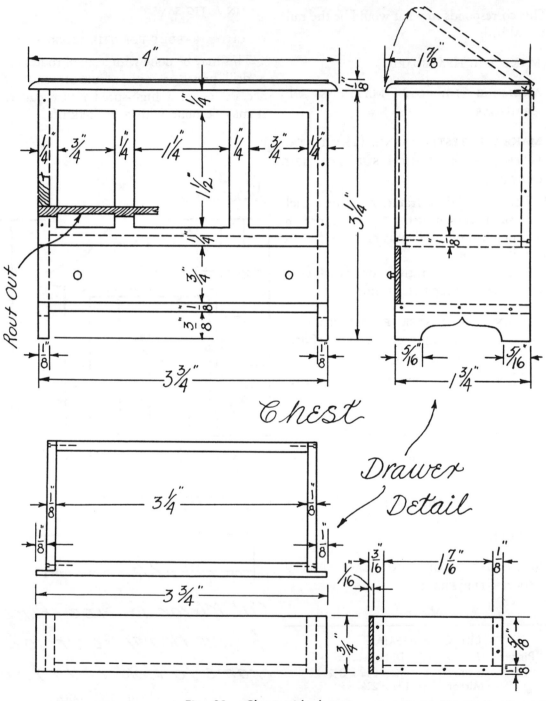

Fig. 21. Chest with drawer.

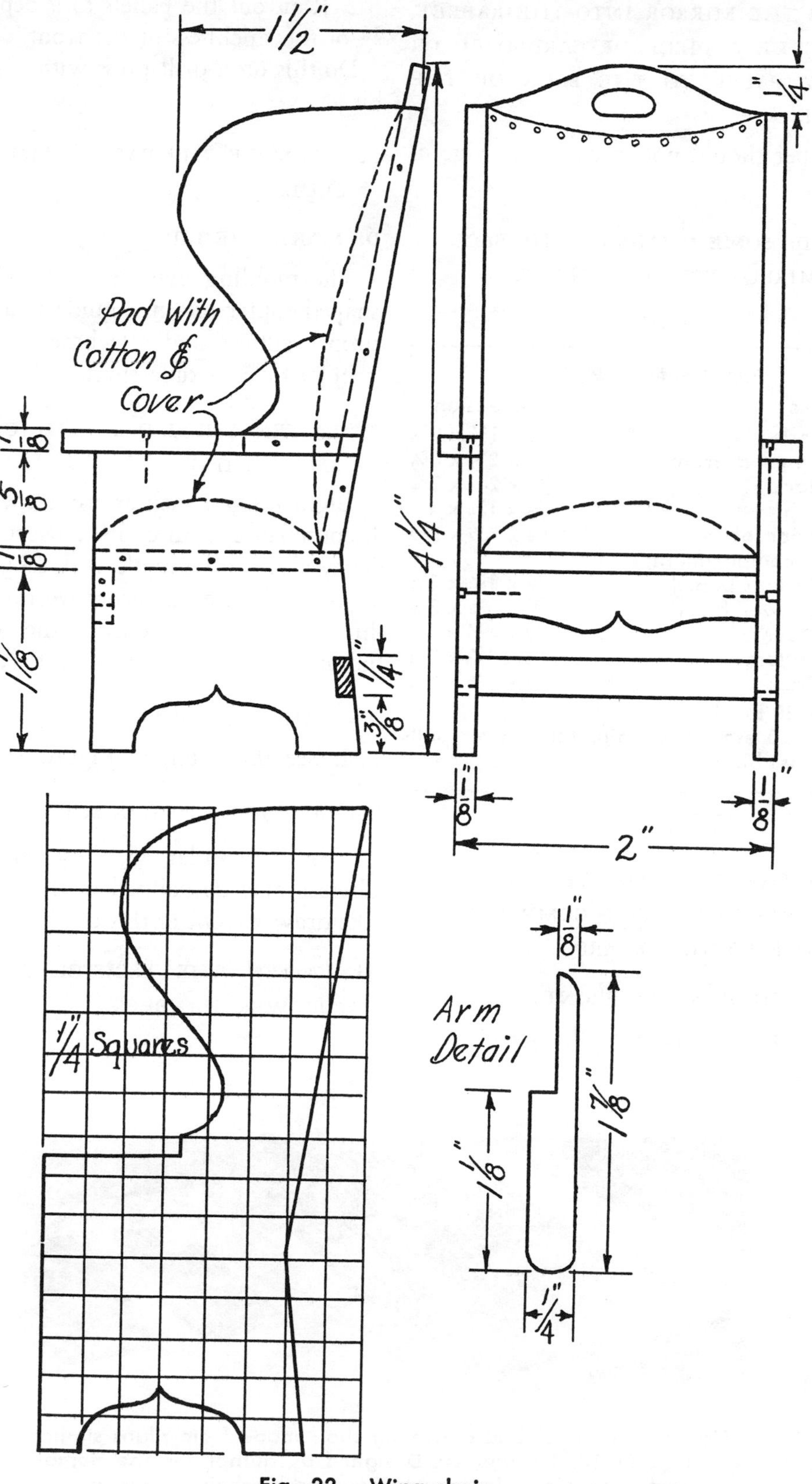

1 1/2"
1/4"
Pad With Cotton & Cover
1/8"
5/8"
1/8"
1 1/8"
4 1/4"
1/4"
3/8"
1/8"
1/8"
2"
1/4" Squares
1/8"
Arm Detail
1 7/8"
1 1/8"
1/4"

Fig. 22. Wing chair.

H. PLACE THE MIRROR INTO THE RABBET, AND GLUE A PIECE OF CARDBOARD OR HEAVY PAPER TO THE BACK OF THE FRAME.

This paper should not come to the edge of the frame.

I. PROVIDE SOME MEANS ON THE BACK OF THE MIRROR FOR HANGING IT.

Chest

BILL OF MATERIAL

Pieces	Use	Dimensions
2	Ends	⅛ x 1¾ x 3¼
1	Paneled front	⅛ x 2 x 3¾
1	Back	⅛ x 2 x 3¾
1	Top	⅛ x 1⅞ x 4
1	Floor of chest compartment	⅛ x 1½ x 3½
1	Bottom board	⅛ x 1¾ x 3½
1	Drawer front	³⁄₁₆ x ¾ x 3¾
2	Sides	⅛ x ¾ x 1¹¹⁄₁₆
1	Bottom	⅛ x 1⁹⁄₁₆ x 3¼
1	Back	⅛ x ⅝ x 3¼

½-in., No. 20 brads
¼-in., No. 20 escutcheon pins for drawer pulls
2 small brass hinges

PROCEDURE

A. MAKE THE TWO ENDS, THE BACK, THE FLOOR OF THE CHEST COMPARTMENT, AND THE BOTTOM BOARD.

B. MAKE THE PANELED FRONT.

1. Lay out the shape of the panels from Figure 21.

2. Rout out the panels to a depth of about ⅓ of the thickness of the front.
Do this on a drill press with a small router bit.

C. ASSEMBLE THE PARTS WITH BRADS AND GLUE.

D. MAKE THE LID.

The molding may be made with properly shaped router bits if a guide is used, or with proper cutters and attachments on a rotary grinder or a flexible shaft.

E. FASTEN THE LID TO THE CHEST WITH SMALL HINGES.

Light hinges, such as are needed here, may be purchased from craftsmens' supply houses. They also can be made with 28-gauge copper or tin and wire. A decorative miniature strap hinge of copper, fastened to the outside of the lid and back, would be attractive.

F. MAKE THE DRAWER.

1. See the detail in Figure 21.

G. GIVE THE CHEST A SUITABLE FINISH.

Designs similar to those on the Welsh dresser may be painted in the panels and on the drawer front of this chest.

H. FASTEN THE ESCUTCHEON PINS FOR DRAWER HANDLES.

Fig. 23. Parts of bed and wing chair made from plans similar to Figures 18, 19, and 20. Designed by author for **The Home-craftsman Magazine** and reproduced by their permission.

BILL OF MATERIAL

Pieces	Use	Dimensions
2	Sides	⅛ x 2 x 4
1	Seat	⅛ x 1½ x 1¾
1	Back	⅛ x 1¾ x 3⁵⁄₁₆
1	Scrolled seat rail	⅛ x ⅜ x 1¾
1	Rear rail	⅛ x ¼ x 2
2	Arms	⅛ x ¼ x 1⅞

Upholstering material to suit
Cotton for padding
½-in., No. 20 brads

PROCEDURE

A. MAKE A PATTERN OF THE SIDES AS SHOWN IN FIGURE 22.

B. SAW OUT TWO SIDES.

C. MAKE THE SEAT, BACK, REAR RAIL, AND SEAT RAIL.

D. ASSEMBLE THE PIECES YOU HAVE MADE, WITH BRADS AND GLUE.

Upholster the seat and back before you fasten the sides to them. Draw the cloth around the edges. When the sides have been fastened, the excess cloth may be trimmed off.

E. MAKE THE ARMS.

Fasten them to the chair.

F. GIVE THE CHAIR A SUITABLE FINISH.

Chair

BILL OF MATERIAL

Pieces	Use	Dimensions
2	Rear legs	³⁄₁₆ diam. x 3
2	Front legs	³⁄₁₆ diam. x 1¼
1	Seat	⅛ x 1½ x 1⅝
1	Front stretcher	⅛ diam. x 1⁵⁄₁₆
1	Rear stretcher	⅛ diam. x 1⅛
2	Side stretchers	⅛ x ¼ x 1
3	Slats	⅛ x ⁵⁄₁₆ x 1⅛

Upholstering material for seat
Cotton for padding
¼-in., No. 20 escutcheon pins for fastening seat cover

PROCEDURE

A. MAKE THE BACK AND FRONT LEGS.

Round members as small in diameter as these are more easily whittled and filed to shape than turned on a lathe. First saw the piece square, then make it octagon shaped, and finally round it.

B. CUT GROOVES INTO THE BACK LEGS FOR THE SLATS.

Clamp a guide to the drill-press table, and use a ¹⁄₁₆-in. router bit. If two legs are made on one stick, end to end, the piece may be more easily held to do this grooving before sawing the legs apart.

C. MAKE THE SLATS, AND GLUE THEM TO THE GROOVES.

Notice that the slats are tapered in section to make them thinner at the top (Fig. 24).

D. DRILL HOLES FOR THE FRONT AND REAR STRETCHERS INTO THE FRONT AND BACK LEGS.

E. FIT THE STRETCHERS TO THESE HOLES, BUT DO NOT GLUE THEM TOGETHER UNTIL AFTER THE LEGS HAVE BEEN SLIPPED INTO THE SEAT HOLES.

F. MAKE THE SEAT.

Drill the back holes at an angle of 97 deg.

G. FIT THE LEGS TO THE SEAT HOLES, AND SPRING THE BACK LEGS APART SUFFICIENTLY TO INSERT AND GLUE THE STRETCHER.

H. MAKE AND GLUE THE SIDE STRETCHERS TO THE LEGS.

I. GIVE THE CHAIR A SUITABLE FINISH.

J. PAD AND UPHOLSTER THE SEAT.

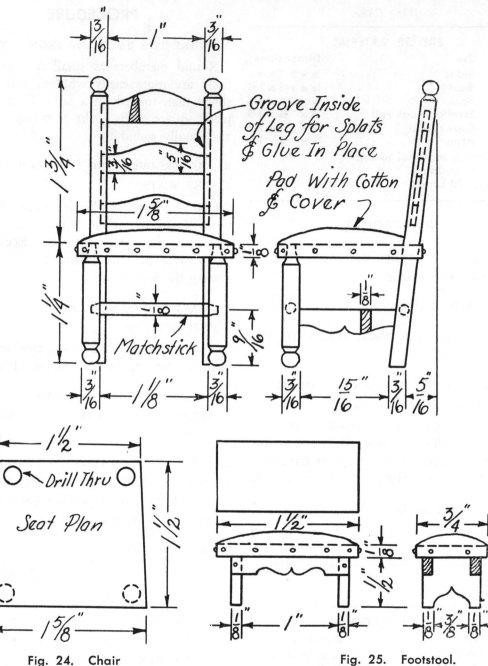

Groove Inside
of Leg for Splats
& Glue In Place

Pad With Cotton
& Cover

Matchstick

Fig. 24.   Chair

Drill Thru

Seat Plan

Fig. 25.   Footstool.

Footstool

BILL OF MATERIAL

Pieces	Use	Dimensions
1	Top	1/8 x 3/4 x 1 1/2
2	Ends	1/8 x 5/8 x 1/2
2	Rails	1/8 x 3/16 x 1 1/4

Upholstering material for seat cover
Cotton padding, and brads

PROCEDURE

A. MAKE ALL OF THE MEMBERS.

B. BRAD AND GLUE THEM TOGETHER, DRILLING SMALL HOLES FOR THE BRADS TO AVOID SPLITTING THE SMALL PIECES.

C. GIVE THE STOOL A SUITABLE FINISH.

D. UPHOLSTER THE SEAT.

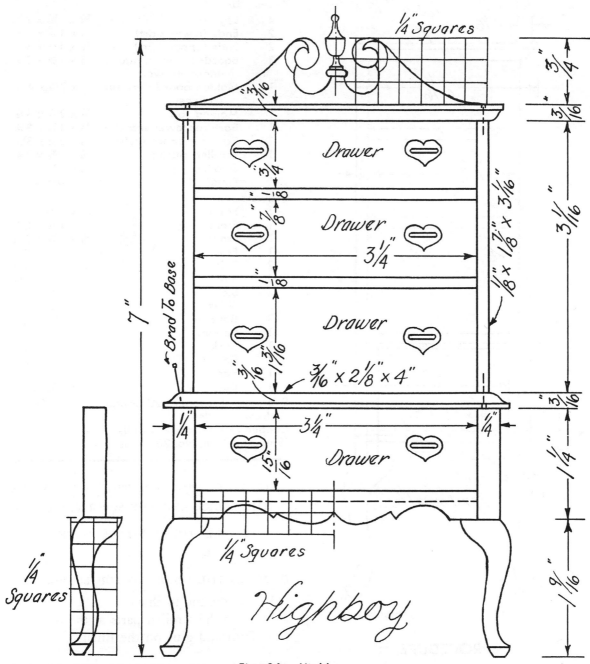

¼" Squares

3"

3/16"

3½"

3/16"

¼"

9/16"

7"

Brad To Base

3/16"

3¾"

⅛"

7/8"

⅛"

Drawer

Drawer

Drawer   3¼"

7/8" × 1⅛" × 3/16"

3/16"   3/16"

3/16" × 2⅛" × 4"

¼"   3¼"   ¼"

15/16"   Drawer

¼" Squares

¼" Squares

Highboy

Fig. 26.   Highboy.

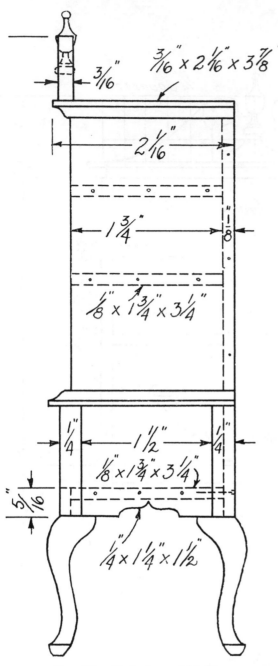

Fig. 27. End view of highboy.

BILL OF MATERIAL

Pieces	Use	
4	Legs	$\frac{3}{16}$ x $\frac{5}{16}$ x $2\frac{13}{16}$
2	Ends (lower part)	$\frac{1}{4}$ x $1\frac{1}{4}$ x $1\frac{1}{2}$
2	Ends (upper part)	$\frac{1}{8}$ x $1\frac{7}{8}$ x $3\frac{1}{16}$
3	Boards between and under drawers	$\frac{1}{8}$ x $1\frac{3}{4}$ x $3\frac{1}{4}$
1	Molded board between sections	$\frac{3}{16}$ x $2\frac{1}{8}$ x 4
1	Molded top	$\frac{3}{16}$ x $2\frac{1}{16}$ x $3\frac{7}{8}$
1	Back for lower section	$\frac{1}{8}$ x $1\frac{1}{4}$ x $3\frac{1}{4}$
1	Back for upper section	$\frac{1}{8}$ x $3\frac{1}{4}$ x $3\frac{1}{16}$
1	Scrolled apron	$\frac{1}{8}$ x $\frac{3}{8}$ x $3\frac{1}{4}$
1	Scrolled top	$\frac{3}{16}$ x $\frac{3}{4}$ x $3\frac{1}{2}$
1	Finial	$\frac{1}{4}$ diam. x $\frac{3}{4}$
Drawers:		
1	Front	$\frac{3}{16}$ x $\frac{15}{16}$ x $3\frac{1}{4}$
1	Front	$\frac{3}{16}$ x $1\frac{3}{16}$ x $3\frac{1}{4}$
1	Front	$\frac{3}{16}$ x $\frac{7}{8}$ x $3\frac{1}{4}$
1	Front	$\frac{3}{16}$ x $\frac{3}{4}$ x $3\frac{1}{4}$
2	Sides	$\frac{1}{8}$ x $\frac{15}{16}$ x $1\frac{13}{16}$
2	Sides	$\frac{1}{8}$ x $1\frac{3}{16}$ x $1\frac{11}{16}$
2	Sides	$\frac{1}{8}$ x $\frac{7}{8}$ x $1\frac{11}{16}$
2	Sides	$\frac{1}{8}$ x $\frac{3}{4}$ x $1\frac{11}{16}$
3	Bottoms	$\frac{1}{8}$ x $1\frac{3}{16}$ x 3
1	Bottom	$\frac{1}{8}$ x $1\frac{11}{16}$ x 3
1	Back	$\frac{1}{8}$ x $\frac{13}{16}$ x 3
1	Back	$\frac{1}{8}$ x $1\frac{1}{16}$ x 3
1	Back	$\frac{1}{8}$ x $\frac{3}{4}$ x 3
1	Back	$\frac{1}{8}$ x $\frac{5}{8}$ x 3

8 pieces of copper, 20-gauge x $\frac{5}{16}$ x $\frac{7}{16}$, for drawer pulls

Copper wire for drawer pulls

$\frac{1}{2}$-in. and $\frac{3}{4}$-in. No. 20 brads

BETWEEN SECTIONS, THE MOLDED TOP, THE BACKS, AND THE SCROLLED APRON.

C. ASSEMBLE THESE PIECES WITH BRADS AND GLUE.

D. MAKE THE SCROLLED TOP BOARD.

1. Saw the top to shape.
2. Carve the scrolled parts at the top.
3. Turn and glue on the finial.

E. FASTEN THE SCROLLED TOP TO THE HIGHBOY.

F. MAKE THE DRAWERS (FIG. 28).

G. GIVE THE HIGHBOY A SUITABLE FINISH.

H. MAKE AND ATTACH THE HARDWARE.

See Figure 29 for instructions.

PROCEDURE

A. MAKE THE LEGS.

Follow the instructions given under *A* in instructions for making the writing desk.

B. MAKE THE ENDS (UPPER AND LOWER), THE THREE BOARDS BETWEEN AND UNDER THE DRAWERS, THE MOLDED BOARD

168

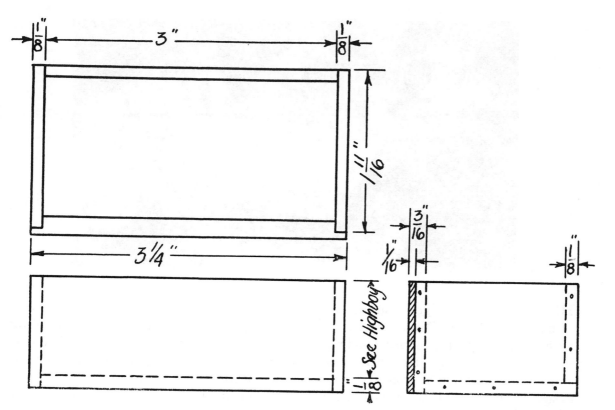

Fig. 28.   Highboy drawer detail.

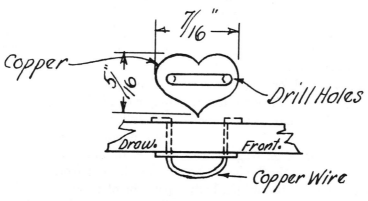

Fig. 29.   Drawer pull.

Conestoga Wagon

THIS type of covered wagon is properly called a Conestoga wagon. These wagons were stanchly built, gracefully formed, and brightly painted. At many places they were strongly reinforced with wrought iron. The undercarriage or running gear was painted a bright red, and the body, blue. The ironwork was black.

On the original wagons, white oak was used for framing, and black or sour gum for the wheel hubs because of its interwoven grain. Hickory was used for the axle trees and double trees, and poplar for the wagon body. Rugged white oak was used for wheel spokes and felloes. The wheels were dished outward from 2 to 3 in., depending upon their diameter.

At the side of most Conestoga wagons was a toolbox, and hung under the body at the rear was a feedbox as long as the wagon body was wide. These may be seen in the frontispiece, but they are not included in the drawings.

MATERIAL.

For the model of the Conestoga wagon, close-grained woods, such as birch, maple, poplar, or white pine should be used. Poplar was used to build the running gear, reinforcing strips, and even the bent hoops of the model shown above. The body sides and ends were made of ¼-in. gum-veneered plywood. The hoops were soaked overnight in water, then in boiling water for a short time just before bending. They were then tacked to one side of the body, and the curve was carefully formed between thumbs and forefingers of both hands to get the proper shape. If hickory is available, it should be used for the hoops, because it is easier to bend than some other woods.

Gum or maple is good for the hubs, and maple or birch makes good spokes.

A bill of material giving the sizes of each piece is not included here, since in most cases several of the small pieces can be more economically cut from a large piece of wood if patterns of paper or cardboard are first made. The drawings should be consulted for sizes.

PROCEDURE

A. MAKE FULL-SIZE PATTERNS OF PIECES A, B, C, D, E, F, G, H, I, J, K, L, M, AND N, THE BODY SIDES, TAIL GATE, AND DASHBOARD (FIGS. 5, 9, AND 10).

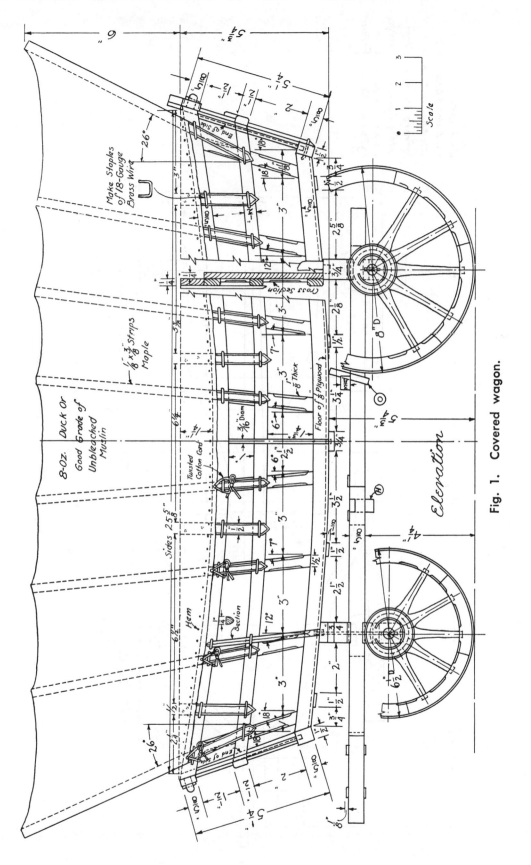

Fig. 1. Covered wagon.

171

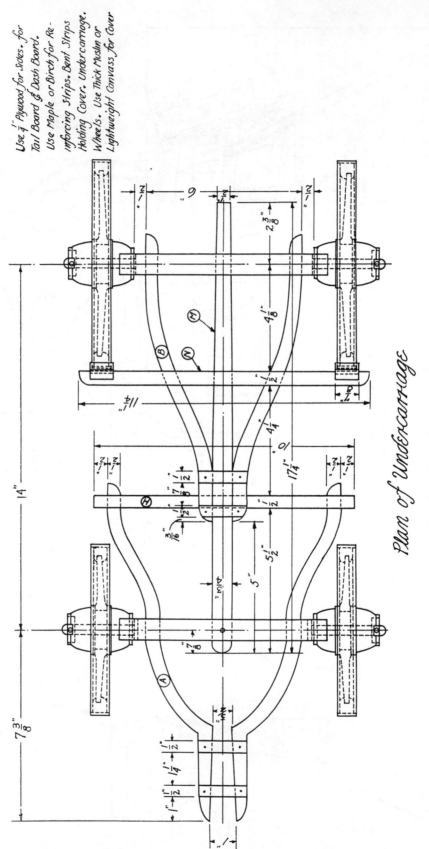

Use ¼" Plywood for Sides, for Tail Board & Dash Board. Use Maple or Birch for Re-inforcing Strips. Bent Strips Holding Cover. Undercarriage. Wheels. Use Thick Muslin or Lightweight Canvass for Cover

Plan of Undercarriage

Fig. 2. Plan of undercarriage.

172

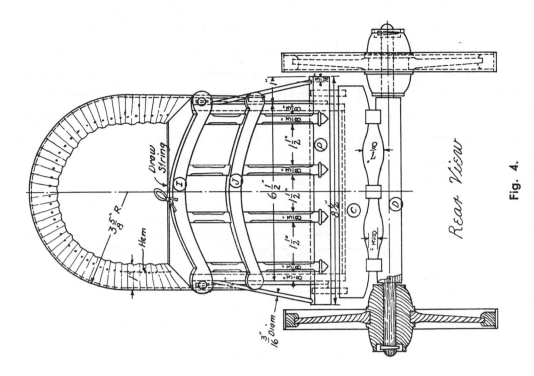

Rear View

Fig. 4.

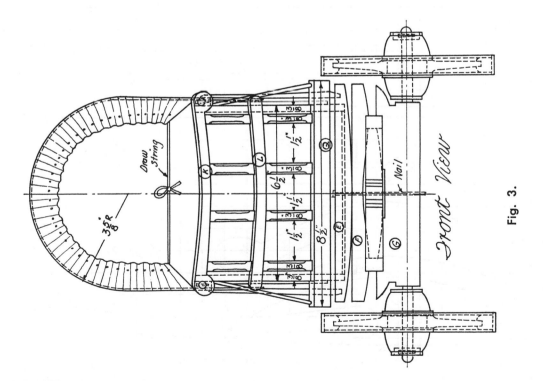

Front View

Fig. 3.

173

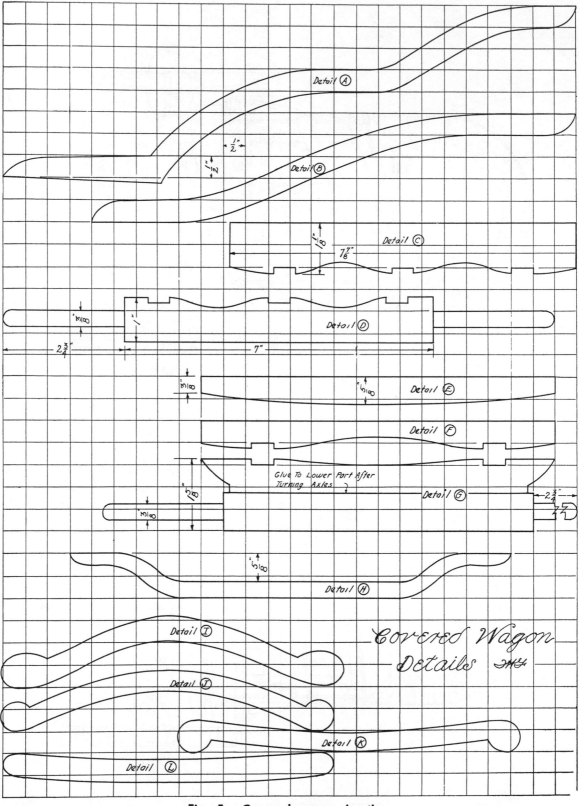

Fig. 5. Covered-wagon details.

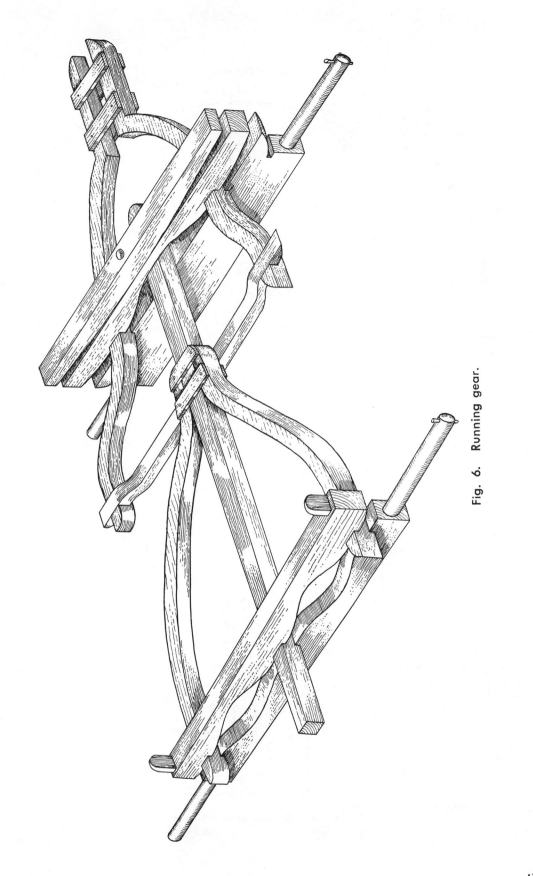

Fig. 6. Running gear.

175

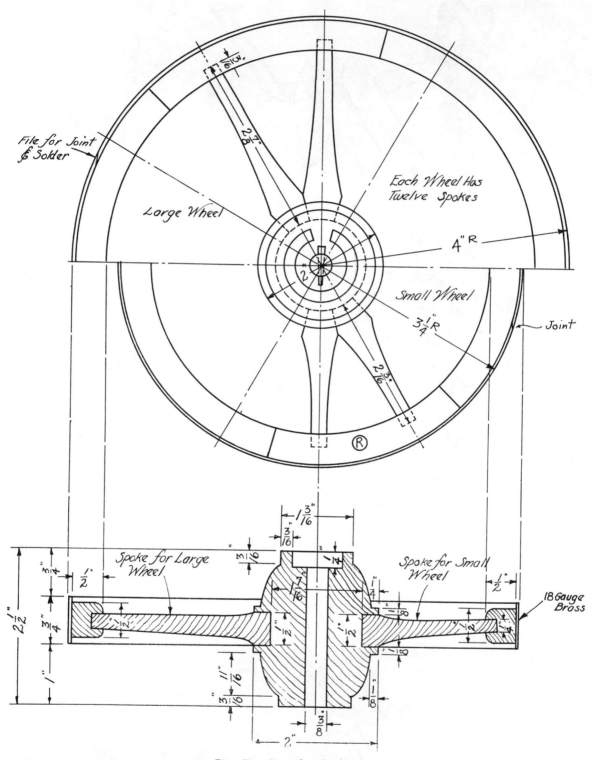

Fig. 7.   Details of wheels.

176

B. CUT OUT PARTS FOR THE RUNNING GEAR (FIG. 5).

1. From stock planed to ⅝ in. thick, saw out two forward hounds, *A;* two rear hounds, *B;* and the coupling pole, *M.* Use a jig saw, a band saw, or a coping saw.

2. From stock ¾ in. thick, cut out the axles and the axle trees, *D* and *G;* bolsters, *C* and *F;* and the bed block, *E.*

3. From stock ½ in. thick, cut out the rubbing strip *H,* and the lower cross beams for the dashboard and tailboard, *P* and *Q.*

C. SHAPE THE PIECES, MAKE THE JOINTS, AND ASSEMBLE THE RUNNING GEAR (FIG. 6).

1. The front axles are turned on the lower part of the axle tree, as shown in detail *G,* and this is then glued to the upper part.

2. Be sure that the dadoes across the axle trees and bolsters are the same distance apart, so as to make good joints with the hounds.

D. LAY OUT AND MAKE THE WHEELS.

1. Turn and drill the hubs (Fig. 7).

2. On a plywood board, make full-size layouts for the front and rear wheel spokes and the felloes.

a) With a compass, draw circles 1⁷⁄₁₆-in. diameter, 2¹¹⁄₁₆-in. radius, and 3³⁄₁₆-in. radius for the small wheel.

b) Draw circles 1⁷⁄₁₆-in. diameter, 3⁷⁄₁₆-in. radius, and 3¹⁵⁄₁₆-in. radius for the large wheel.

c) Divide each of these circles into 24 sectors. These show the center lines of the twelve spokes, and the boundary lines of the spokes and felloes (Fig. 7).

d) Lay out the exact shapes of the spokes and felloes, so that they may be properly fitted together to make the wheel.

3. Out of a piece of ¼-in. plywood, cut a disk 7⅞-in. diameter, and from another piece cut a disk 6⅜-in. diameter, as shown in Figure 8.

4. Tack the pieces of plywood from which the disks have been cut to fit over the wheel layouts to make a jig.

5. From stock ½ in. thick, cut and fit together the spokes and felloes in these jigs. Each joint must be carefully made so the wheel can be assembled.

First saw the spokes to the shape shown in Figure 7; then, with a sharp knife, a file, and sandpaper, round the spokes.

6. Drill holes into the felloes, and make a trial assembly of each wheel. Place a pencil mark at the end of each spoke where it joins the felloe, to prevent driving it in too deep when gluing.

7. Glue and assemble the wheels.

a) It is best to glue the spokes to the felloes first before gluing them to the hub.

b) Glue two spokes to each felloe.

c) Note that the wheels are *dished* outward. This may be accomplished by properly shaping the spokes so that the tires are ⅛ in. closer to the outside of the hub than to the inside. Another method is to slightly bevel the hub end of the spokes on the inside of the wheel, and then, making a jig to hold the rim of the wheel at the proper elevation, press the hub down with a clamp to get the proper dishing.

8. Cut tires of 18-gauge, or thinner, brass or copper.

Measure the circumference carefully with a strip of paper, allowing for a joint as shown in Figure 7. Clamp the tire to a slab of marble, and solder the joint. Solder the tire to fit the wheel tightly, then slip the tire on the wheel.

E. FIT THE WHEELS TO THE AXLES, AND HOLD THEM IN PLACE WITH LINCHPINS.

Note the openings in the ends of the hubs for removing the linchpins.

F. FROM THE PATTERN SHOWN IN FIGURE 9, CUT OUT THE SIDES OF THE BODY.

G. FROM THE PATTERNS FOR THE DASHBOARD AND TAILBOARD, CUT AND SHAPE THESE PARTS (SEE FIG. 10).

H. MAKE THE VERTICAL AND HORIZONTAL REINFORCING STRIPS FOR THE SIDES, THE DASHBOARD, AND THE TAILBOARD. Glue these in place as shown in Figures 1, 3, and 4.

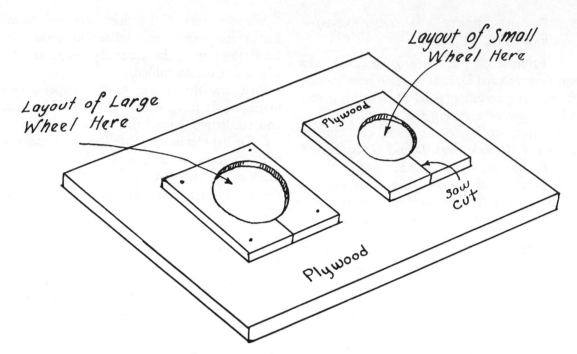

Fig. 8.   Jig for wheel assembly.

I. ASSEMBLE THE BODY WITH BRADS AND GLUE.

J. FASTEN THE BOARDS TO THE TOP OF THE BODY.

These boards have been made from pieces sawed from the sides, and come flush with the outside of the upper reinforcing strip. The vertical strips holding them to the body are fastened to the sides with thin wire staples hammered into tiny holes which have been drilled on each side of them. These staples may be easily formed from thin wire, with thin-nosed pliers. The wire may be steel, brass, or copper.

K. MAKE THE HOOPS FOR THE COVER.

1. Clamp a long enough piece to the workbench, and plane it to the proper thickness.

2. Soak the piece overnight, and then immerse it in boiling water for a short time before bending it to shape. By band-sawing the end of a board which is 7¼ in. wide, to the proper shape, a form for each hoop may be made. If the strips are clamped to these forms until dry, they will hold their shapes.

3. Line up the tops of all hoops so they will more or less follow the curve of the body.

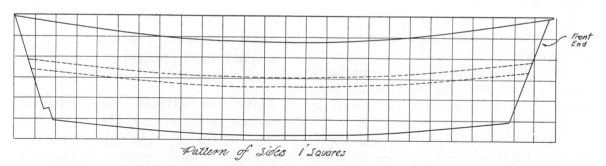

Fig. 9.   Pattern for sides of covered wagon.

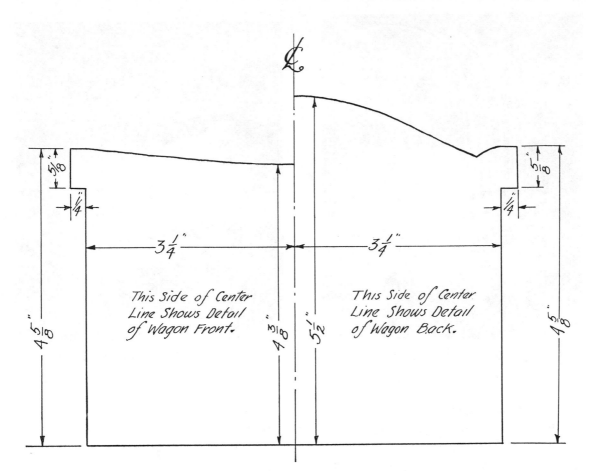

$\mathcal{C}$

$\frac{5}{8}''$

$\frac{5}{8}''$

$\frac{1}{4}''$

$\frac{1}{4}''$

$3\frac{1}{4}''$

$3\frac{1}{4}''$

This Side of Center
Line Shows Detail
of Wagon Front.

This Side of Center
Line Shows Detail
of Wagon Back.

$4\frac{5}{8}''$

$4\frac{5}{8}''$

$3\frac{1}{8}''$

$5\frac{1}{2}''$

Fig. 10.   Patterns for front and back.

Fig. 11.   Front view of covered wagon.

Fig. 12.   Rear view of covered wagon.

Fig. 13.   Front detail of top.

Fig. 14.   Rear detail of top.

L. PAINT THE WAGON.

1. Paint the running gear crimson.

2. Paint the body blue.

3. Use black paint on all parts on which iron reinforcing bands naturally would be placed. Such parts are the ends of the hubs, the strips joining the hounds together, the top of the rubbing strip, the top of the front bolster, etc.

M. MOUNT THE BODY ON THE RUNNING GEAR.

N. MAKE THE COVER, AND TIE IT TO THE WAGON.

Use 8 or 10-oz. duck.

1. Make a pattern of paper.

2. Sew hems for the draw strings.

O. MOUNT THE WAGON ON A BOARD OR BASE.

Practice Block

IN ALL woodwork, certain fundamental operations must be mastered before anything worth while can be built. In order that many of these A B C's of woodworking may be mastered in the shortest possible space of time, this practice block has been designed. In making the block, the student may learn each operation without being bothered with such construction difficulties as he might meet in a project. Any mistakes he may make will waste little material. The steps, as they are presented here, follow each other in logical sequence; that is, the things which ordinarily would be done first on a project also are first in making the practice block.

The advantages gained in making such a practice block should prevent waste of material on subsequent projects. It also should teach a proper sequence of operations on more complicated work and confidence to perform the operations required to build more difficult projects encountered later.

The most serious disadvantage in making the practice block is that it can be put to no practical use after it has been completed, and, therefore, may seem a waste of time to the young beginner. In his own classes, covering all age groups from the seventh grade through the graduate school of a large university, the author has found the following to be true: In junior high school classes, all but the best students lose some interest in continuing the operations which go beyond planing and squaring the block. Therefore, it has become a practice of the author's not to require any of the work given under Roman numeral II of this group, but instead to follow the instructions under Roman numeral I with the making of simple projects in which the subsequent operations are included. Most of the older groups of beginners will follow through without losing interest. Also, the more advanced the students are in years, the more they can be made to appreciate the value of taking the

TOOLS AND MATERIALS
1 piece of clear, kiln-dried poplar, ⅞ in. or over in thickness, by 3¼ in. wide, by 7¼ in. long
1-ft. ruler
Try square with an 8-in. blade
Smooth plane or jack plane
½ and ¾-in. socket firmer chisels
Marking gauge
Compass or dividers
Mallet
Brace and bits
Hand screw (woodworker's clamp)
Backsaw
Coping saw
Bench hook
Workbench equipped with woodworker's vise, vise dog, and bench stop

time necessary to learn these fundamental operations before undertaking a project of more practical value.

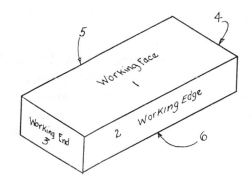

Fig. 1. The sides are numbered in the order in which they are to be done.

PROCEDURE

I. Plane the block square and to size.

A. NUMBER THE SIDES.

1. The better wide side or face is No. 1; the better edge is 2; the better end is 3. Opposite of 3 is 4; opposite 2 is 5; opposite 1 is 6. NOTE: The sum of opposite sides always equals 7 (Fig. 1).

1. Be sure the plane is sharp and properly set. To sharpen a plane iron or a chisel, use the following instructions:

Fig. 2.   Grinding a plane blade.

a) To grind a plane blade, hold the blade as shown in Figure 2, with the bevel on a grindstone or emery wheel. The bevel should be considerably wider than the thickness of the blade, straight, and at right angles to the side of the blade. Move the blade sideways, back and forth over the stone until a smooth, slightly concave bevel has been formed. Keep from burning the cutting edge by dipping the blade into water frequently or by using light pressure when holding it on the stone.

b) After a plane blade has been ground to shape on an emery wheel or grindstone, it must be whetted to make it sharp. To do this,

Fig. 3.   Whetting a plane blade.

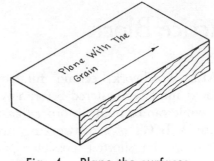

Fig. 4.   Plane the surfaces with the grain.

hold it as shown in Figure 3 with the bevel flat on the oilstone. Use machine oil thinned with kerosene on the oilstone as a lubricant and to keep the surface of the stone from glazing. Whet the plane iron by moving it over the entire surface of the oilstone with a circular motion. Exert considerable downward pressure on the blade while whetting. Remove the wire edge formed by whetting, by reversing the blade and laying it flat on the stone with the bevel on top and then moving it back and forth over the stone several times. Repeat these processes as often as necessary until the wire edge has been entirely removed and the edge is keen and sharp.

Fig. 5.   Correct method of laying plane on bench.

2. Decide the direction to plane by determining which way the grain runs.

Plane the grain lines found on the edge of the block, *uphill* (Fig. 4).

Fig. 6.   Keep plane parallel
to edge.

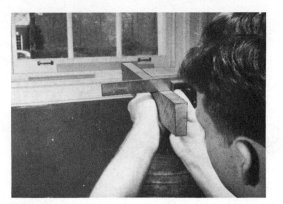

Fig. 8.   Testing edge for squareness.

3. Fasten the block in a vise, and plane. Begin planing the side at the edge closest to you.

4. Test the side for flatness (Fig. 7). Do no sanding.

Fig. 7.   Testing board for
flatness.

C. PLANE EDGE 2.

1. Place the block in a vise as nearly level as possible.

2. Keeping the plane in line with the block (not angled), and holding it as level as possible, plane the edge.

3. Test for squareness with side 1 and for flatness (Fig. 8).

D. PLANE END 3.

1. Place the block in a vise as nearly level as possible, and with one edge turned toward you and the other toward the bench, clamp the block low so that the end is just above the vise.

2. Check the plane for sharpness, and set the blade to cut a fine shaving.

3. Grasp the plane firmly, keeping the wrists fairly stiff.

4. Plane only a little over halfway across the end until fairly smooth; then reverse the edges and smooth the remainder of the end. NOTE: If you were to plane all the way across the end, splinters of wood would be broken off on the far edge.

E. MEASURE AND MARK OFF THE LENGTH
   TO WHICH YOU WANT TO PLANE YOUR
   BLOCK.

Saw and plane the block to this line.

1. Place the ruler on the block as shown in Figure 9, and mark the length, which should be 7 in.

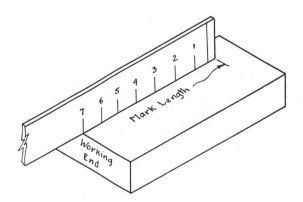

Fig. 9.   Mark length with ruler.

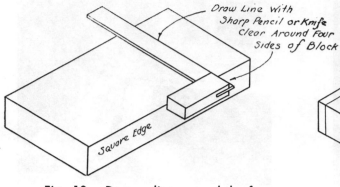

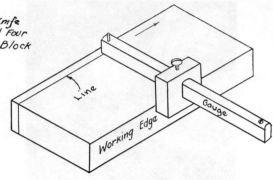

Fig. 10. Draw a line around the four sides of a block.

Fig. 12. Mark width of block.

2. With a try square held tightly against the squared edge of the block, draw a fine pencil line or make a knife line at the 7-in. mark. Continue squaring it clear around the sides and edges of the block as shown in Figure 10.

3. Clamp the bench hook into the vise, lay the block on it as shown in Figure 11, and saw off the end on the waste side of the line.

4. Plane end 4 to this line, going through the steps given under *D*.

F. MARK THE BLOCK FOR WIDTH, AND PLANE IT TO THIS LINE.

1. Set the gauge to the 3-in. mark.

2. Place the hand with which you will push the gauge so that the index finger is on one side of the gauge block and the middle finger

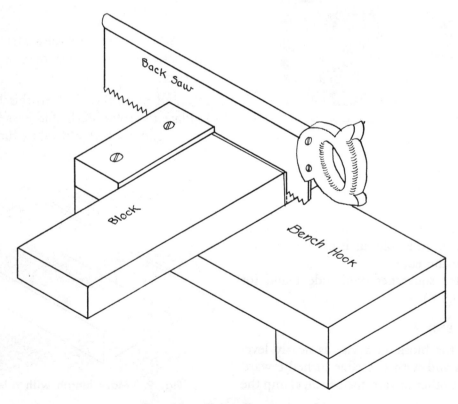

Fig. 11. Saw off waste end.

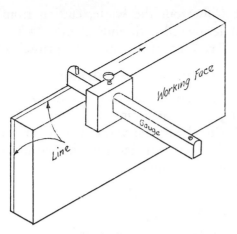

Fig. 13.   Mark thickness of block.

is on the other side. With the thumb on the beam, push the gauge away from you to mark the width of the block (Fig. 12). Plane the block to this line.

Follow steps under *C*.

G. MARK THE BLOCK FOR THICKNESS, AND PLANE IT TO THIS LINE.

1. Set the gauge for ¾ in.

2. Tilt the gauge slightly forward and, holding it as before, gauge a line around the block as shown in Figure 13.

3. Plane to this line until the line disappears, and test for flatness. Follow the steps under *B*.

H. HAVE THE INSTRUCTOR CHECK AND GRADE THE BLOCK AT THIS POINT.

II. Draw all lines and layouts for cutting the mortise, rabbet, gain, etc., which appear on the block (Fig. 14).

A. USE A TRY SQUARE AND A SHARP PENCIL OR KNIFE FOR ALL LINES ACROSS THE GRAIN.

B. USE A GAUGE FOR MARKING ALL LINES GOING WITH THE GRAIN.

C. USE A COMPASS OR DIVIDERS FOR ALL CURVED LINES.

D. USE A TRY-AND-MITER SQUARE (FIG. 7) FOR LAYING OUT THE 45-DEG. ANGLE.

III. Cut the mortise, rabbet, gain, and other members.

A. CUT THE MORTISE.

1. Bore two ⅝-in. holes through the block. Bore only halfway through from each face.

2. Chisel the hole. Pare away the wood a little at a time, using a slicing cut.

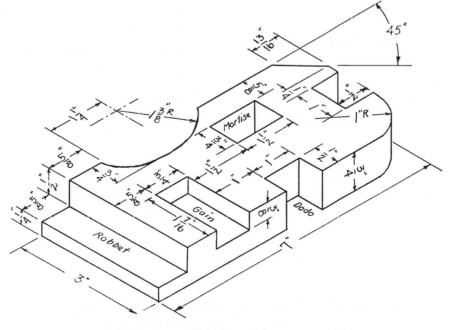

Fig. 14.   Draw all lines and layouts on block.

3. Check the walls of the mortise for squareness.

B. CUT THE GAIN.

1. Drive the chisel, lightly, straight down all around, about ⅟₁₆ in. in on the waste sides of the lines. The flat side of the chisel should be next to the lines when doing this. Use a mallet to hammer the chisel.

2. Trim out the waste by hammering the chisel from the center of the gain toward the first cuts made, holding the chisel with the beveled side down.

3. Repeat steps 1 and 2 until the proper depth has been attained.

4. Complete chiseling the gain by trimming with the flat side of the chisel.

C. CUT THE RABBET.

1. Saw on the waste side of the line with a backsaw, sawing across the face side of the block.

Do not saw entirely to the bottom of the rabbet, but allow a little wood to remain for trimming.

2. Chisel out the waste. Begin near the surface, and work down gradually to the line. Finish the rabbet by chiseling across the grain. Turn the bevel of the chisel up when doing this.

D. CUT THE DADO ON THE EDGE OF THE BLOCK.

1. Saw from the edge of the block nearly to the line opposite the edge. Stay on the waste side of the lines going across the grain.

2. Chisel out the waste, cutting from the middle toward both ends of the block.

3. Trim the edges with slicing chisel cuts.

E. CUT THE DADO ON THE END.

1. Saw from the end nearly to the line going across the grain.

2. Chisel out the waste, a little at a time, cutting from both faces of the block toward the center of the end.

3. Trim the edges.

F. CUT THE MITER.

1. Saw off on the waste side of the line.

2. Trim to the line with a plane or chisel.

G. CUT THE OUTSIDE CURVE.

1. Saw on the waste side with a coping saw.

a) The teeth of the coping-saw blade should be pointed toward the handle of the saw.

b) To hold the saw properly, take the handle in the right hand, and place the left hand over the right. Keep the blade level while sawing.

2. Trim to the line with the chisel, using the flat side of the chisel.

H. CUT THE INSIDE CURVE.

1. Saw on the waste side with a coping saw.

2. Trim to the line with the chisel, using the beveled side of the chisel.

NOTE: Do not sandpaper the practice block.

IV. Have the block checked by the instructor.

A. NO DIMENSION SHOULD BE OFF MORE THAN ⅟₃₂ IN.

Wood Finishing

MUCH of the beauty of a project made of wood will depend upon the quality of its finish. Some brief instructions on wood finishing are deemed necessary in a book of this kind. While it is true that other things enter into the making of a quality project besides the finish, it can be stressed that unless the finish is good, the best made project will appear no better than second rate when judged for quality.

SANDING.

After a project has been completed and the time has arrived for finishing, the project should first be carefully inspected for blemishes, such as file marks, dents, plane or machine marks, scratches, etc. Most projects made in the school or home workshop may be sanded with No. 1 flint paper and finished with No. 1/0 flint paper, or the project may be sanded with No. 2/0 garnet paper and finished with No. 4/0 garnet paper. All sanding should be rubbed parallel to the direction of the grain. Sometimes it is necessary to sand a joint across grain on at least one member of it, until a level surface has been obtained, but to complete the sanding, each member of the joint should be sanded parallel to the grain.

STAINS.

The next operation will depend somewhat on the kind of wood and the type of finish being used. Usually, the first finishing coat to be applied is stain, unless the project is to be painted. There are exceptions, however, which we will note.

Some kinds of wood, as maple and oak, take stain very unevenly, the hard spots absorbing very little stain while the soft spots absorb a great deal. This undesirable feature sometimes can be overcome by giving the surface of the wood a wash coat of thin shellac before staining it. Regular 4-lb. cut shellac should be thinned with equal parts of alcohol for this wash coat.

Three kinds of stains are commonly used. They are water, spirit, and oil stains.

WATER STAIN.

Water stains are good and are the cheapest of the three. They are excellent where the colors are carefully controlled by proper mixing according to formulas, and where quantity production under skilled and careful supervision is being carried out. If water stains are used, the grain first must be raised by sponging with water. After the surface has dried, it must be sanded smooth again.

SPIRIT STAIN.

Spirit stains usually are alcohol stains, and are difficult for an amateur to use. Many of them fade badly, and therefore are not recommended for projects made in the school or home workshop.

OIL STAIN.

Of the three types, oil stains are the best all-around coloring agent for the methods and facilities usually available in the small shop. They can be obtained in a wide variety of colors at fairly reasonable prices. They mix readily with fillers, are easily applied, and are reasonably durable. Oil stains may be bought ready mixed in colors such as mahogany, walnut, maple, etc. Painters' pigments also may be bought in small cans, and any color may be easily mixed or matched if the person doing it has some knowledge of what combination of pigments make the different colors. Since most stains are of a brown, red, or amber tint, the color range in mixing stains usually is not very great.

To obtain browns, such as walnut, Adam brown, brown mahogany, etc., burnt umber, burnt sienna, Van Dyke brown, French ocher, and lamp black, mixed in various proportions according to taste, and thinned with some vehicle, such as turpentine or mineral spirits, usually will make economical and satisfactory stains.

For red maple stain, dark Venetian red should be used as a base, with burnt umber and yellow ocher added to it.

An organic dye, such as para red, will produce the best results in obtaining a satisfactory red mahogany. Since this is not always available at local paint stores, however, satisfactory substitute mahogany colors may be mixed by using various proportions of dark Venetian red, burnt sienna, tinted with either chrome yellow orange, American vermilion, or dragon red, depending upon how brilliant a red is desired.

Golden oak and light browns can be obtained with a very light mixture of burnt umber and turpentine.

FILLERS.

On open-grained woods such as mahogany, oak, or walnut, it is necessary to follow the stain with filler. This is done to close the open pores of the wood, so that the surface will be more nearly level and the pores will not absorb more than their share of the surface coating which follows. Silex fillers in paste or liquid form generally are used. These fillers may be mixed with a sufficient amount of the stain which has already been applied to the wood so it will not change the color of the surface to which it has been applied. Filler of the consistency of heavy cream must be rubbed into the pores of the wood by applying it thickly to the surface with a brush, and then rubbing it well into the pores with burlap, Spanish moss, or even coarse cloths. Too large a surface must not be attempted at one time, because all filler remaining on the surface must be removed before it sets too hard.

SHELLAC.

Close-grained woods, such as maple, pine, poplar, and birch, need no filler, and the stain coat may be followed with a coat of shellac or varnish after drying for twenty-four hours. A coat of shellac over all stained or filled surfaces is recommended. However, the 4-lb. cut shellac should be thinned with about half as much alcohol, or even as much alcohol as shellac to allow it to be brushed on more evenly. Denatured alcohol and not wood alcohol should be used, since the poisonous fumes of the wood alcohol may cause blindness.

As a general rule, the most difficult surfaces should be done first in all finishing operations, and the most exposed or most accessible surfaces should be done last. Stain should be wiped off with a soft cloth as it is being applied, to give it a more even tone. Stain may be brushed or wiped on in almost any direction, but shellac or varnish must be finished off with the grain on the final strokes of the brush. Shellac should be brushed as little as possible; just enough to spread it smoothly and evenly, otherwise it will gum up the surface with a sticky, unsightly film which can hardly be removed.

Red stains, such as mahogany, will bleed through varnish unless the surface has been first coated with shellac. Browns are not so likely to do this.

A shellac coat should be thoroughly steel-wooled after it has dried for twenty-four hours. This should leave the surface smooth with all gloss removed, and ready for the next coat. No. 00 steel wool should be used for this operation, and the entire surface should be well dusted before the next coat of finishing material is applied.

All finishing operations should be as clean and neat as possible in order to get satisfactory results.

A good surface may be built up with two or three more coats of shellac, thinned as before. Each one must be wooled down before the next one can be applied. Shellac, however, is a more brittle finish than varnish, and is more readily attacked by moisture, chemicals in everyday use about the home, the direct rays of the sun, etc., than is a good floor varnish. So, for the next coat, after one of shellac, a good grade of floor varnish is recommended.

VARNISH.

Varnish is of two kinds, glossy or flat. Even if a flat varnish is to be applied for the final coat, which will obviate the necessity of rubbing the final coat with pumice stone and oil, the coat following the shellac coat should be glossy varnish. Varnish should be applied in a room with a temperature of not less than 70 deg., and the room should be as nearly dust free as possible. Varnish should be brushed much more while it is being applied than was the shellac. Very often it is brushed on across the grain, and finished off with the grain. This insures good coverage. Even the quick-drying varnishes, commonly known as four-hour varnish, should be allowed to dry about 48 hours before steel-wooling or pumice-stoning. Two coats of varnish should be applied over the shellac, and three coats make a better surface for rubbing down with pumice stone and oil.

The last coat of varnish, if glossy varnish is used, should be rubbed down with pumice stone and rubbing oil (a light mineral oil). Pumice stone and water also can be used. This cuts a little faster, but leaves the surface more dulled. The surface should be rubbed until it is smooth like a mirror. The abrasive action of the rubbing compound tends to level down all of the little ripples which even the best varnished surface has after the varnish has dried.

The pumice-stone rub should be followed by a rub of rottenstone and oil, which gives the surface a high luster. This completes the finishing operations.

CARE OF BRUSHES.

Good work cannot be done unless the proper tools, carefully maintained, are at hand. For our purposes we are assuming that only the better grades of China-bristle brushes, with bristles rubber set, are being used. Cans and other receptacles, in which the ingredients are poured for use, must be kept thoroughly clean. So must brushes. This means that, as soon as a particular operation has been completed, the receptacle and the brush must be thoroughly cleaned.

Mineral spirits, kerosene, turpentine, and various other thinners may be used to clean stain, paint, or varnish brushes. Various brush cleaners, specifically designed for the purpose, also are on the market.

Denatured alcohol is used to clean shellac brushes.

After cleaning a brush with one of these liquids, a good lathering in hot water and soap suds should remove the last traces of grease and dirt, leaving the bristles soft and clean for the next operation or job.

PAINTS.

If the project is to be painted or enameled, a different procedure must be followed.

The project should be just as carefully sanded as if it were to be stained and varnished. Even so opaque a substance as paint seldom hides sloppy work, and it pays to do a good sanding job.

For indoor work, flat wall paint or enamel undercoat is used. Two coats usually are sufficient. Each coat should be sanded down with fine sandpaper, No. 1/0 or finer, before the next coat is applied. The second base coat may be heavier, or it may be thinned down less than the first or priming coat. Only turpentine or some cheaper paint thinner should be used, but it should be one which has been recommended by the manufacturer. Over the second base coat, one or more coats of enamel should be applied. It is always best to match the colors of the base and enamel coats as nearly as possible before the work is begun.

In painting, the whole gamut of colors is used. The best thing for one who is unfamiliar with color mixing is to buy ready-mixed paint. However, it will not be long before a painter wants to match colors with something he has seen, or something he particularly wants, and for which he cannot buy ready-mixed paint. If a formula chart is not available, he must then seek the advice of an experienced person, or do some experimenting of his own. Since experimenting usually is quite expensive, it is advisable to buy ready-mixed paint. A great many colors are available. Some are not as permanent as others, and some have much stronger tinting power than others.

BRIEF SUMMARY OF OPERATIONS TO BE FOLLOWED IN FINISHING A PROJECT.

1. Sandpaper smooth, and remove all blemishes.

2. Stain, and wipe with soft, clean cloth. Allow to dry for 24 hours.

3. Apply filler colored with stain previously used. Rub well into the pores of open-grained woods. Wipe all residue off the surface. Close-grained woods do not need filler.

4. Apply a coat of shellac. If a 4-lb. cut is used, thin it in the proportion of 2 parts shellac to 1 part alcohol. Brush with the grain and only enough to apply it smoothly.

5. Steel-wool the shellac after it has dried 24 hours.

6. Apply a coat of glossy floor varnish. If the object is to be exposed to the weather or to damp places, use spar varnish instead of floor varnish.

7. Steel-wool the first varnish coat after it has dried at least 48 hours.

8. Apply a second coat of varnish.

9. Rub the final coat of varnish with FF or finer powdered pumice stone and rubbing oil, using a felt pad where possible, or a cloth for the purpose.

10. Follow the pumice-stone rub with a rub of rottenstone and oil.

BOARD MEASURE

Width in Inches — Lengths in Feet. — All lumber figured as being 1" thick.

Width	1'	2'	3'	4'	5'	6'	7'	8'	9'	10'	11'	12'	13'	14'
18	1.5	3.	4.5	6.	7.5	9.	10.5	12.	13.5	15.	16.5	18	19.5	21.
17	1.42	2.83	4.25	5.66	7.08	8.5	9.92	11.33	12.75	14.17	15.58	17	18.42	19.83
16	1.33	2.67	4.	5.33	6.67	8.	9.33	10.67	12.	13.33	14.67	16	17.33	18.66
15	1.25	2.5	3.75	5.	6.25	7.5	8.75	10.	11.25	12.5	13.75	15	16.25	17.5
14	1.17	2.33	3.5	4.67	5.83	7.	8.17	9.33	10.5	11.67	12.83	14	15.17	16.33
13	1.85	2.17	3.25	4.33	5.42	6.5	7.58	8.67	9.75	10.83	11.92	13	14.08	15.17
12	1.	2.	3.	4.	5.	6.	7.	8.	9.	10.	11.	12	13.	14.
11	.91	1.83	2.75	3.67	4.58	5.5	6.42	7.33	8.25	9.17	10.08	11	11.92	12.83
10	.83	1.67	2.5	3.33	4.17	5.	5.83	6.67	7.5	8.33	9.17	10	10.83	11.67
9	.75	1.5	2.25	3.	3.75	4.5	5.25	6.	6.75	7.5	8.25	9	9.75	10.5
8	.67	1.33	2.	2.67	3.33	4.	4.67	5.33	6.	6.67	7.33	8	8.67	9.33
7	.58	1.17	1.75	2.33	2.92	3.5	4.08	4.67	5.25	5.83	6.42	7	7.58	8.17
6	.50	1.	1.5	2.	2.5	3.	3.5	4.	4.5	5.	5.5	6	6.5	7.
5	.42	.83	1.25	1.67	2.08	2.5	2.92	3.33	3.75	4.17	4.58	5	5.42	5.83
4	.33	.67	1.	1.33	1.67	2.	2.33	2.67	3.	3.33	3.67	4	4.33	4.67
3	.25	.5	.75	1.	1.25	1.5	1.75	2.	2.25	2.5	2.75	3	3.25	3.5
2	.17	.33	.5	.67	.83	1.	1.17	1.33	1.5	1.67	1.83	2	2.17	2.33

Index